THE I TATTI
RENAISSANCE LIBRARY

James Hankins, General Editor

CYRIAC OF ANCONA
LIFE AND EARLY TRAVELS

ITRL 65

CYRIAC OF ANCONA
✦ ✦ ✦
LIFE AND EARLY TRAVELS

EDITED AND TRANSLATED BY

CHARLES MITCHELL
EDWARD W. BODNAR

AND

CLIVE FOSS

THE I TATTI RENAISSANCE LIBRARY
HARVARD UNIVERSITY PRESS
CAMBRIDGE, MASSACHUSETTS
LONDON, ENGLAND
2015

Series design by Dean Bornstein

Library of Congress Cataloging-in-Publication Data

Ciriaco, d'Ancona, 1391–1452, author.
Life and early travels / Cyriac of Ancona ;
edited and translated by Charles Mitchell, Edward W. Bodnar
and Clive Foss.
pages cm — (The I Tatti Renaissance library)
ISBN 978-0-674-59920-8 (alk. paper)
1. Ciriaco, d'Ancona, 1391–1452 — Correspondence.
2. Ciriaco, d'Ancona, 1391–1452 — Travel.
I. Mitchell, Charles, 1912–1995.   II. Bodnar, Edward W.
III. Foss, Clive.   IV. Title.   V. Series: I Tatti Renaissance library.
PA8485.C53Z46 2015
930.1092 — dc23   2014032675

Contents

ॐS९५

· CONTENTS ·

Introduction

ᛒᛇᛒ

Merchant, accountant, politician, traveler, antiquarian, spy, Cyriac di Filippo de' Pizzicolli of Ancona (1391–ca. 1452) has been called the father of archaeology because of his careful recording of antique sites and inscriptions and his belief that the physical record of the past was as important as the literary. His early life—the first forty-five years—is known from the text that occupies most of this volume, the life written by his friend Francesco Scalamonti. Remains of Cyriac's correspondence and diaries illuminate his later years, but few of those exist for this earlier period. Scalamonti presents the career of a man who started as the son of an impoverished widow and rose to become one of the best known and influential humanists of his age. His apprenticeship to a merchant made him a keen and successful businessman, while his training as an accountant influenced his meticulous treatment of the records of antiquity. Early travels in Italy stirred a curiosity that led him to combine exploration of ancient sites with profitable business trips around the Aegean and Levant. A surviving Roman arch in his native Ancona stimulated the desire to understand the ancient world by learning Latin through the text of Vergil's *Aeneid* and then to undertake Greek also. Financial success, good connections, and his revelations of the ancient world enabled Cyriac to enter the highest circles: he became a familiar of the king of Cyprus, the pope, the Holy Roman Emperor, the emperor of Byzantium, and even the Ottoman sultan. He urged all of them to preserve antiquities and became a successful advocate of the union of the Roman and Greek churches and of a Western crusade against the Turks. On his travels, Cyriac's interests were not one-sided: he constantly recorded not only ancient inscriptions but also information about the Ottoman state and its military capacities with a view to informing the pope and his European allies.

All this is to be found in Scalamonti, whose narrative has been supplemented and contextualized by modern biographies, but remains fundamental.[1] Despite the title it carries, however, it is less than correct to refer to it as a life. In fact, it presents itself as materials for a fuller biography that was to have been composed by the Venetian aristocrat and humanist Lauro Quirini.[2] Failing Cyriac himself, Quirini could hardly have found a better informant to give him reliable materials for his proposed biography. Knight, lawyer, and diplomat, Francesco Scalamonti (d. 1468) was descended from a French family that migrated from Arles to Ancona in 1114.[3] Guillaume de Chaumon, the founder of this branch of the family, married an Anconitan in 1124 and changed his name to Scalamonti. Francesco is thus presented by our sources as the scion of a noble family that had been settled in Ancona for three centuries. The date of his birth is not known, but since he stated in his dedicatory letter to the *Vita* that he had known Cyriac from his earliest childhood, we can safely presume that they were more or less of an age. On February 16, 1436, Francesco was named as Count Francesco Sforza's *luogotenente* in Fabriano, a post he held for two years. He then was sent as an ambassador of Ancona to Sforza, who was then besieging Tolentino and in need of the small force that Francesco brought along. On September 17, 1438, from Ancona, Cyriac wrote a very warm reply to two letters from Scalamonti. The latter had urged him to write the history of Venice and of the Milanese duke (Filippo Maria Visconti, d.1447), to put aside his taste for pagan literature, and to read more of the sacred writings of the orthodox Catholic faith.[4] Cyriac modestly refused the first charge on the grounds that he could not rival the great historians of antiquity, but he promised to do something about the second without, however, neglecting the *veneranda disciplina* and the *auctoritas optima* of the gentile pagans. In 1441 Scalamonti was *podestà* of Norcia, as he informed Cyriac in a letter of December 30 of that year, when he complained that Cyriac had not been corresponding with him as he was wont to do.[5] In 1450 Scalamonti was sent by Ancona on a diplomatic mission to the pope, and on another to Venice in 1452, when he was characterized as *il nobile cavaliere . . . dottore di legge e soggetto di molte qualità* (the noble knight, . . . doctor of laws and a man of parts). Among his humanist friends was Francesco Filelfo, a friend also of Cyriac's, who addressed five letters to Scalamonti that we know of.[6] Another of Filelfo's letters, dated June 22, 1468, informed a mutual friend that Scalamonti had died that year of the plague in his native Ancona.[7]

Lauro Quirini, to whom Scalamonti directed his work, though much younger than the latter and unable to claim such familiarity with Cyriac and his family as Scalamonti enjoyed, was not unqualified, as a youthful admirer, to attempt Cyriac's biography.[8] Born probably around 1420, Quirini sprang from one of the twenty-four most ancient patrician families of Venice, a city with which Cyriac had close connections, not least through his powerful Venetian patron Gabriele Condulmer (later Pope Eugenius IV). Quirini studied in Padua, where he won his doctorate in Arts on April 26, 1440, and in Civil Law on March 16, 1448. In the following year, having in 1445 been refused membership in the Paduan College of doctors *in artibus*, he returned to Venice, where, perhaps on his own account, he gave a course of public lectures on Aristotle's *Ethics*.[9] In 1451 and 1452 he was a *lector* in rhetoric and moral philosophy at Padua University, but he resigned his post in the latter year, and at the end of it returned to Crete, where he seems to have spent the rest of his life. He died in 1480 or 1481.

While still a student at Padua, Quirini made contacts with many humanists and embarked on a literary career. In 1441, when Eugenius IV, driven from Rome, held court in Florence, Quirini lodged there in the house of Cardinal Bessarion, and in that year he wrote a lost Latin commentary on a vernacular sonnet composed by Cyriac. The latter Cyriac had contributed to the famous *Certame Coronario* organized in Florence by Leon Battista Alberti.[10] It was very likely this encounter with Cyriac that prompted Quirini to undertake his biography. The fact that Quirini was a Greek scholar himself—he translated the anonymous Greek tractate *De sacerdotio Christi* transmitted in the *Suda* as well as a speech of Caesar's from Dio Cassius—no doubt played its part in fostering his desire to record the doings of so passionate a rediscoverer of antique Hellas. As for his other original compositions, Quirini wrote a *De politia* in two books; on the occasion of the abortive second *Certame Coronario* (on the theme of Envy) he wrote a Lucianic *Dialogus de gymnasiis Florentinis* in 1442;[11] between about 1446 and 1450 he composed three pieces on nobility—a letter, a polemical tractate, and a legal *consilium*—opposing the argument of Poggio's *De nobilitate* of 1440.[12] Quirini there defended the Venetian idea that nobility derived from both ancestry and virtue against Poggio's more radical position that nobility was based on virtue alone. In 1447 Quirini wrote another Lucianic dialogue, *De pace Italiae*. A number of other works, occasional eulogies and letters, also survive from his pen.

How did Scalamonti compile the materials for his *Vita*? As he explicitly states in his dedicatory letter to Quirini, he drew his information from Cyriac's mother and relatives, and from Cyriac's own mouth and from his numerous writings. We have no means of distinguishing precisely what Scalamonti received orally, but the *Vita* again and again gives the impression of repeating or paraphrasing Cyriac's own records, and Scalamonti tells us more than once in his text that he had original *commentaria* of Cyriac's before him. Unfortunately, however, none of these notebooks, relating to the years covered by the *Vita* (down to 1434 or early 1435), has come down to us. But we need not rely entirely on Scalamonti's testimony that such *commentaria* did once exist, at least for the later period dealt with in the *Vita*, for Torelli Sarayna, writing in the sixteenth century, gives an account of the amphitheater in Verona, inspected by Cyriac in 1433–34, which clearly is taken almost word for word from Cyriac's travel journal.[13]

Further verbal correspondences, moreover, exist between passages in Scalamonti's *Vita* and two of Cyriac's surviving set pieces, namely his *Anconitana Illyriacaque laus et Anconitorum Raguseorumque foedus*, about the trade treaty concluded between Ancona and Ragusa in June 1440,[14] and the so-called *Itinerarium* addressed to Eugenius IV, which refers to the *Certame Coronario* that took place in Florence on October 22, 1441, and therefore was written after that date. It has been argued that verbal coincidences between passages in the *Vita* with corresponding passages in the *Laus et Foedus* and the *Itinerarium* prove a dependence of the *Vita* on these later documents; but it is preferable, granted Cyriac's habit of mining his own notebooks for passages usable in letters, to assume that *both* the *Vita* and the *Itinerarium* and *Laus et Foedus* are dependent on the lost notebooks, and that therefore the *Vita* is not necessarily dependent on either the *Itinerarium* or the *Laus et Foedus*.

When did Quirini conceive his idea of writing Cyriac's biography? On this question our only internal evidence is the beginning of Scalamonti's dedicatory letter to Quirini, where he says that he had recently read a letter, written by Quirini in Padua to Cyriac in Florence, about the projected life. Quirini's initial proposal, which Cyriac had evidently welcomed, must have been made quite some time previously, because a later part of Scalamonti's letter makes it clear that Cyriac had been dilatory in supplying the materials Quirini had asked for, so that Scalamonti felt obliged to compile them himself. All we know for certain is that Quirini made his request some time before the death of Cyriac. Absent new evidence, pinning the composition down to a particular year is difficult. The narrative ends in late 1434 or early 1435, but it contains some apparent anachronisms that point to a date later than 1435. (These passages will be pointed out and discussed in the notes to the translation as they occur in the *Vita*.)

This volume also includes Cyriac's earliest surviving work, a long letter to Pietro Bonarelli, as well as his epistolary exchanges with Leonardo Bruni, the chancellor of Florence and the most famous Greek scholar and literary figure of Cyriac's day. The epic account of *The King's Naval Battle* (*Naumachia regia*), datable to 1435 and addressed to Scalamonti, has also been added. In principle, the volume also includes as appendices all documents from the period covered by Scalamonti, 1391–1435, including captions for now-lost illustrations of St. Sophia in Constantinople, since Cyriac's first visit there is described by Scalamonti (Appendix II), and some letters of Francesco Filelfo to and about Cyriac (Appendix III). A few later works are also included as related to texts in this volume: the famous "Caesarean letter" to Leonardo Bruni of 1436, whose point of departure was their first exchange of 1432; a further letter to Bruni inquiring whether the "Caesarean letter" has arrived; a response to Cyriac's Caesarean letter from Poggio, addressed to Bruni; Cyriac's note on constitutions illustrating the political terminology used in his discussions with Bruni (Appendix IV); and a letter of a certain Antonio di Leonardo to Felice Feliciano, the copyist of the lone copy of Scalamonti's *Life*, who included the letter with his copy (Appendix V). A chronology of the events in Cyriac's life as documented by Scalamonti and other sources has been compiled for the convenience of the reader (Appendix I).

The letter to Pietro Bonarelli was written during an otherwise undocumented journey in 1423 from Ancona to Venice by way of Fano and Rimini. In it Cyriac justifies his attention to pagan authors by reference to Dante's *Purgatorio* (6.119–20), where Christ is called *Giove crocifisso*. The wider context is the defense of studying pagan poetry in Christian societies, a recurrent theme of humanist literature going back to the beginnings of the movement.[15] The literary form is that of an imagined dream in which the debate takes place, with Mercury pleading Cyriac's cause. The poetic cast of the language and numerous grammatical errors typical of the autodidact fully bear out Scalamonti's report (*Life* §53) that Cyriac had only recently begun to learn and write Latin via an unusual method: the close study and imitation of Vergil. Vergilian echoes are especially prominent, as if Cyriac were showing off his newly acquired learning.[16]

Cyriac's important correspondence with Leonardo Bruni consists of two parts: an exchange of letters, probably in 1432/33, and a long composition addressed to Bruni in the form of a letter, the so-called Caesarean letter, dated 1436. The first letters deal with politics, spurred by Cyriac's question, apropos of the newly installed Holy Roman Emperor Sigismund III, whether the title of king or of emperor should be considered the higher one. Bruni replies, basing his argument primarily on Roman history, that the title "king" was far more distinguished than that of emperor. To us today his argument appears specious, for he deliberately ignores the profound differences between the two meanings of the Latin word *imperator*. In the Roman republic, *imperator* was an honorific title conferred upon a victorious commander by acclamation of his troops; the *imperator* would then, presumptively, be entitled to celebrate a triumph in Rome. The title expired after the end of the triumph and conveyed no executive power or role in the government. In this sense it could certainly be considered as inferior to the title of king or dictator, as Bruni claims. But when Augustus came to power, after the Battle of Actium in 31 BCE, he took on *imperator* as a personal title in perpetuity. By the second century CE it had acquired a meaning something like our modern term "emperor"—that is, the ruler of the Roman Empire, who *eo ipso* was superior to kings and other dignitaries. In late antiquity it unambiguously denoted the supreme authority in the Roman world, as it has ever since. For Charlemagne, for instance, the position of Roman emperor was plainly superior to the kingships he held over the Franks and Lombards. In Sigismund's time, the Holy Roman Emperor was called *rex Romanorum* after he was elected and before being crowned by the pope. Only after being crowned by the pope was he, properly speaking, the *imperator*, though he was sometimes accorded the title by courtesy before his coronation. In other words, the imperial title was plainly superior to the royal in the fifteenth century. Bruni's answer showed he considered the linguistic usage of the old Roman republic, before the Augustan principate, to take precedence over late Latin and the living Latin of his contemporaries.

Cyriac's "Caesarean letter" of 1436 is really a long essay, set in the context of a voyage to the Dalmatian coast, defending the reputation of Julius Caesar against the aspersions of Poggio, who preferred to elevate Scipio Africanus over Caesar. As in his letter to de Bonarellis of 1423, Cyriac brings in the Roman gods.[17] Calliope appears to him in a dream and takes up his cause with Jupiter, who agrees to send Mercury to Cyriac's aid. The god, disguising himself as Calliope, addresses the assembled savants. Ranging widely through Roman history, he expounds the merits of Caesar and explains the fall of the Roman Empire. Style and imagery track those of the earlier letter, from which several phrases are repeated.

In this second round of correspondence with Bruni, Cyriac involved himself in a major intellectual controversy that involved some of Italy's leading humanists. The debate ostensibly was about the relative merits of two ancient Roman commanders, Scipio Africanus and Julius Caesar. It began when Scipio Mainente of Ferrara, later bishop of Modena and a close friend of Pope Eugenius IV, wrote to Poggio Bracciolini asking whether Scipio or Caesar were greater. In April 1435, Poggio replied in detail, comparing their careers, praising Scipio Africanus for his *virtue*, the only criterion that made men worthy of glory and praise; Caesar only for his *deeds*. He argued that Caesar, by destroying Roman liberty, also created an atmosphere that was not conducive to good writing; hence the inferiority of the authors of the Empire to those of the Republic.[18]

That same summer, Leonello d'Este, marquess of Ferrara and duke of Modena, visited Pope Eugenius, then living in exile in Florence, where he acquired a copy of Poggio's letter. On his return to Ferrara, he turned it over to Guarino of Verona, the famous humanist educator and the marquess' trusted agent. In June, Guarino replied at length to Poggio, in defense and praise of Caesar's deeds *and* virtue, basing his arguments on a vast range of classical authors and writing in a generally moderate tone, though affecting to pity Poggio for his errors.[19]

Poggio, in turn, in October 1435, composed a very long letter, not to Guarino but to the Venetian statesman Francesco Barbaro, who had studied with Guarino, sending him the entire correspondence and asking him to act as arbiter.[20] He lamented the vehemence of Guarino's attack and replied in detail to the points he had raised, blaming Guarino for misunderstanding and misrepresenting his sources.

Cyriac now (January 1436) entered the fray—the self-taught neophyte Latinist, plunging headlong into debate with the greatest scholars of the day. His letter, presented here, is of a very different nature from the others. Instead of a somber refutation of Poggio's arguments, Cyriac turns to mythology and impersonates the god Mercury in order to make the case for Caesar, stressing all his accomplishments, especially that of laying the foundation for the stable and long-lasting Roman Empire. The Roman republic itself would have been forgotten had it not been for the founding of the imperial system by the Julio-Claudians, says Cyriac; and he does not omit to include the traditional argument, going back to the Church Fathers of Christian antiquity, that God chose to be incarnated as Christ under the peace of the empire, not amid the turbulence of the republic (§17).

Poggio, now thoroughly exasperated at the intervention of someone he considered a rank amateur, wrote a blistering invective, not to Cyriac himself but to Bruni, on March 31, 1436. This was an *ad hominem* attack, no longer so concerned with Caesar or Scipio as with sneering at Cyriac's pretentious Latinity and mode of presentation. Finally, in 1440, Pietro del Monte, a former pupil of Guarino and a correspondent of Cyriac's, wrote to Poggio in support, deploring Guarino's excessive sharpness.[21]

Poggio's anger at Cyriac seems to have cooled a bit by May 1438, when he agreed to write a letter of recommendation for him,[22] nor did it deter Cyriac from later boasting of his acquaintance with Poggio in a letter to Pope Eugenius IV (October 1441)[23] or from writing to Poggio still later in a friendly vein (1442). Poggio, for his part, could not resist taking one more brief shot at Cyriac in his *Facetiae*.[24]

At first sight, all this might seem like the pettiest of antiquarian squabbles, debating subjects long dead, but in fact it had real contemporary relevance. The exchanges were part of an ongoing debate about the respective merits of republican government as opposed to a monarchy in a land, Italy, largely divided between those two forms of government.

Scipio, who defeated Hannibal, and Caesar, who conquered Gaul, were probably Rome's greatest generals, but their careers were very different. At the height of his glory, following the utter defeat of Carthage, Scipio could easily have accepted offers of special powers that would give him lifelong control of the Republic. Instead, he virtually withdrew from public life, returning to military command only at the specific request of the Senate. Caesar, however, used his military success to invade Italy, against a decree of the Senate, starting a civil war, and acquired for himself supreme power and the unprecedented title of Perpetual Dictator. Scipio defended the Republic; Caesar overturned it.

The two Romans, then, were highly relevant to discussions of political systems in Renaissance Italy. Scipio stood for republics, Caesar for autocracies. This is generally agreed, though there are varying refinements; some, for example, believe the debate had a subtext related to current politics in Florence, a republic fallen under the sway of a single family, the Medici.[25]

The King's Naval Battle was a grandiose composition, presented in the form of a letter to Scalamonti, that describes in epic terms the naval battle at Ponza, where the side Cyriac and the pope favored was badly defeated. The main figures in the conflict were Alfonso V, king of Aragon (1416–58) and the republic of Genoa, then under the control of Filippo Maria Visconti, duke of Milan (1412–47). The battle, which took place on August 5, 1435, was the result of a dispute over the succession to the Kingdom of Naples. The queen of Naples, Joan II, childless and last of her line, had adopted Alfonso in 1421, then changed her mind several times, alternating between him and Louis III of Anjou. After Louis' death she switched to his brother René, an adoption that was opposed by Pope Eugenius IV, the traditional feudal lord of Naples. Consequently, when Joan died in 1435, war broke out between Alfonso and René, who was joined by Filippo Maria, himself related by blood and marriage to the late queen. Alfonso, already king of Sicily, was also disputing control of Sardinia with the Genoese.

Queen Joan and Genoa had taken Naples from Alfonso's brother Ferdinand in 1424. After failing to recapture the city in 1432, Alfonso seized the opportunity seemingly offered by Joan's death. With substantial local support, Alfonso captured Capua and laid siege to the coastal stronghold of Gaeta. Filippo Maria then sent a well-equipped Genoese fleet against Alfonso, whose ships met defeat at Ponza, one of the great naval battles of the early Renaissance.

Although the king and his three brothers were captured in what appeared to be a real disaster, the aftermath was not drastic. The Genoese received their captives with great honor, and Alfonso convinced Filippo Maria that it was not in his interest to oppose Spanish control of Naples. This left Alfonso free to retake Capua and establish his base at Gaeta. Naples finally fell after a long siege in 1442, Alfonso took over the whole kingdom, and four years later he finished conquering Sardinia. By that time, the Milanese had been driven out of Genoa by a popular revolt in 1435, not long after Ponza. The Spaniards, despite their shattering defeat, wound up dominating all of southern Italy.

This volume is principally the work of Fr. Edward Bodnar, S. J., who regrettably did not live to see its completion; he passed to his eternal reward in November 2011 at the age of ninety, just short of celebrating sixty years in the Jesuit Order. Fr. Bodnar, whose kind nature endeared him to all he met, devoted his long scholarly life to the study of Cyriac. His 1958 Princeton PhD in classics, which focused on Cyriac's description of Greece, was published as *Cyriacus of Ancona and Athens* in 1960. Extensive travel in the lands Cyriac visited followed, leading to *Cyriacus of Ancona's Journeys in the Propontis and the Northern Aegean, 1444–1445* (1976) and the text included here, Scalamonti's *Vita Viri Clarissimi et Famosissimi Kyriaci Anconitani* (1996), both of these in collaboration with a distinguished art historian, Charles Mitchell of Bryn Mawr. Most recent was Cyriac's *Later Travels* (2003), published in the I Tatti Renaissance Library. Fr. Bodnar went on working, leaving behind the texts included here and materials for a planned third volume, to comprise the period 1435 to 1444.[26]

In this volume, the Scalamonti text, translation, and notes as well as the Bonarelli correspondence are the joint product of Bodnar and Mitchell. Fr. Bodnar left behind a critical edition (which he never published) of Cyriac's "Caesarean" letter to Bruni (1436), as well as draft translations of it and the *Naumachia*. The undersigned editor is responsible for translations of all the inscriptions, the letter of Poggio denouncing Cyriac, and various parts of the Appendices; he has revised as well all the other translations and introductions, and condensed Fr. Bodnar's notes to suit the requirements of this I Tatti series (though he has also, occasionally, added to them). Wherever possible, Fr. Bodnar's original language has been maintained.

In their 1996 edition of the Scalamonti *Life* (pp. v–vi), Fr. Bodnar and Prof. Mitchell expressed their special thanks to Augusto Campana, who had contemplated an edition of Scalamonti's *Vita Kyriaci*, but, learning of Bodnar and Mitchell's work, agreed that they should take over the project. They were grateful to Cecil Grayson for editing the Italian poems that occur in the *Vita*, and to Nelia Saxby for translating them. In addition, they thanked an array of learned organizations, universities, and Jesuit bodies that had supported the project from 1965 to 1983, and librarians and colleagues whose help and advice had contributed to this work.

The present editor would add his thanks, first to Fr. Bodnar, for inviting him to participate in the preparation of *Later Travels*; to Fr. Eugene Nolan S. J., for giving him full access to Bodnar's research materials; to James Hankins, for encouragement to undertake and complete this work; to Roger Tomlin, for advice on Latin inscriptions; and to Jacob Tulchin, whose unerring instinct for Latin idiom improved the translations of Cyriac's correspondence.

C. F.
Cambridge, MA
November 2012

NOTES

1. For a fuller introduction to Cyriac's life and works, see the introduction to *Later Travels* in this I Tatti series (ITRL 10), which covers the years 1443 to 1449, the final period of Cyriac's life. For a detailed modern treatment of Cyriac's career, see Colin, *Cyriaque d'Ancône*, and the more popular work of Belozerskaya, *To Wake the Dead*. (References given in short form in this Introduction and in the Notes to the Translation can be found in full in the Bibliography; for Abbreviations see the headnote to the Notes on the Translation, p. 315.)

2. See *Life* §3. The rest of this and the subsequent paragraphs down to p. xviii are adapted from Bodnar's Introduction to Scalamonti, 1–18, and the headnote to Scalamonti, 166 (Appendix I).

3. For the details of his life that follow, see Spadolini, "Il biografo," who obtained the family history from a manuscript book lent him by a Count Scalamonti of Camerata Picena.

4. Moroni, *Epigrammata*, 41–42; *Itinerarium*, 73–76.

5. The correspondence is preserved in Florence, Biblioteca Nazionale Centrale, MS. Naz. II.IX.15, pp. 258–59; Volterra, Biblioteca Guarnacci, MS. 5031, fols. 32v–33r. Cited in part (from the Volterra manuscript) by Spadolini, "Il biografo," 71b, and by De Rossi, "De Cyriaco," 361a, n. 3 (from the Florence manuscript).

6. Filelfo, *Epistolarum familiarium* (Venice: Iohannes et Gregorius de Gregoriis, 1502), ff. 34r–34v (September 29, 1444); 36v (October 31, 1444); 71v (September 5, 1452); 190r (January 31, 1467); and 191v (June 27, 1467). All are addressed to "Francisco Scalamonti equiti aurato." (This edition may be consulted online through the Bayerische Staatsbibliothek in Munich.)

7. Babinger, "Veneto-kretische Geistesstrebungen," 67.

8. The following summary of Lauro Quirini's life is from P. O. Kristeller's introduction to *Lauro Quirini umanista*, 27. For a more detailed chronology of Quirini's life and writings, see the "Cronologia" by Seno and Ravegnani in the same volume, 11–18; for his treatise on true nobility, see *Knowledge, Goodness and Power*, with further biographical material.

9. He had earlier, in 1441, challenged the elderly Leonardo Bruni to a debate on the subject of Aristotle's *Ethics*, which Bruni had translated from the Greek. See Hankins, "Addenda to Book X," 414–16.

10. The sonnet was on the theme of friendship, the topic Alberti had set for the *Certame*. Cyriac mentions Quirini's commentary on his sonnet in a letter to Pope Eugenius IV, the so-called *Itinerarium*, 13–14. See also the letter of Iacopo Zeno to Cyriac (Bertalot and Campana, "Gli scritti," 369). For Cyriac's and Quirini's participation in the *Certame Coronorio*, see Mancini, *Vita di Leon Battista Alberti*, 202, who says that Cyriac did not compete for the prize (a silver crown), but recited a sonnet, preserved in MS. Naz. II.V.160 of the Biblioteca Nazionale Centrale in Florence, f. 33. See also Gorni, "Storia."

11. Published in Bertalot and Wilmanns, "*Lauri Quirini Dialogus*," 483–93.

12. *Lauro Quirini umanista* gives editions of all three works; they are translated in Rabil, *Knowledge, Goodness and Power*, 143–81.

13. See the parallel passages cited in Scalamonti, 9–10.

14. Published, along with the archival text of the treaty itself, by Praga, "Indagini e studi . . . Ciriaco de' Pizzicolli," 270–78.

15. Ronconi, *Le origini*.

16. For the many errors in spelling and grammar, see Scalamonti, 167–75. For the Vergilian echoes, see the relevant notes to the translation.

17. There are in fact frequent borrowings in Cyriac's 1436 letter to Bruni from his own earlier letter to Bonarelli; these are tracked in detail in Cortesi's edition of the 1436 letter, in "La *Caesarea laus*," 53–65.

18. Critical edition by Crevatin, "La politica," 309–26; see also pages 281 to 298 for the sources and development of Poggio's views of Caesar and Scipio. The themes of Poggio's letter are related to his treatise on true nobility, translated in *Knowledge, Goodness and Power*, 53–96; the Whiggish charge that the death of republican liberty had led to cultural decline was a major theme in the work of Poggio's older friend Bruni.

19. Canfora, *La controversia*, 119–40. Canfora's work does not deal with Cyriac, who only appears in a footnote.

20. Ibid., 141–67.

21. Bracciolini, *Opera omnia*, 4:617–39.

22. Letter to Jacopo Foscari, from Ferrara, May 15 [1438], in Bracciolini, *Epistularum familiarium libri*, 2:294, no. 11.

23. *Itinerarium*, 10–13.

24. Bracciolini, *Opera omnia*, 1:442.

25. A useful summary and analysis of the controversy is found in Oppel, "Peace vs. Liberty"; and for the controversy and its interpretations, see Cortesi, "La *Caesarea laus*," 9–19; Pade, "Guarino and Caesar," 80–82; and Pade, *The Reception of Plutarch's Lives*, 1:235–54, with further bibliography.

26. To be published in this I Tatti series. For the works of Fr. Bodnar referred to, see the Bibliography.

FRANCESCO SCALAMONTI

THE LIFE OF
CYRIAC OF ANCONA

Vita Clarissimi et Famosissimi Viri
Kyriaci Anconitani
Feliciter Incipit

1 Franciscus Scalamontius eques Anconitanus Lauro Quirino Veneto patricio viro claro salutem dicit.

2 Cum hisce diebus nuper apud Anconem patriam elegantem illam epistolam tuam quam exacto tempore e Patavina urbe Florentiam Kyriaco Anconitano nostro destinasti vidissem, clarissime Laure, tui ex ea nobilitatem animi extimare coepi. Quom te tam rarissimi hominis vitam cursumque describere deligisse perceperam, rem certe bene merentem et honorificam sui et tuae dignam facundiae duco, nec te hac ipsa in re Italos inter doctissimos homines dormitante quippe ingenio consideravi. Nam quis clariorem sibi nostro aevo materiem politiorem iucundioremve in scribendo deligere posset quam singularis viri vitam peregrinationemque memoriae litterisve mandare? Qui solus in orbe post insignem illum geographum Claudium Ptolemoeum Alexandrinum ab Hadriani Caesaris tempore per tria atque decem annorum centena orbem totum percurrere, regionum provintiarumque situs et qualitates, montes, nemora, fontes fluviosque, maria et lacus atque nobilissimas urbes et oppida per Graeciam, Asiam et Aegyptum perque Ionicas insulas et Aegaeas visere indagareque sui quadam animi magnitudine et generositate ausus est. Et quicquid in his dignum nobilia inter venerandae veternitatis monumenta comperuit, Latine Graeceve honeste non in vulgaribus quidem litteris emendavit, et denique, ut saepe suo audivimus ore, quicquid in orbe reliquum est ad extrema Oceani promontoria et ad Thylem usque insulam et abmotas quascunque alias mundi partes videre scrutarique indefesso nempe animo proposuerat, suis quibusque incommodis, laboribus atque vigiliis omnibus expertis posthabitisque.

Here Begins
the Life of the Learned and Famous
Cyriac of Ancona

From Francesco Scalamonti, knight of Ancona, to the distin-   1
guished Lauro Quirini, patrician of Venice, greetings.

When I was recently at home in Ancona, most distinguished   2
Lauro, I read that elegant letter you wrote from Padua some time
ago to our friend, Cyriac of Ancona, in Florence; and from it I
began to appreciate the nobility of your character. This choice of
yours to write about the life and career of such an extraordinary
man seems to me well worth the while and likely to do honor both
to him and to your own eloquence. Moreover, in the matter of eloquence I did not consider you to be an idle talent among the
learned men of Italy. For who could choose a more splendid, re-
fined, and happy subject to write about in these days than to hand
down to posterity a record of the life and journeys of this singular
figure? Cyriac is the only man in thirteen hundred years, since the
time of the great Alexandrian geographer Claudius Ptolemy in the
age of Hadrian, whose expansive nature and highborn temper gave
him the courage to travel all over the world — through Greece,
Asia, Egypt, and the Ionian and Aegean islands — to survey and
investigate the sites and characteristics of its territories and provinces, its mountains, woodlands, springs and rivers, its seas, lakes
and noblest cities and towns. Whatever fine monuments of venerable antiquity he found worthy of note in these places, he faithfully recorded, not in the common language, but in Latin or
Greek; and, as we have often heard him say himself, his inde-
fatigable resolve, regardless of all discomforts, toils and sleepless
nights the task involved, was to inspect and examine whatever ancient remains were to be seen in the world as far as the last rocky
heights jutting into Ocean, to the island of Thule, and any other
remote parts of the earth.

3   Equidem, vir clare et vere Musarum decus virentissime Laure, ipsum te verum hac in parte Quirinum et Quirini nominis dignissimum possessorem exornatoremque cognosco, dum te tam dignam et honorificam provinciam cepisse conspicio, tam diligentem scilicet Latini nominis exornatorem ornare atque insignia sua quaeque ornamenta insigniter perennia facere te primum omnes inter Italos providentissime decrevisse. Igitur honeste ut late magis et integre opus perficere posses, ab eo ea ipsa in epistola vitae suae cursum omnem a natali die certo ordine tibi certius describere flagitabas. Qua in re cum eum tardiorem vidissem (nam in alienis potius quam propriis in rebus laudibusve solertem esse cognovi) et me sibi in primis ab ineunte aetate et a teneris, ut aiunt, unguiculis amicicia, consuetudine et domestica omni familiaritate iunctum plane cognovissem, id mihi honestum et honorabile munus honos ipse atque honestas iniungere videbatur; quod equidem abnuere nefarium duxi. Pro igitur munere suscepto calamum cepi, et Kyriaci Anconitani nostri originem vitamque et peregrinationis cursum, et horum quaeque memoratu digna visa sunt, et quae carae parentis ab ore suorumve relatu, et ab eo ipso et sui plerisque litteris intelligere, noscere atque videre et percipere potui, hisce benivolentiae dignissimae tuae brevissimo ordine describendum atque hisce transmittendum curavi.

4   Vale et Kyriacum ipsum lege.

5   Kyriacus Anconitanus Anconitana patria ortus, quae civitas in Adriaco ad sinistrum Italiae littus in extremo Apenini montis promontorii capite sita est insigni portu a divo Traiano condito aliisque vetustatum egregiis ornamentis ornata et dignum Picenni provinciae caput habetur. Hic honesto genere natus patrem habuit Philippum ex patricia nobili Picennicollensi familia, matrem vero

Indeed, I recognize that in this matter, Lauro, you who are a   3
distinguished man and truly a verdant laurel glorifying the Muses,
have shown yourself to be a true Quirinus[1] and eminently worthy
to possess and adorn the name "Quirinus," inasmuch as you have
undertaken the honorable and worthy endeavor to be the first Italian notably to record for all time every notable achievement of
Cyriac, to adorn him who has so diligently adorned the Latin
name. Accordingly, in order to be able to write the life faithfully
and as comprehensively and completely as possible, you asked
Cyriac in your letter to write out a complete and orderly account
of his whole career from the day of his birth. But when I realized
that he was rather slow in complying (for I know that he is always
better at promoting other people's affairs and praise than his own),
and since from my earliest youth, from my baby toenails as the
saying goes, we have been close friends and familiar neighbors,
honor and decency seemed to lay on me this decent and honorable
duty, which it would be very wrong to refuse. In discharge of this
obligation, I have therefore taken up my pen and have seen to it
that the enclosed materials should be written out in summary
form and sent to you, giving an account of the lineage, life and
travels of our friend Cyriac of Ancona, taking my information
from his mother, his relatives, and his own mouth and numerous
writings. These materials I enclose herewith for your friendly use.

Farewell, and read Cyriac himself.   4

Cyriac of Ancona was a native of Ancona, a city situated on the   5
left, or Italian, shore of the Adriatic Sea, at the very head of a
promontory of the Apennines. Distinguished by its port built by
the divine Trajan and by other splendid ancient structures, it is
considered a worthy capital for the province of Piceno. Cyriac was
the legitimate son of Philip, a scion of the noble patrician family
of the Pizzecolli. His mother was Masiella, the daughter of the

Masiellam, Kiriaci Silvatici viri famosi filiam, quem peperit pridie
K. Aug. Bonifacio IX pont. DXLII olympiadis anno III.[1] Is enim
infans annum iam VI agens patrem amisit paulo ante tribus nau-
fragiis binisque piratum incursionibus non sine pernicie aere non
modico expoliatum. Mater igitur vidua angusta in re domi in-
fantem simul binis cum aliis minoribus natu parvulis, fratre Cincio
et Nicolosa sorore, non sine labore atque vigiliis educavit.[2] Ac eos
bonis moribus litterisque erudire quoad licuit operam dedit. Interea Kiriacus, puer iam fere novenis, ingenti et innata visendi orbis cupiditate, fatali quadam sorte et divino quodam afflante numine, Kiriacum Silvaticum tum forte per Adriacum Venetias rei
suae causa petentem invita parente avum quidem avide sequitur.

6   Nam tam celebris amplissimae civitatis fama iam tenerum pueri
atque fatalem animum excitarat. Quam demum Idibus Aprilis
Michaele Stenno duce splendidissimam vidit et admiratus est mi-
rificentissimam urbem. Et quemadmodum fata dederant inclytam
hanc et insignem Italiae civitatem tantae sibi indagationis principium fore praedignam, ita eam ipsam avidius diligere amareque
semper et ingenti laude attollere exornareque conatus est.

7   Exinde puer ipse Kiriacus Kiriaco avo ipso ducente Patavinam
adivit antiquam Enetum et egregiam urbem, quam, Francisco Ca-
rario principe, magnam et triplici circundatam muro viderat et
pleno undique flumine ablutam. Inde nobilem eiusdem civitatis
arcem et ornatissimam principis aulam vidit, in qua primum in
claustris vivos deambulare leones conspexisse memorabat.

8   Exinde vero patriam suosque revisit et dilectissimam genetri-
cem, quae summo studio puerum Francisco Zampeta paedagogo

noted Ciriaco Selvatico. She gave birth to him on the 31st of July in the third year of the 653rd Olympiad in the pontificate of Boniface IX.[2] When he was six years old, that son lost his father, who shortly before that had been ruined financially, stripped of his wealth by three shipwrecks and two pirate raids. Cyriac's mother, a widow of slender means, by dint of hard work and sleepless nights, brought the child up at home, along with two other younger siblings, a brother, Cincio, and a sister, Nicolosa, and did whatever was possible to educate them in good manners and letters. Cyriac was now about nine years old; born as he was with an immense craving to see the world and impelled by a kind of divinely inspired destiny, he eagerly, against his mother's wishes, accompanied his grandfather, Ciriaco Selvatico, who was then by chance about to make a sea voyage on business up the Adriatic to Venice.

For the fates had already fired the boy's young mind with the 6 fame of this great and populous city, and when he first saw it on the 13th of April, when Michele Steno was doge,[3] he was filled with admiration for its marvelous splendor. And just as destiny had decreed that this renowned and important Italian city should be the fit starting point for a life of such great discoveries, so he always especially loved it and did all he could to exalt and adorn it with generous praise.

Next, the young Cyriac, under his grandfather Ciriaco's guidance, went to Padua, the ancient and noble city of the Eneti, which was ruled by Francesco Carrara.[4] There he looked round the great city, surrounded by triple walls and washed on all sides by a deep river, and he viewed the prince's noble castle with its large painted hall, where, as he used to recall, he saw for the first time live lions walking around in their cages.

After that he returned home to rejoin his relatives and his 8 dearly loved mother, who had carefully arranged for him to be taught his letters by the schoolmaster, Francesco Zampetta.

docente litteris erudire curaverat. Sed anteaquam duodecimum
aetatis suae annum puer exactum vidisset, et Kiriacum avum ad
Ladislaum regem maturare certis indiciis percepisset, expretis omnibus et charae parentis precibus, avum sequi terra marique constituit.

9   Et sic ex Piceno per Mauricinos, Brucios et Salentinos campos
perque Apuleos, Sannitas, Lucanos atque Campanos Neapolitanum omne nobilissimum regnum percurrit, plerisque egregiis ur-
bibus oppidisque visis, in quis pleraque vetustatum monumenta
conspectare iam coeperat, inter quae apud antiquam Thetidis urbem Achilei capitis simulachrum vetusto de marmore vidit. Sed
primum ipso in regno apud Theanum oppidum per dies consedere
eiusdem optimo cum principe, Geophedra Aliphi comite et magno
totius regni camerario; exinde in Suessa apud ipsum Suesanum
ducem Scyllaceique in Calabris comitem, grandaevum et regni
maritimarum rerum omnigenum praefectum, ambo praeclara
Martiana de domo fratres, quibus inclytis principibus Kiriacus
avus antiqua familiaritate notus et carissimus erat, et cum his in
Pannonia ab Karoli regis tempore versatus.

10   Exinde vero regiam Neapolitanam nobilissimam Campaniae civitatem venere, ubi Ladislaum ipsum regem, inclytum atque perstrenuum armis principem, inter parandam fabrifaciundamve classem in ipso urbis navistacio conspexere. Sed inde paucos post dies,
insignibus tantae civitatis inspectis, Calabres petentes oneraria
nave devecti, apud Salernum civitatem serenissimum ipsum regem
secus mare hastiludium hippodromaleve spectaculum celebrantem
florentissima stipatum militia respexere.

11   Exinde, urbe conspecta, per cymbam Lucania littora radentes et
floridos laetosque Melphetanos Paestinosve Lucaniae colles de-
super inspectantes, tandem exoptatis Calabrum oris incolumes
applicuere, in quis Turpiam, Laconiam Maydemque oppida deve-
nere. Et cum in Mayde Ciriacus avus consisteret, ex ea puerum

Nevertheless, before his twelfth year was out, observing evident signs that his grandfather was in a hurry to visit King Ladislas, Cyriac made up his mind to accompany him on land and sea, despite all his mother's entreaties against it.

So leaving Piceno he journeyed through the whole of the most 9
noble kingdom of Naples, through the country of the Mauricini, the Bruttians, the Salentines, and of the Apulians, the Samnites, the Lucanians and Campanians. On his way he saw many remarkable cities and towns where he now began to notice their numerous antique monuments, including an antique marble bust of Achilles that he saw in the ancient city of Thetis. Their first halt in the kingdom itself was at the city of Teano, where they stayed for some days at the court of its lord, Count Geoffredo Alife, the Grand Chamberlain of Naples. They next stopped at Aurunca, where they visited the Duke of Sessa and his aged brother, the count of Squillace in Calabria, grand admiral of the Regno. These two lords, of the noble family of Marzano,[5] were old and dear friends of Ciriaco, having been with him in Hungary in King Charles' time.[6]

Finally they arrived at the most noble and royal Campanian city 10
of Naples, where they saw the famous martial prince, King Ladislas, building and fitting out a fleet in the shipyard of the city. After a few days in Naples, where they saw the sights of the great city, setting out for Calabria, they took ship in a merchantman and disembarked at Salerno where they again saw the king surrounded by his splendid bodyguard, attending a tournament and a horse race by the sea.

Then, after viewing the city, they took passage in a small boat, 11
down the Lucanian coast, looking up at the charming sight of the well-cultivated hills of Amalfi and Paestum, until they arrived safely in Calabria, their destination, where they visited the cities of Tropea, Laconia and Maida. At Maida Ciriaco Selvatico settled down, putting his grandson to school to continue his study of

nempe ad perdiscendas litteras Palphi Scyllacaei civis amici sui
tutelae commisit, ubi puer primum grammateis in ludis primos
primae artis canones coeperat intelligere.

12　　Sed ibi posteaquam per annum moram traxere, avus suus ex
Mayde rebus exactis (nam et eo in loco divinam omnem historiam
materni eloquii carminibus peregregie traduxerat), patriam denique remeare constituens, Neapolim iterum Tyrrenno remenso
aequore revisit, ubi Anconitanam trirerem, ut Bonifacium pontificem ad balnea duceret, ab Anconitanis Marcone Torelliano praefecto missam invenere.

13　　Sed ubi exacta re inde concesserant, Suessam repetentes, aliquot per dies apud Suessanum ducem degere. Cuius in regia Kiriacus ipse puer puero inclyti ducis filio Ioanni Antonio tanta se
consuetudine et familiari benivolentia iunxerat, ut nullo inter se
discrimine apud patriam maiestatem haberi se videbantur. Nam
una eadem pueros adoleverat aetas parumper sed moribus doc-
trina dispares. Ast enim vero avus interea talibus posthabitis ho-
noribus, ut fidem potissimum filiae servaret, Kiriacus puerum ad
patriam charamque parentem exoptatum reduxit.

14　　Reversi quidem in patriam civitatem, cum plerosque per dies
avus puerum a suis multum deplausum blandiciis cognovisset,
puerique mentem inertem consistere nolle plane scivisset, ac civitatem totam non liberalibus studiis sed mercemoniis potissimum
maritimisque exercitationibus deditam intellexisset, ac his artibus
cives quamplures ditiores ope auctos sane novisset, et puerum ipsum ex paupere ditiorem evadere cupiens, de consensu matris
quoidam ex affinibus suis diviti negociatori, viro quidem in civitate
praestanti et patricio nobili, Petro magistri Iacobi physici clari filio,
puerum ipsum Kiriacum iam decimum quartum aetatis annum

letters under the care of his friend, Palfo of Squillace, where the boy first began to learn the first rules of grammar, the first of the arts.

But then, after a year's stay in Calabria, Cyriac's grandfather 12 wound up his affairs in Maida (including an outstanding translation of all sacred history into Italian verse) and decided at last to return to his home; so, recrossing the Tyrrhenian Sea, he sailed back to Naples, where they found an Anconitan galley under the command of Marcone Torelliano which had been sent by Ancona to convey Pope Boniface [IX] to the baths.

Having finished their business there, they then returned to 13 Sessa to stay for a few days with the duke, at whose court the young Cyriac became such good friends with the famous duke's young son, Giovanni Antonio, that one could not distinguish which of the two the duke regarded as his own child — for the two boys had quickly reached the same degree of maturity, though quite different in education and upbringing. However, the grandfather felt that it was time for them to put these courtesies behind them and to keep his promise to his daughter; so he brought his grandson home to the boy's dear mother, who eagerly awaited his return.

For many days after their return, Ciriaco Selvatico watched his 14 grandson being welcomed and petted by the family, but the boy, he knew, was obviously eager to occupy his mind. As Ancona was a place wholly given over, not to liberal studies, but to trade and shipping, which had enriched so many of the citizens, and as he wanted to raise the boy from poverty to wealth in that kind of enterprise, he arranged, with the mother's consent, to apprentice the boy, now aged fourteen, for seven years to a rich merchant relative of his, namely the prominent citizen and noble patrician, Pietro, son of the eminent physician Messer Iacopo. The young Cyriac applied himself to the business and soon clearly

agentem septenale per tempus in negociariae rei servitium dederat. Qui posteaquam puer hisdem se deditum exerciciis cognoverat, non arithmeticae modo praecipuam artem, quin et geometricam et plenam denique negociariae rei disciplinam, nullo docente, se ingenii sui praestantia solertiaque fretus, brevi tempore, exemplaribus tantum inspectis, didicisse manifestum ostendit; et tanta demum fide, integritate, diligentia, vigilantia atque solertissima cura in eiusdem patroni sui negotiis die noctuque gesserat et domi forisque, assiduis laboribus vigiliisque omnibus expretis, ut vixdum exacto biennio Petrus iam Kiriacum ad omnem rem gerendam paratum idoneumque existimans, ut publicae rei negociis quibus frequens cum consulari potestate sevir, tum regulatoria dictatoriave trevir electus, inter patricios cives liberius habiliusque vacari posset, omnem sibi puero suae rei curam non modo domi mercisque omnigenae, quin et agrariae utique rei administrationem reliquit. Et sic puer ipse rem quodammodo magnam virili quodam animo suscipiens, ita per quinquennium mercaturam omnifariam exercuerat, ut divo et catholico genio suo ea utique in parte favitante Mercurio, non modice patroni sui opes augendo concreverat; et ita in his se aeque gessit, ut non suis modo ⟨a⟩ civibus, sed ab extraneis plerisque, qui tum forte saepius Anconitanis negociabantur, Perusinis, Florentinis, Venetisque laudatus est.

15 Adolescens praeterea, anteaquam servicii tempus explicuisset, patrono potissimum curante optumo, nondum aetate idoneus primum ad consularem seviratus dignitatem, mox ad senatoriam extra comitiorum ordinem ascendit, in quis se semper pace belloque egregie eximia cum laude gessit. Exacto sed enim cum patrono constituto tempore, etsi materna pietas adolescentem ad se paupere in casa reduxerat, nunquam se tum ab honesta patroni optumi consuetudine et benivolentia separavit.

16 Sed enim interea quamquam in civitate puer expertus et non mediocriter eruditus se publicis privatisque negotiis exercere sua cum dignitate et utilitate potuisset, animus tamen nobilis, qui eum

demonstrated that he had learned, not only the basic art of arithmetic, but also geometry and all the mercantile skills; and this he achieved in a very short time, without any teacher, but by studying the way things were done and by relying on his own extraordinary quickness of mind. He labored day and night, regardless of long hours and lack of sleep, and was so trustworthy, diligent, and skillfully attentive to his duties, in and out of the office, in discharging his master's business, that within two years Pietro considered him perfectly capable of looking after the whole business on his own. Pietro had more than once been elected, not only as one of the six *anziani* but also as one of the three *regolatori*[7] of the city. Now, as a patrician, he wanted to have more time and leisure for local politics, so he handed over to Cyriac the management, not only of all his mercantile business in Ancona, but also of his country estates. The lad manfully shouldered this huge task and for five years conducted the whole complex enterprise so successfully—favored by his divine and catholic genius, Mercury[8]—that he considerably increased his master's wealth, and his fair trading won the praise, not only of his fellow citizens, but of the many outside merchants from Perugia, Florence and Venice who were then doing business with the people of Ancona.

Meanwhile, before he had finished his term of apprenticeship 15 and although he was still not of proper age, the young man was raised, with the strong backing of his master, first to consular rank as one of the six *anziani* and later, by exception, to the Senate;[9] and in these offices he never failed admirably to discharge his duty both in peace and war. When the seven agreed years of his apprenticeship were over, Cyriac's concern for his mother took him back to her simple house, but he never ceased to enjoy the honest company and kindness of his excellent master.

By this time the young man had acquired considerable practical 16 experience in civic affairs, and was perfectly well qualified to take a responsible and useful part in public and private business in

ad visendas mundi oras impellebat, peregrinis maritimisque negotiis immisceri compulerat, et ita se primum Ciucio[3] Picennicoleo
consanguineo suo Alpheriae cuiusdam onerariae navis patrono se
navigationis principio scribam minorem iunxit.

17   Qua cum bona navi fructuum onerata ex Ancone per hyemem
Illyrico superato altum per Ionium, Creta magni Iovis insula procul inspecta, vasto denique demenso Libyco Aegyptiacove freto,
Alexandriam insignem Aegypti civitatem venit. Ubi primum ingentia Phariae praecelsae olim turris vestigia, regias ex Numidico
lapide portas, maximum Philadelphi regis obiliscum, et magnam
ex Dinocrate architecto Alexandri Macedonis columnam, quam
hodie vulgus Pompeianam appellat, inspexit, ac alia pleraque vetustatum insignia monumenta; et ibi primum kamelos, dromeda-
rios, struthiocamelosque nec non mymones et novos gentium
habitus vocesque admiratus est. Vidit exinde ibi Sultaneum principem magna eunuchorum servorum omnigenum caterva stipatum
advenientem ingenti splendore, pompa eximioque honore a suis et
externis hominibus in urbe susceptum.

18   Sed navis ibidem, Stephano demum Quirino Veneto patricio
nobili curante, rebus omnibus exactis, ex Alexandria Rhodum, ex
Rhodo vero Chium venerat, ex qua quidem nobili et Aegaea insula
Kiriacus adolescens, scriba maior creatus, Samium Ichareamque
vidit, egregias et fama celebres in Asia insulas. Et tandem ad Ioniam veniens Milesiam vidit, olim nobilem et nunc dirruptam vetustate urbem. Sed eiusce maximi amphiteatri et pleraque alia suae
maiestatis eximiae conspectantur vestigia, quae hodie Graeciae
vulgus palatia vocitare solent.

19   Exinde vero Kariae Ciliciaeque littora perlegentes, Cyprum
opulentissimam olim insulam venere, ubi Kiriacus e navi esiliens
Cyrinum oppidum veterem, Paphum, Amacostem atque regiam

Ancona; but now his noble spirit drove him to see the world, and
to engage in maritime business abroad, so he attached himself as a
minor clerk to his relation Ciucio,[10] who had chartered a merchantman belonging to a certain Alfieri, which was about to start a journey.

In this good ship, laden with a cargo of fruit, he left Ancona —   17
it was winter time — and sailed down the Dalmatian coast, through
the Ionian Sea; he had a distant view of Crete, the island of great
Jupiter, and finally, after a long crossing through Libyan and Egyptian waters, arrived at the famed Egyptian city of Alexandria.
There he had his first sight of the huge remains of what was once
the tall lighthouse of Pharos, the royal gates of Numidian[11] stone,
the great obelisk of King Philadelphus, the tall column of Alexander of Macedon designed by the architect Dinocrates, now popu-
larly called the column of Pompey,[12] and many other remarkable
antique monuments; and it was there that for the first time he saw
with wonder camels, dromedaries, ostriches, and apes, as well as
new peoples with their strange garments and accents. In Alexandria, too, he saw the Sultan[13] arriving with great splendor attended
by a band of eunuch servants of all races and ceremoniously received in the city by his own people and by visiting foreigners.

When, through the good offices of Stefano Quirini, noble pa-   18
trician of Venice, all the business had been done in Alexandria, the
ship sailed to Rhodes and from Rhodes to Chios; from which
noble Aegean island, having now been promoted to senior clerk,
the young Cyriac had a view of the famous islands of Samos and
Icaria off the coast of Asia. His next stop, as he came into Ionia,
was Miletus, a city once illustrious, but now fallen in ruins, where
he viewed the remains of the great theater and of numerous other
monuments of its former greatness, which the present-day Greeks
call palaces.

Then, sailing past the coasts of Caria and Cilicia, they arrived   19
at the once immensely wealthy island of Cyprus, where Cyriac
went ashore and visited the ancient cities of Kyrenia, Paphos,

Leucosiam mediterraneam civitatem vidit. Inde Syriam navigantes Berutum venit; ex qua demum Italiam repetens et Caietam urbem per Scylaea Carybdaeaque perniciosa vada, Regium Iulii nobilem Calabrum et antiquissimam civitatem venit.

20   Inde Messanam insignem Siciliae civitatem et praeclaram viderat ac pulcherrimam urbem. Exinde vero per Tirrenum navigantes, Caietam antiquam et memorabilem Campaniae civitatem venit, ubi exonerata repparataque navi Castrum ad Mare venerat.

21   Et inde castaneis avellanisque oneratis, Alexandriam iterum repetentes, Tyrrenum inde transfretantes, per Aeolias insulas ingenti ad IIII Kalendas Martias acti procella, ad Drepani portum ex Ustica insula maris noctu perniciem evasere, quam et antiquissimam urbem ut memorabilem Dardanidis Anchisae sedem conspectare maluerat. Et tandem extra moram, ad Beatae Nuntiatae Virginis aedem solutis nauticis de more votis concedentes, inde Vulcaneam inter insulam et sinistrum Sicaniae littus Scyllaea rursus formidanda per vada transmeantes Aegyptiacam iterum Alexandriam revisere.

22   Ubi demum exactis Ioanne cum Michaele Veneto rebus, Anconem patriam repetentes per Illyricum, Dalmatica Ragusio nobili urbe et antiqua pulcherrimaque Epidauri colonia visa, et tribus demum semestribus peractis, Anconitanum portum suosque et proprios lares rerum experientia doctior opulentiorque revisit, ubi paucos post dies Nocolosam, sororem iam maturam viro et a matre conubio pactam, Bartholomaeo Libori filio Brondello

Famagusta and, inland, the royal city of Nicosia. They then set
sail for Syria, landing in Beirut, and then turned back to make for
Gaeta in Italy. On the return voyage they passed the dangerous
straits of Scylla and Charybdis and made landfall at the noble and
most ancient Calabrian city of Reggio.

From there he visited the famous and most beautiful city of   20
Messina in Sicily. Finally, sailing up the Tyrrhenian Sea he arrived
at the ancient and renowned Campanian city of Gaeta, where they
unloaded and repaired the ship and then stood over to Castellamare.

There they took on board a cargo of chestnuts and filberts and   21
then set sail again for Alexandria. But on the 26th of February,
while they were attempting to cross the Tyrrhenian Sea, they were
driven westward by a violent storm through the Aeolian islands by
way of the island of Ustica, and during the night they escaped the
perils of the sea by taking shelter in the port of Trapani, the ancient and famous city once ruled by the Trojan Anchises, which
Cyriac had much desired to see. Thence, when the sailors, as
usual, had said their prayers of thanksgiving in the Church of the
Annunciata, they set sail without delay and, passing between the
island of Vulcano and the northern shore of Sicily, once more
navigated the dangerous straits of Scylla and so got back to Alexandria in Egypt.

There they settled their affairs with Giovanni Michiel of Venice   22
and then reembarked to return home to Ancona. The voyage took
them up the coast of Illyricum, giving them a sight of the ancient
and beautiful Dalmatian city of Ragusa, a colony of Epidaurus;
and so, after one and one-half years away, Cyriac arrived back at
the port of Ancona, more experienced and richer than when he
had set out, to rejoin his relatives and home. While he was away,
his mother had arranged for the marriage of his sister, Nicolosa,

desponsatam, aucta de se dote, honorifice dederat, et ubi Kiriacus in urbe aliquod per tempus tum privatis tum et publicis rebus intentus versaretur.

23 Interea patria, hostilibus armis incaute Nonis Octobribus noctu moenibus iam furto sublimiori in parte captis, oppressa, una aliis cum civibus cumque Petro suo optimo olim patrono ad expellendum hostem civitatemque liberam incolumemque servandam non exigua quidem pars fuerat; quam vero rem ipse primum materno quidem eloquio litteris haud inepte mandarat. Nam et in his quandoque sub patrono media inter negotia ingenium exercuerat, cum saepe Dantis, Petrarchae, Boccaciique poemata per ocium lectitare maluisset.

24 Quibus de facultatibus cum doctiores inter viros verba aliquando non vulgariter habuisset, civis quidam ex his nomine Crassus, facundus quidem vir et eruditus, Kiriaci adolescentis ingenium admirans, haec denique nostro idiomate carmina sibi media sua inter se vice misit.

> Siegui il tuo stille e non guardar al folle
>> Vulgo insensato: siegui quel valore,
>> Kiriaco mio, di quegli el cui splendore
>> Sé eternando, el nome e'l tempo extolle.
> Lassa la cura d'este cose molle,
>> Ov'è ville il dilecto et vano amore.
>> Natura siegui, el tuo divin auctore
>> Natura [è] che al cielo el capo tolle;
> e virtù quella che, honorato in fama
>> Fa salir l'hom per arme o per scïenza;
>> Poi di eterna dolzeza il ciel l'adombra.

who was now of suitable age, and a few days after his return Cyriac, augmenting her dowry himself, gave her away with due honor to Bartolomeo Brondello, the son of Liborio, to whom she was betrothed, after which he settled down for a time in the city to devote himself to private and public business.

Meanwhile the city was under enemy attack and, on the night 23 of the seventh of October, the upper walls were unexpectedly captured by a surprise stratagem.[14] Cyriac, along with other citizens and his own former good patron, Pietro, played an important part in driving back the enemy and safely freeing the city—an event which he not unskillfully recorded in his native speech,[15] his first literary composition. For he had already begun to write when he was still in the intervals of learning his trade under his master Pietro and spent a good deal of his leisure reading the poems of Dante, Petrarca, and Boccaccio.

He sometimes had civilized discussions with his more educated 24 friends about poetry writing; and a learned and eloquent citizen of Ancona called Crasso,[16] who admired young Cyriac's talent, in the course of their poetic exchange sent him the following sonnet in our language:

> Follow your style and take no heed of the mad
> insensate rabble; follow that excellence,
> Cyriac mine, of those whose splendor
> is in itself immortal and fame and time extol.
>
> Abandon concern for these degenerate matters
> which it is vile to delight in and futile to love.
> Follow Nature; your divine authority
> in Nature which takes its preeminence from Heaven;
>
> and Virtue, the power that, bringing honorable repute,
> causes man to distinguish himself in arms or knowledge,
> and after, Heaven restores him with immortality's sweetness.

E te che al suo cantar le muse chiama,
  Non parvipender la divin' semenza
  Per fructo trar di quel che poi tutto umbra.

25   Quoi deinde Kyriacus talia per verba eodem carminum ordine
respondit:

Non per seguir lo stil che a l'alto colle
  Di Parnaso ce pingie, — il suo valore
  Sempre hai seguito et hor ti rende honore
  Sì come a quel che meritando il volle, —
Spargo l'inchiostro delle nostre ampolle,
  Ma per seguir il mercatal labore:
  Scrivendo e canzellando, el dibitore
  Per poesia nei mei libri s'incolle.
Hor la virtù che sol da te s'indrama,
  Movendo verso me per sua clemenza,
  Me mostra usir di quel che tanti adombra.
Ma perché più longo ordo e magior trama
  M'è oppo a ringratiar Tua Reverenza,
  De ciò narrar fia qui mia rima sgombra.

26   Et talia pleraque eiusdem generis carmina, ternarios, cantilenas
et sextinas variis quidem temporibus edidit, et diversis per Latium
viris claris et peritissimis misit; quae quom primum nostra in provintia iuvenis facundissimus ille Albertus Fabrianensis intellexisset, haec illico sibi elegantissime scripsit:

Hor serato si vede il fonte Arpino.
  Mantua, Smyrne, Corduba e Sulmona,
  Et tu Delpho, Parnaso et Helicona,
  Posto hai silentio al tuo cantar divino,
Ché, conspirante el summo Seraphino,
  Un tal tra noi dal ciel organo sona,

20

And you, whom the Muses call to join their song,
do not belittle the seed of your divine gift,
to warrant, after, oblivion's all-engulfing shade.

To him Cyriac replied with another sonnet with the same   25
rhyme scheme:

Not so as to follow the style which to the lofty hill
of Parnassus urges us — for its excellence
have you ever pursued, and this now does you honor,
like a man who wished to possess it by merit —
  do I shed the ink of our ampoules,
but to follow my commercial labor:
I write and cancel out, and the debtor,
instead of poetry, is nurtured in my books.
  The virtue now, which from you alone flows forth
and is bestowed on me by its own clemency,
would show me as exempt from that all-engulfing shade.
  But since a longer form and greater substance
are needed to thank properly Your Reverence,
let my rhyme be here exonerated from that telling.

He also wrote from time to time many other sonnets as well as   26
verses in *terza rima*, songs and sestinas, which he sent to various
famed and skilled men in Italy, and when an eloquent young local
poet, Alberto of Fabriano,[17] heard of this, he immediately wrote
him the following elegant sonnet:

Now is seen closed the font of Arpino,
of Mantua, Smyrna, Cordoba and Sulmona,
and you, Delphi, Parnassus and Helicon,
silence have imposed on your immortal song;
  for while there lives on earth the mighty Seraphino,
there resounds among us such heavenly organ chant,

21

> Che fa il lume Atheniese e quel d'Ancona
> Favilla spinta sotto fin rubino.
> Dunque prehendi da Daphne l'alme fronde,
>   E pon con tua corea, Apollo divo,
>   Sacro diadema in cossì digne come.
> E tu, mare Adrian, aquieta l'onde,
>   E mostra pace, e ben poi dir 'son vivo
>   E morte voi altre aque senza nome.'

27   Verum et quae sibi decentia eodem ordine dicta reddiderat omittam. Sed quae deinde Leonardo Iustiniano Veneto patricio, nobili et eloquentissimo viro, scripserat, hac in parte praetereundum non censui.

> Quel che con summa providentia et arte
>   Volgie col moto più alto e festino
>   La sancta mola del ciel christallino,
>   Movendo gli altri ciel di parte in parte,
> Vole del suo splendor tale adornarte
>   Qual circonscripto in oro fin rubino,
>   Unde non poteria mai mio picolino
> Stil, quanto converia, tanto exaltarte;
>   Perché del fior del tutto el marin piano
>   Se stende fino al ciel con care piume
>   La fama del valor Justiniano,
> Che come chiaro spechio di costume
>   Cossì la vita del bel viver humano
>   Mostra, facendo a tutti gli altri lume.

28   Quibus talia statim Leonardus ipse eodem ordine respondit:

> Quelle ample lode mie che in brieve carte
>   Conchiude in stille altiero e pellegrino,
>   In te sol si converte ivi, e il divino
>   Inzegno tuo traluce in mille parte.

that makes the brilliance of Athens and Ancona
but a dead spark under a fine ruby.
    Therefore, seize from Daphne the sacred boughs,
and place, in your melodious dance, O divine Apollo,
a sacred diadem upon your most deserving locks.
    And you, O Adriatic Sea, be still your waves
and take on tranquil mien, and say, for well you may, "I live
and you, you other nameless waters, are dead in fame."

I will not quote the appropriate sonnet Cyriac sent back in re-   27
ply; but I cannot here omit to cite the one he later wrote to that
noble and eloquent Venetian patrician, Leonardo Giustiniani:[18]

    He who with mighty foresight and skill
turns with the utmost power and motion
the holy millstone of the Crystalline Sky,
and moves the other Heavens from side to side,
    wishes to surround you with his splendor, like
a fine ruby which is circumscribed in gold,
whence to these heights never could my childish style,
as would be fitting, elevate you so;
    because from the Flower of the whole sea-lapped plain
there reaches up to Heaven with loving wings,
the fame of Giustiniani's glorious excellence,
    which, like of his mores a bright mirror,
reflects the beauty of his human state
and acts as lit beacon to all others.

To which Leonardo immediately replied using the same meter: 28

    Those ample praises of me which in brief compositions
you enclose with excellent and polished verse,
are here to you alone redressed, for your immortal
intellect shines forth in a thousand parts.

E già gran tempo le tue laude sparte
    Quanto si calcha il bel terren latino,
    Con tutto il cuor mi fero a te vicino
    E d'un caldo disio vago ad amarte.
Se cierchi in me virtù, troppo luntano
    Dal ver ti allonghi, ché'l celeste nume
    Non, come scrivi, a me larga la mano.
Ma se amor cierchi, un abondante fiume
    Vi trovarai, dil tuo valor soprano:
    Virtù honorando a sé virtù risume.

29   Et subinde haec eadem ilico dicta subiecit:

Qual sparir suole matutin pianeta
    Al pander de le come aurate e bionde
    Del sol che a men nocturna faza asconde
    Con l'alma lampa sua diurna e lieta,
Tal dal suave suo stil vinta si aquieta
    La sparsa fama tua, né già risponde
    A l'alte rime, unde si stilla e fonde
    Accenti di ogni digno e gran poeta.
Sì suave hermonia tua voce rende,
    Che quasi Orpheo, Apollo et Amphione
    Le labra a più bel canto mai non sciolse.
Quanto donque mia prima oppinione
    Dal vero è vinta, tanto più si accende
    L'amor che già gran tempo ad te mi colse.

30   Quibus et Kyriacus ipse statim haec de more respondit:

In fin che i fiumi al mar seguir lor meta
    Non resta, o l'ombre render monti e fronde,
    E che le vaghe stelle il ciel circonde,
    Convien tua fama al mondo esser cometa;

For a long time now, your praises spread,
wherever the lovely Latin land is pressed,
with all my heart have me made close to you,
and with strong desire to love you, eager.

If you search for virtue in me, too far
do you wander from the truth, for the heavenly Lord
does not, as you say, extend to me his hand.

But if you seek love, an abundant flow
will you find, for your supreme excellence:
by paying honor to virtue, virtue gets back itself.

And he added the following sonnet: 29

Just as the morning globe is wont to disappear
at the spreading of the golden and the yellow locks
of the sun, and to be concealed by the less nocturnal aspect
of the sun's life-giving lantern of the cheering day,

so, overcome by its own sweet verse, is hushed
your own widespread repute, nor yet does it correspond
to the noble rhymes in which are distilled and fused
the tones of every great and worthy poet.

Such sweet harmony does your voice make,
that hardly Orpheus, Apollo and Amphion
ever did loosen their lips in more beautiful song.

As strongly, therefore, as my first opinion
by truth is overthrown, so strongly is ignited
the love that has long gathered me to your side.

To which Cyriac, in his customary fashion, at once replied: 30

For as long as rivers do not rest to reach the sea,
their goal, or turn boughs and mountains into shade,
and as long as the sky surrounds the lovely stars,
your fame must needs be like a comet unto the world.

Ché l'alma rima tua dolce e ripleta
   De l'alta symphonia che mi confonde,
   Move dal pegaseo sì suave unde
   Che di gustarle omai sempre mi asseta.
Ma quando ad humiltà tanto discende
   Che'l mio stil basso al summo Hyperïone
   Extolle tra i cantor che'l canto extolse,
Non me puote honorar, ma son coronee
   Et vostre alme virtù che tanto splende
   Quanto largir tra noi Peana volse.

31   Sed posteaquam binos fere per annos in civitate tum privatus tum consulari potestate sevir ⟨di⟩versis in rebus egregie se exercuerat, ad navigationem iterum intentus navim conscendit, suis nonnullis et Petri olim patroni sui mercemonialibus rebus advectis; et denique Lucinio Brunellio praefecto per Liburneam Tharsatica Seniaque visis Siciliam iterum revisit, nobilissimam insulam. Sed antea in Calabris Scyllaceum conscenderat celebre promuntorium.

32   Exinde Aethnaeo praecelso et fumifero Sycaniae monte procul inspecto, Thauromenium venerat, arduum atque vetustissimum oppidum, ubi et ingentia plura vetustatum monumenta conspexit; et inde Scyllaea rursus immania per vada, porthmo iterum formidabili superato, Messanam praeclarissimam civitatem revisit; et Pellaeo deinde promuntorio remenso Panormum venit, antiquam et insignem Sycilliae urbem, ubi exonerata abietibus nave plerosque per dies versatus est. Et ipsa in amplissima urbe primarios inter et generosissimos viros Jacobo Pizinga, Rogerio Spatafora equiti et Ioanni de Vintimillia comiti honorifica se familiaritate coniunxit, quibus cum humanissimis viris nobiles scenas, quas Toccos dicunt, sacra et superis ornatissima templa et magnificentissimi Armirati Clari Montis insignia regia vidimus, et

For your noble rhymes, so sweet and so full
of that elevated concord that confounds my senses,
move from the Pegasean font waves so enticing
that ever do I thirst to taste them.

But when they descend so lowly
as to praise my base style up to mighty Hyperion,
among the singers that the song extolled,

they can do me no honor, but they are crowns
and yours, noble virtues, that shine forth so greatly,
so greatly as Apollo wished to bestow them among us.

After nearly two years in Ancona, where he was variously en- 31
gaged both in his private affairs and as one of the six *anziani* of
the city, he decided to go to sea again; so having loaded a ship,
commanded by Lucinio Brunelli, with his own and his old master
Pietro's merchandise, he sailed via Liburnia, sighting Rijeka and
Senj[19] and returned once more to the noble island of Sicily, disem-
barking on the way at Squillace in Calabria and climbing its promontory.

Then after a distant view of the lofty, smoking volcano of 32
Etna, he arrived at the steep and ancient town of Taormina,
where he inspected many large, ancient monuments; next, having
once more negotiated the dangerous straits of Scylla, he revisited
the splendid city of Messina; and finally, turning the headland
of Pella, he fetched up at the ancient and splendid Sicilian city
of Palermo, where he unloaded his cargo of fir trees and made
a stay of many days. Among the leading nobility of this great
city he was honorably and cordially received by Iacopo Pizinga,
Ruggiero Spadafora, knight, and Count Giovanni da Ventimi-
glia,[20] in whose humane company we inspected[21] the fine porticoes
known as the Tocci, the richly decorated churches, the splendid
palace of the Grand Admiral Chiaramonte and the remarkable

conspicuum in arce regiumque sancti Petri sacellum lapidum por-
phyritum et mirae artis musaycae perornatum.

33   Sed extra civitatis moenia uberos inter et melifluos campos
apud Montem Regalem conspicuam et insignem viderat Beatae
Virginis aedem, in qua ornatissimas ex aere portas et nobile de
marmore claustrum vidit et preciosa optumi Guglielmi aliorumque regum monumenta. Praeterea Clarissima in Valle repositum
Sancti Martini pontificis monasterium una optumo cum viro et
amicissimo nostro Trintio Foroflaviniano vidit, et deinde secus
praefatam urbem Alcimon, nobile Bernardi Emcaprarei et inex-
pugnabile oppidum, inspexit.

34   Et denique Panormum remeantes, cum ibi navis illa aeris alieni
causa venundata mansisset et per idem tempus in Panormitano
portu quattuor Venetum onerariae triremes, Nicolao Donato imperatoria potestate praefecto, ex Britannia Venetias repetentes applicuissent, Kiriacus a Panormo quam celeriter expeditus, hisdem
longis navibus, rebus suis impositis, triremem Iohanni Magnimpe-
rio patrono conscendens, Venetias petiere.

35   Et ex itinere in Illyrico, cum Iaderam insignem Liburnorum
urbem venissent, ibidem Sanctum Venerium equitem clarum et
Petrum Loredanum insignem virum pro Venetis ea in civitate correctores convenimus, a quis perhumane et honore eximio suscepti,
primum de Martini quinti pontificis maximi in synodo Con-
stantiensi creatione, ut laetum unionis nuntium, laete grateque
perceperant.

36   Sed postea Venetiis cum applicuissent, Kiriacus exoneratis navibus expediri se quam primum operam dedit, et e mercibus aere
exacto, Anconem et ad suos incolumis remeavit, cum alii ex navigatione socii per Neapolim terrestri itinere patriam per multa in-
commoda revisissent.

Royal Chapel of St. Peter in the palace with its porphyry marble and marvelously worked mosaics.

At Monreale, in the fertile, mellifluous countryside outside the walls of Palermo, he visited the remarkable Church of the Blessed Virgin and admired its ornate bronze doors, its noble marble cloister and its fine monuments of William and other Norman kings. He also, in the company of our common friend, Trintio Foroflaviniano, inspected the monastery of St. Martin in Chiaravalle and the nearby impregnable town of Alcimon,[22] the seat of Bernardo Emcaprareo. 33

Finally, they returned to Palermo to find that their ship had been sold to cover its owner's debts. Four Venetian shipping galleys, however, on their voyage home from England, under the high command of Niccolò Donato, had just arrived in the port, and Cyriac as quickly as possible loaded his goods into them, himself boarded the galley owned by Giovanni Magnimperi and thus left Palermo for Venice. 34

On the way home up the Dalmatian coast they stopped at Liburnian Zadar and we[23] met and were graciously received by the Venetian representatives there, Santo Venier, knight, and Pietro Loredan,[24] who gave them the first news — a happy augury for the reunification of the Church — of the election of Martin V as pope by the Council of Constance.[25] 35

In Venice he did all he could to get his merchandise unloaded from the ships as speedily as possible and to sell it. This done, he returned safely to his family in Ancona, while his other associates in the voyage had made a hard land journey home by way of Naples. 36

37   At enim vero postea quam per dies in patria cum suis moratus est, desiderans denique Bizantium magnamque Constantinopolitanam civitatem ⟨videre⟩, onerariam navim Pasqualino patrono et consanguineo suo scriba Kiriacus ipse conscendit et tandem, Illyrico superato, Liburneis Dalmateisque plerisque insulis visis, ad Illyrici sinus fauces Suasnam et Ceraunia Epyri promuntoria Idibus Septembribus advenere. Exinde Corcyram ad insulam coryphaeas *Phaeacum et aereas arces* videre. Inde Cephalonicas Zacintheasque insulas et Leucatae formidabile promuntorium conspexere et demum per Ionicum Strophades, antiquas et memorabiles Arpiarum domos procul adnavigantes videre. Et Mallea denique promuntoria superantes, Peloponesiaca montana Archadiae prope colles visa posthabitaque, Cythara procul inspecta, et sparsas per Aegaeum insulas transfretantes, sacram inter Cycladas et nobilissimam Dellon vatidici Apollinis insulam invisere. Exinde Miconem inter et Tinem transeuntes, Lesbeam secus insulam transvecti, Tenedum ad Hellesponti fauces conspexere, et angustum fretum die noctuque transmeantes, hinc Asiae Frigiaeque fines radebant, hinc pinguem prope conspexerant Europam. Et ibi primum ad dexterum Thraciae littus Hellesponticam, Caliepolim prope, dirruptam vetustate Sexton venere, ubi primum Kiriacus pileatos et longipedes Teucros inspexit; et demum, Lelio Freducio egregio negociatore curante, expeditis rebus concedentes, inde Propontiacum per aequor Proconesiam videre procul, marmoream insulam, et tandem Bizantium Threiciam et insignem ad Bosphorum civitatem incolumes Nonis Octobribus applicuere.

38   Ubi posteaquam insigni et amplissimo in portu consederant, Kiriacus primum ea in urbe convenerat Philippum Alpherium, consanguineum suum et egregium ibi pro Anconitanis civibus consulem, quo duce quaeque civitatis insignia et imperatoriam Manuellis Palaeologi maiestatem vidit.

Cyriac then remained at home with his family for some time,   37
but, desiring at last to see the great Byzantine city of Constantinople, he embarked as clerk on a merchant ship chartered by
his relative, Pasqualino. They sailed past Illyria seeing many
Liburnian and Dalmatian islands on the way and arrived on the
thirteenth of September at Saseno[26] and the Epirote promontory
of Acroceraunia, at the jaws of the Illyrian Gulf. The next leg of
their voyage gave them views of the Phaeacians' steep and "aery
citadels"[27] of Corfu, the islands of Cephalonia and Zante, and the
dangerous promontory of Leukas, the Strophades in the Ionian
Sea, the fabled, ancient home of the Harpies, which they saw
from afar. Then they rounded Cape Mallia and the upland mountains of Arcadia in the Peloponnese, passing Cythera at a distance,
and sailing through the scattered islands of the Cyclades in the
Aegean, went ashore at Delos, the renowned and holy island
of prophetic Apollo. Thence they sailed between Myconos and
Tinos, passed close by Lesbos, had a sight of Tenedos and then,
during a day and a night, passed through the narrow strait of the
Hellespont, where the coast of Asia and Phrygia on the one hand
and fertile coast of Europe on the other come close together. At
the ancient, ruined city of Sestos, near Gallipoli, on the southern
shore of the Hellespont opposite Thrace, they went ashore and
Cyriac had his first sight of the Turks with their turbans and long,
pointed shoes; there, having settled their affairs with the aid of the
excellent merchant, Lelio Freducio, they reembarked, saw the marble island of Proconnesus in the Propontis from a distance, and
finally arrived safely on the seventh of October at the renowned
city of Byzantium on the Thracian side of the Bosporus.

The first man they met in that city, after settling down in the   38
renowned and very spacious port, was Cyriac's kinsman, Filippo
Alfieri,[28] the eminent consul of Ancona in the city, who showed
them some of the sights,[29] a tour during which they saw the emperor, Manuel Paleologus, in all his majesty.

39   Et inde primum ea ex amplissima trigonia urbe viderat ingentia atque nobilia ex cocto latere moenia maritimum a duobus partibus littus alteramque circumdantia terciam et mediterraneam partem; vidit et insignem illam et regiam de marmore Portam Chryseam a divo Theodosio conditam duabus marmoreis turribus munitam; et a facie prima ab extra marmoreae primae parietes ornatae videntur antiquis ex Phidia operibus ibidem ab eo principe aliunde deductis. Ibidem vero arma a Vulcano Achilli Thetidis gratia edita arte fabrefactoris eximia conspectantur, ⟨quae⟩ hinc inde columnis pulcherrimis exornata viderat.

40   Deinde in urbe primum sacra divis ornata atque ingentia delubra, et ante alia insigne illud et maximum a Iustiniano Caesare Divae Sophiae conditum et admirabile templum, ingenti testitudine marmoreisque crustatis parietibus et pavimento conspicuo nec non porphyreis serpentineisque magnis et innumeris sublime columnis viderat; et ante ipsum venerabile templum alta columna Heracleam illam mirificam aeneam equestrem statuam, arduum quippe et conspicuum opus.

41   Sed non longe sublimiori in parte vidit nobile illud hippodromale theatrum marmoreis a capite in convexu columnis epistyliisque perornatum, ac in medio lapideis obilyscis aeneisque draconibus et speculatoriis plerisque marmoreis insigne, sed in primis illum ingentem unico ex Numidico lapide obilyscum Phoenicibus caractheribus omni ex parte insignitum, quem ex Latinis Graecisque litteris Theodosium principem Proculo architecto curante cognoverant erexisse.

42   Viderat et binas deinde per urbem Theodosinas cocleas et insignes de marmore columnas Taurinam Xerolophaeamque eximiae altitudinis; et intra architectorum opere conspicuas et alias plerasque per urbem inspexerat immanes marmoreas porphireasque columnas, nec non aeneas et plurigenum lapidum statuas, basses et epigrammata, nymphaea, fontes et arduos cocto de latere aquae ductus; et denique ornatissima viderat diversa per sacra et

Then he viewed the fine brick walls surrounding the two sides   39
facing the sea and the third one facing inland, of the huge, trian-
gular city, and the splendid, royal Golden Gate with its two marble
towers built by divine Theodosius and adorned on its external,
marble facade with ancient sculptures by Phidias imported by that
emperor from elsewhere. There too he inspected the finely wrought
arms made on behalf of Thetis by Vulcan for Achilles flanked by
beautiful columns.

Next, inside the city, he first inspected its great ornate churches   40
and, especially, the huge and magnificent temple of Hagia Sophia
founded by Justinian[30] with its vast dome, its marble-faced walls,
its remarkable pavement and its numerous tall, weighty porphyry
and serpentine columns, and in front of it the marvelous bronze
equestrian statue of Heraclius,[31] conspicuously placed on the top
of its high column.

A little higher up in the city he saw, too, the noble hippodrome   41
adorned with its convex arrangement of marble columns and architraves at the head, and its stone obelisks and bronze serpents in
the middle, and its many marble stands for the spectators; and
most of all he admired the enormous obelisk made from a single
block of Numidian stone, and inscribed on all sides with hieroglyphs which, as they learned from the Greek and Latin inscriptions below, was erected to the order of the emperor Theodosius
by the architect Proculus.[32]

And after that he saw the two remarkably tall spiral marble   42
columns of Theodosius, one in the Forum Tauri, the other near
the hill of Xerolophos.[33] He saw in the city many other great
and remarkably designed marble and porphyry columns as well as
statues of bronze and various kinds of stone, bases and inscriptions, nymphaea, fountains and lofty brick aqueducts.[34] He also
saw many libraries famous for their many gold-illuminated and

pulcherrima monasteria bybliothecas plerasque Graecis sacris et
gentilibus litteris auro imaginibusque insignes.

43   Exinde alia ex parte ad ulteriorem portus ripam viderat Galatheam illam Peram, nobilem pulcherrimamque in conspectu
Constantinopolitanae urbis coloniam, turritis moenibus, aedibus
sacris negociatoriis scenis, praetoriis et altis undique civium pala-
tiis perornatam. Cuiusce portus et optimi emporii littus frequens
cetearum onerarium navium multitudo compleverat.

44   Deinde vero Kiriacus rebus exactis eadem cum navi Anconem
iterum patriam remenso aequore remeavit. Ubi posteaquam apud
suos per aliquot tempus moratus fuerat, Polam antiquissimam in
Histria secus Italiae fines civitatem visere cupiens, naviculum conscendit et Illyrico transfretato eam ipsam venerat Polensium civitatem, quam magna ex parte dirruptam vetustate conspexerat. Sed
nobilia pleraque suae antiquitatis vestigia vidit. Et Salviae Postu-
miae Sergi duoviri aedilis clari filiae egregias portas et aedificia
pleraque ingentia viderat, et nobile ac magnis editum lapidibus
amphitheathum, quod Polenses voti sui compotes Lucio Septimio
Severo et Antonino divis et caesareis fratribus dicavere; viderat et
innumera per urbem et extra ad mare usque lapidea sepulchra,
quorum pleraque nobilia exceperat epigrammata, Andrea Contareno tum pro Venetis praetoria potestate comite curante favitanteque.

45   Exinde vero cum paucos post dies Anconem patriam revisisset,
ex ea denique plerisque navigationibus Chion, Calliepolim, Bizantium revisit, Alboneo in Liburnea primo ad mare oppido con-
specto.

46   At et cum in patria diversis intentus negotiis versaretur, et Petro optimo olim patrono suo defuncto, Ioannes Lucae Tollentineus
aromatarius nostra in civitate primarius, mortuo Nicolao Cossi
Florentino qui libros suae societatis mercemonales curabat, ad hos

pictured Greek manuscripts, both sacred and profane, in diverse monasteries.

Then he went over to the farther bank of the port and walked 43 round Galata in Pera,[35] the splendid colony to be seen from the city of Constantinople, across the water, with its turreted walls, its churches, its merchants' warehouses and offices and its many tall public and private palaces. This splendid trading port was crowded with a host of cargo ships.

Finally, having finished his business, Cyriac voyaged back once 44 more in the same ship to his native Ancona, where he stayed for some time. He now had a desire to visit the ancient city of Pola in Istria, close to the Italian frontier, so embarking in a small ship to cross the Illyrian Sea, he arrived there to find the city largely ruined. But he did see many evidences of its noble past, including the splendid gates of Salvia Postumia, the daughter of the aedile Sergius,[36] as well as many large buildings and the fine amphitheater built of large stones that the people of Pola gratefully dedicated to the imperial brothers, Lucius Septimius Severus and Antoninus. He also saw, both inside the city and outside its walls down to the sea, numerous stone tombs, many of whose epitaphs he transcribed,[37] being accompanied and much helped by Andrea Contarini, who was then the Venetian governor of the city.

Then, after these few days in Pola, he returned home to An- 45 cona, after which he made a number of voyages to Chios, Gallipoli, and Byzantium, having previously inspected the coastal city of Labin in Liburnia.

While Cyriac was in Ancona engaged in various business,[38] his 46 old master, Pietro, having died, Giovanni di Luca of Tolentino, the leading spice dealer in the city, engaged him to balance his books, since Niccolò Cossi, a Florentine, the former accountant of the firm, was dead, and since none of his commercial associates was

in finalem calculum redegendos, cum et periti in mercemonalibus
socii illos bene deducere nequivissent, Kyriacum adolescentem
huiusce rei peritum conduxit; qui cum difficile quodammodo esset
et laboriosum opus, nam ad quattuordecimum annum res actae et
interminatae permanserant, omnes tum ingenii praestantia sui Kiriacus ad verum summumque rationis calculum libros egregie ter-
minatos redegit, et Ioanne mortuo heredibus dedit eiusdem.

47   Interea Gabriel Condulmarius, reverendissimus cardinalis Senensis pro Martino quinto pontifice legatus, in Piceni provintia
Anchonem venerat, correctoriam pontificiaque potestate provintiam curaturus, qui cum paucos post dies Anconitanum portum
reparare decrevisset, et ob id civitatis introitus exitusque et aerarii
curatores in melius redigere maluisset, cum plures in urbe aerarii
constituti essent, unum ex omnibus universalem in civitate aerarium deligendum per senatus consultum curavit. Itaque treviri,
quaestores patritios inter cives creati, ratiocinatores quaestorianos
fidos et peritissimos cum tota ex urbe deligere decrevissent, Paulo
Iuliano generali aerario delecto, ratiocinatores Nicolaum Luctare-
lium virum praestantem et hisdem in rebus iam diu exercitatissi-
mum Kiriacumque ipsum adolescentem designavere; quo in nego-
tio ita se diligenter et provide gesserat adolescens, ut expleto
semestri tempore collega abdicato solus ipse magna cum laude tam
diu eo officio praestiterat, quam diu Gabriel ipse nostra in civitate
et provintiae legatione permanserat, auxiliatoribus scribis quos
ipse delegerat adiuvantibus; quo in tempore et fere biennio Kiriacus adolescens ipse publicus omnes eiusdem quaestoriae rei generis libros ac plerosque eiusdem negotii ordines meliorem in formam facilioremque redegit. Ac rem publicam ipsam, multis et
inexplicandis diu gravatam foeneribus et absque Aegidii cardinalis

competent to do the job properly. Cyriac, young as he was, was a skilled accountant, and though it proved a particularly difficult and laborious task, since the ledgers had not been accurately kept and balanced for fourteen years, his superior intellect enabled him to close the books in a thoroughly true and comprehensive fashion and to hand them over to the heirs of Giovanni di Luca, who by this time had died.

Meanwhile, Gabriele Condulmer, cardinal of Siena and legate   47
of Pope Martin V, had arrived in Ancona to become rector of the province of Piceno on behalf of the Holy See; and he very soon resolved to repair the port of Ancona. This involved introducing better regulation of the import and export taxes and of the officers of the treasury; and the cardinal caused the senate to decree that one single treasurer should be elected in place of the existing system of several city treasurers. Accordingly, a board of three men constituted from among the wellborn citizens to control the finances, decreed that trustworthy and experienced accounting officers should be chosen from among the whole population, having already elected Paulo Giuliano to be general treasurer. And the accounting officers they chose were: Niccolò Luttarelli, who had been an excellent financial officer for a long time, and the young Cyriac, who performed his task with such diligence and foresight that his colleague stood down after six months, leaving him to carry on alone — a duty he performed to the satisfaction of all, with the help of assistant clerks chosen by himself, so long as Gabriele remained in the city as legate of the province. The young Cyriac was in this office for almost two years, and during that time he reduced all the financial records and many of the financial regulations to a better and more convenient form; and he also, by his extraordinary attention and industry, with the assistance of a number of leading citizens, freed the city from a large number of

tempore, sua potissimum cura et industria, civibus plerisque optumis iuvantibus, potissima ex parte liberavit.

48   Etenim cum Gabriel cardinalis Martino iubente pontifice Flamminiae provintiae legatus Bononiam concessiset, Kiriacus se statim nostro sexviratu coram sponte abdicavit officio, cum non hisdem vulgaribus torpescere et implicari negotiis sed potius eum ad orbem omni ex parte visendum generosus animus concitabat. Atque cum, paulo anteaquam ex Ancone legatus Gabriel excesisset, Seraphinus Urbinas ⟨et⟩ Memmius Gazarius Senensis, iurisconsulti ac primarii apud legatum praestantioresque viri et summa cum Kiriaco benivolentia coniuncti, pleraque invicem materni eloquii carmina misissent, ad hanc ipsam orbis explorationem fatalem adolescentis animum excitarunt; quorum potissima eum inter et Seraphinum missa hisce reponenda delegi, et haec quae primum Kiriacus Seraphino misit:

49   Quel spirito gientil, che Amor conserva
          Nella presaga mente al suo camino,
          Me pinse al summo del colle apollino,
          L'orme seguendo d'una biancha cerva,
      Dove Thersicor con la sua caterva
          Scorsi d'intorno al fonte caballino
          Condur in forma humana un seraphino
          Coperto da le fronde di Minerva.
      Indi veder uscir di tal fontana
          Diana nuda in come a l'aura sparte
          Mi parve, e sotto un lauro Daphne e Peana;
      Poi d'un boscheto uscir Venere e Marte
          E, vista di costui la fronte humana,
          Cingierla e coronarla di lor arte.

unexplained interest-bearing debts that had gravely burdened it
since the time of Cardinal Egidio.³⁹

But when Cardinal Gabriele, at Pope Martin's behest, left An-   48
cona for Bologna to become legate in the province of Flaminia,⁴⁰
Cyriac at once tendered his resignation to the six *anziani* of the
city; for his noble spirit, no longer content to risk stagnation in
these common involvements, now impelled him, rather, to travel
and to see the whole world. Shortly before the legate Gabriele departed from Ancona, two of the senior lawyers on his staff, Serafino of Urbino and Memmio Gazario of Siena, with whom Cyriac
had struck up a warm friendship, exchanged Italian poems with
him; and these friends further aroused the young man's feeling
that his destiny was to explore the world. Here, then, I quote
some of the best of these poems exchanged between him and Serafino, beginning with one from Cyriac:

That gentle spirit, which Love keeps,   49
   in his all-seeing mind, on the chosen path,
urged me to the peak of the Apollonian mount,
   in pursuit of the tracks of a white doe.
There, Terpsichore with her troop
   did I see, round about the equine font,
lead a Seraphim in human guise,
   who was covered in the boughs of Minerva.
Here it seemed to me that from this font I saw
   naked Diana issue forth with windblown locks,⁴¹
and underneath a laurel tree Daphne and Apollo;
   then from a thicket Venus and Mars emerge,
and seeing of the Seraphim the human brow,
   encircle it and crown it with their art.

50   Quibus peregregie deinde talia Seraphinus ipse respondit:

Le rissonante rime in chui si serva
    Omne habito suppremo et pellegrino
    Che me corona, e fra'l ceto divino
    Con summa intelligentia me preserva,
Ricerchan miglior lyra e miglior nerva,
    Simile a quelle di Dante o Petrarchino.
    Ma quanto può mio ingiegno picolino,
    Rengratio prima, et priego che proterva
Fortuna e invidia te ritrovi vana
    sì, che i posterior legan tue carte
    E la tua fama resti integra e sana.
Tanto duri il tuo nome in omne parte,
    Quanto si moverà l'opra mondana
    E vegia nei dì nostri laurearte.

51   Ad quae ilico mutato et invicem alternato versus ordine repli-
cando respondit:

Qual circuncinto in oro fin rubino,
    In cui raggio di sol fulgente serva,
    O qual diamante di magior conserva,
    Perla, ballasso, smiraldo o zaphino,
Qual chiare stelle in color celestino,
    Rose con zigli verdigianti in herva,
    Più vaghe si miran con l'alma serva
    Dal primo senso human per color fino,
Tal nel secondo fia quasi coharte
    L'alme al sentir de la diva e soprana
    Tua rima digna di perpetuarte.

Whereupon Serafino replied with an excellent sonnet: 50

The resounding rhymes in which you have enclosed
every supreme and rare quality
which encrowns me, and in the company of the Immortals
with great intelligence, have enshrined me,
    require response from a better lyre and greater vigor,
like those of Dante and of our Petrarch;
but as my small intellect is able to do,
I firstly give you thanks, and pray that you may find
    contrary Fortune and Envy so powerless against you,
that future generations will bind your works
and your reputation remain whole and unharmed.
    May your name last in every country
for as long as worldly creation has movement
and may I see you in our lifetime with the laurel crowned.

To which, changing the order of the rhymes, Cyriac rejoined: 51

As a fine ruby when in gold encased,
wherein a ray of the flashing sun is locked,
or as a diamond amid a mighty store
of spinel, emerald, sapphire, or pearl,
    as the bright stars against heaven's blue,
as roses and lilies in the green-leaved grass
more keenly are admired for their color fine
when the soul's in thrall to the first human sense,
    so by the second sense is the soul almost compelled
to listen to your poems, divine, transcending all,
and worthy to raise you to the eternal stars.

E benché da me volli alta e luntana
　　Sua voce, pure al son compresi in parte
　　Esser via digna più che Mantuana.

52　　Quibus et talia utique Seraphinus eodem carminis ordine dicta remisit:

Bench'io comprehenda esser venuto al chino
　　Il viver nostro in cui virtù si enerva,
　　E veggia l'età nostra facta serva
　　De vicii e de ignorantia, pur oppino
Che'l celico motor, che è tutto pino
　　Di voler iusto e sancto, a te risserva
　　Resuscitar le Muse e sua catherva
　　⟨Per⟩ decreto ⟨di⟩ spirital distino.
Dovunque l'acque Adriace ne fian sparte,
　　O circuisse anchor l'onda occeana,
　　Veggio celebre via per eternarte.
Fuggi la turba inerte e tanto insana,
　　Che vol ne l'altre cure enlaquearte,
　　E fa' la mente tua da lor prophana.

Quae quidem vatisona amicissimi hominis dicta innatam sibi generosam animi cupiditatem perbellissime confirmarunt.

53　　Verum eodem legati tempore Kiriacus suo ab amicissimo Marco Pistoriense, egregio Anconitanae rei scriba, persuasus Latinam intelligere facultatem operam dare coepit; nec, ut saepe novi clerici solent, a primis grammaticae partibus incoharat, sed magno quodam et virili animo, ut et melius Dantis poema, de quo satis eruditus erat, intelligere posset, sextum Maronis librum a Thoma Camaerense grammatico insigni, quem et Senecam dicunt, audire ausus est. Is enim ea tempestate Thomas nostra in civitate

And though to me his voice sounds distant far
still at their sound I understand in part
their worth to be greater than Vergil's art.[42]

And Serafino's answering sonnet followed the same rhyme   52
scheme:

Although I understand that on the downward slope
our human state is set and in it virtue is weak,
and although I see our age become enslaved
to vice and ignorance, yet do I maintain
    that the Mover of the Heavens which is all full
of just and holy will, reserves the task to you
of resuscitating the Muses and their company,
by decree of spiritual destiny.
    Wherever spread the Adriatic waters,
or even where the oceanic wave might lap,
I see the path to make you in fame immortal.
    Flee the diseased and listless mob
That wants to ensnare you in other cares,
And to make your mind profane like theirs.

These prophetic words of his good friend powerfully strengthened
Cyriac's noble, inborn desire.

It was during this time, when the cardinal was still legate in   53
Ancona, that Cyriac, at the instigation of his close friend, Marco
of Pistoia, the secretary of the city, began to pay serious attention
to acquiring facility in Latin. He did not start in the usual be-
ginner's way, with the rudiments of grammar, but, having more
grown-up ambitions and wanting better to understand Dante's
Divine Comedy, of which he already had considerable knowledge,
he was bold enough to begin by reading the sixth book of Vergil's Aeneid with the notable scholar, Tommaso of Camerino,[43]
commonly known as Seneca, who at that time was the professor

43

paedagogus et bonarum litterarum praeceptor publice auditores docebat. Sed eo extra ordinem cum Kiriaco foedere pactus, ut praeceptor ipse discipulo Virgilium, discipulus vero praeceptori ipsi Dantem lectitare deberet. Sed anteaquam invicem rem pactam absoluissent, diverso separati itinere hinc inde se disiunxere. At enim vero Kiriacus, cum divinam illam Maronis facundiam ea qua in parte audierat degustasset, tanto ardore animi ingeniique praestantia Maronis Aeneam ab se omnem percurrere enixe conatus est, ut non modo Virgilii operis elegantiam et facultatem intelligere et familiarem poetam habere coeperat, quin et ab eo latinitatem ipsum facile perdiscere, intelligere exercerique peregregie visus est. Et ut ad Maronis notitiam per Dantis poemata venerat, per Maronem ad Homeri magni poematis Graecaeque facundiae cupiditatem notitiae nobilem convertit animum.

54   Interea cum apud Anconitanum ⟨portum⟩ insignem illum marmoreum divi Traiani Caesaris arcum diligentius inspexisset, mirificum opus admirans, cognovit a superiori parte deficere et auream illam equestrem statuam, quam inclytus olim ille Senatus Populusque Romanus huic optumo principi, huiusce saluberrimi portus providentissimo conditori, conspicuas inter divae Marcianae sororis Plotinaeque coniugis imagines mira quidem architectorum ope dicarat; cuius vero splendentem iconis effigiem ipse deinde optumus imperator huic tam egregiae maritimas inter ad Adriacum civitati civibus omne per aevum honorabile signum gestare regia pro sua liberalitate donavit. Quae hodie per egregia publicaque civitatis loca ac purpurea praetoriana vexilla saepe per Latium et Ausonicas urbes enitescere videntur conspicue. Sed ex eo denique mirifico arcu hoc ipsum epigramma conscriptum est:

and teacher of literature in the city, where he gave regular public lectures. Cyriac arranged with Tommaso to become his private pupil, their arrangement being that Tommaso should read Vergil to him, while he read Dante to Tommaso; but before they had come to the end of their mutual agreement, they had to leave Ancona in different directions and part company. Cyriac, however, found such relish in the divine eloquence of Vergil as far as his study of the poem [with Tommaso] had gone, that he zealously embarked—so keen and capable was his intellectual grasp—on reading the whole of the *Aeneid* on his own. Thus he not only began to comprehend the elegance and mastery of the poem and to become thoroughly familiar with the poet, but also, from his study of Vergil, he admirably learned both to read and to write Latin. And just as Dante's poems had led him to the knowledge of Vergil, so the reading of Vergil aroused in his mind a noble desire to win knowledge of Homer's great poem and of the Greek tongue.

Meanwhile he had been diligently and admiringly studying the splendid marble arch[44] of Trajan Caesar, which stands prominently at the port of Ancona, and he recognized that the upper part of it lacked its original golden equestrian statue, which the ancient Senate and people of Rome, with the help of fine architects, had dedicated to this excellent prince, the farsighted founder of their life-giving port, a statue which was flanked by conspicuous images of his sister, Marciana, and his wife, Plotina. This good emperor, with royal bounty, later bestowed on the citizens of Ancona, which held so prominent a place among the Adriatic ports, the perpetual privilege of bearing a splendid copy of this image as their badge of honor; and we still see it today publicly displayed throughout the city and often adorning the purple standards of Anconitan *podestàs* through the cities of Latium and southern Italy.[45] This is the inscription itself as transcribed from the arch:

54

45

IMP.CAESARI
DIVI NERVAE
TRAIANO.OPT
VMO.AVG.GE
RMANICO.DA
TICO.PONT.MAX
TR.PON.XVIIII.

PLOTINAE.	IMP.IXI.COS.VI.	DIVAE.MARTIANAE.
AVG.	.P.P.PROVIDENT	AVG.
CONIVGI.	ISSIMO.PRINCI	.SORORI.AVG.
AVG.	PI.SENAT.P.Q.R.	
	QVOD.ACCESSVM	
	ITALIAE HOC.ETIA	
	M.ADDITO.EX.PE	
	CVNIA.SVA.PORTV	
	TVTOREM.NAVIG	
	ANTIB.REDDIDERIT.	

Hoc ipsum tam ingens et mirabile architectorumque conspicuum opus, et ipsum et tam grave Latinis insignibus litteris epigramma, generoso Kiriaci adolescentis animo ad reliqua per orbem nobilia vetustatum monumenta perquirenda scrutandaque, ut suo saepius ore percepimus, primum quoddam idoneum atque praedignum seminarium fuerat.

55   Et sic se statim Romam inclytam ad urbem, ut ex ea primum maxima rerum atque potissima nobilium in orbe monumenta videret, quam avidissime contulit, Martino quinto pontifice, eiusdem pontificis anno octavo[4] et ad III Nonarum Decembrium diem, ubi paulo antea Gabriel cardinalis ex Bononia abdicatus legatione venerat. Ad illum Kiriacus apud Sanctum Laurentium in Damasco se contulerat, a quo tempore quam laete benigneque susceptus, quater denos per dies apud eum in urbe moratus, quotidie magnam per urbem niveo suo devectus equo, quicquid tantae

The Senate and
people of Rome [*dedicated this
arch*]
to the foresighted emperor,
Nerva Trajan the Best,
son of the deified Nerva,
conqueror of Germany

To the Empress Plotina Wife of the Emperor — and Dacia, High Priest, with the tribunician power for the nineteenth time [114 CE], proclaimed *imperator* nine times, Consul for the sixth time, because he made the approach to Italy safer for sailors by building this port also at his own expense.[46] — To the deified empress Marciana, sister of the emperor

This remarkable great work of architecture, with its important, well-lettered Latin inscription, was the first, seminal inspiration to Cyriac — and a suitable and eminently worthy one at that — to search out and examine all the other noble memorials of antiquity in the world, as we often heard from his own lips.[47]

It was not long, therefore, before he eagerly set out for the famous city of Rome in order to view the world's greatest and most significant historical monuments. He arrived there on the third of December, in the eighth year of Martin V's pontificate.[48] Shortly before this, Cardinal Gabriele had himself arrived in Rome from Bologna, his legateship being ended; so Cyriac visited him at San Lorenzo in Damaso, when he was joyfully and kindly welcomed. He then stayed for forty days as a guest in the cardinal's house, and he daily rode round the city on his white horse closely and

civitatis reliquum extaret venerandae suae veternitatis, templa, theatra, ingentiaque palatia, thermas mirificas, obyliscos et insignes arcus, aquae ductus, pontes, statuas, columnas, basses, et nobilia rerum epigrammata incredibili diligentia sua viderat, exscrutarat exceperatque et, ut postea ex his quandoque digna conficere commentaria posset, fide quoque suis ordine litteris commendavit.

56   At et cum maximas per urbem tam generosissimae gentis reliquias undique solo disiectas aspexisset, lapides et ipsi magnarum rerum gestarum maiorem longe quam ipsi libri fidem et notitiam spectantibus praebere videbantur. Quam ob rem et reliqua per orbem diffusa videre atque litteris mandare praeposuit, ut ea quae in dies longi temporis labe hominumve iniuria conlabuntur, et memoratu digna visa sunt, penitus posteris abolita non sentiat.

57   Sed enim vero interim cum adolescens ille Martini pontificis nepos, inclytus Antonius Salerni princeps, ad venationem quamdam una cum Aloysio Verme et aliis plerisque ex urbe nobilibus iuxta Salarium pontem ivisset, cardinalis vero humanissimus Kiriacum una cum Petro Baduario affine suo ad eam ipsam venationem inspectandam misit; quibus equitando contigerat ut una cum Agabito Columna viro quoque docto arcum ex Capitolio Severi et Antonini divorum fratrum suspicerent, quibus ultima in parte inscriptum erat:

.OB.REM.PVBLICAM
RESTITVTAM
IMPERIVMQ.
POPVLI ROMANI
PROPAGATVM
INSIGNIBVS

diligently inspecting, examining and taking note of whatever venerable antiquities survived in that great city—temples, theaters, vast palaces, marvelous baths, obelisks, and arches, aqueducts, bridges, statues, columns, bases and historical inscriptions. These he faithfully recorded exactly as they were written, so that some day later on he would be able to put them together properly in his *commentaria*.[49]

It appeared to him, as he looked upon the great remains left   56
behind by so noble a people, cast to the ground throughout the city, that the stones themselves afforded to modern spectators much more trustworthy information about their splendid history than was to be found in books. He accordingly resolved to see for himself and to record whatever other antiquities remained scattered about the world, so that he should not feel that the memorable monuments, which time and the carelessness of men had caused to fall into ruin, should entirely be lost to posterity.

One day at this time the noble young prince of Salerno, Anto-   57
nio, the nephew of Pope Martin,[50] rode out of the city with Luigi dal Verme[51] and a band of other nobles for a hunting expedition near the Salarian Bridge, and the cardinal was kind enough to send Cyriac in the company of his kinsman, Pietro Badoer, to watch it. As they were riding alongside Agapito Colonna, a learned man, they looked up at the arch beside the Capitoline of the imperial brothers Severus and Antoninus to whom there was a dedicatory inscription, the latter part of which said:

> The Senate and People of Rome
> [*dedicated this*]
> because the republic
> was restored
> and the power of the Roman People
> enlarged

VIRTVTIB.

EORVM DOMI FO

RISQ. S.P.Q.R.

Quibus perlectis cum Kiriacus ad Agabitum amice dixisset: pote-
ratne aetas haec iners Romanum principem suscitare quempiam,
cui digne talia inscribenda forent? Qui tum adolescentem inspi-
ciens: hunc ipsum fata puerum nostrae collapsae iam diu civitati
praestare admodo possent, qui ex nobilitate Romana ortus Martinum pontificem patruum favitorem potissimum habet. Ex quo
cum ex venatione domi eodem die revertissent, Kiriacus puero ipsi
Antonio haec statim eundem per Agabitum carmina ab se hac ipsa
de re condita misit:

58

Driza la testa omai, inclyta Roma.
　Mira el tuo Marte e suoi nati gemelli,
　Che fur primi martelli
　A fabricar el cerchio de' tuoi colli.
　Orna e racolli la già inculta coma,
　Ché questi vol che in te si rinovelli
　Fabii, Scipii e Marcelli,
　Che tanto hai çerchi già con gli occhi molli,
E vol che omai ritolli
　Quel sceptro sotto el qual domasti el mondo,
　Che' è 'l don dil summo Iove a Citharea
　Promisso per Aenea.
　Vol che omai torni col gran sexto al tondo
　Quando sotto ogni pondo
　Di tua famiglia due colonne tonde
　Han sostenuto in te l'ultime sponde.

by their outstanding
manly virtues
at home and abroad.[52]

When they had read these words, Cyriac in his friendly way
turned to Agapito and asked, "Could this indolent age of ours have
produced any Roman prince worthy of such an inscription?" Agapito glanced over toward the young prince Antonio and replied:
"The fates may well have given this young man to our long de-
cayed city, for he springs from a noble Roman family and enjoys
the powerful favor of Pope Martin, his uncle." Whereupon that
same day, having returned home from the hunt, Cyriac immediately sent the young prince Antonio, by hand of Agapito, a copy of
verses he had composed on this very subject.[53]

58

Hold up your head at last, O glorious Rome.
Look upon your Mars and his born twins
who were the first hammers
to fabricate the circle of your hills.
Adorn and gather up your long neglected locks,
for Mars wills that in you shall be renewed
Fabii, Scipii and Marcelli,
for whom you have long searched with tear-stained eyes;
    and wills he too that at last you should regain
that scepter under which you tamed the world,
which is the gift of mighty Jove to Cytherea
and by him promised for Aeneas.
He wants you, with great guidance, to turn at last full circle
to the time when two round Columns of your family
supported the world's weight to its furthest reaches.

L'una nel divin foro el summo reggie
    Ha stabillito perché al ministero,
    Che fu concesso a Piero,
    Torni sua sposa al seggio laterano
    Per congregar quella smarita gregie,
    Che, vedendola tanto in adultero
    Star senza sposo vero,
    Serà dispersa al fin del occeano.
Hor l'ha conducto in mano
    Di Martin quinto, al chui governo sancto
    Dil pescator la già submersa nave
    Con quelle summe chiave,
    Che concesse li fu sotto 'l gran manto
    son già drizate intanto
    Che foecundarà sì la fè christiana
    Che al tutto fia submersa la prophana.
L'altra nel temporal human governo
    Ha già directa il nepo suo gientile,
    Che in età puerile
    Monstra dil gran valor pregiati segni,
    Inclyto, illustre prince di Salerno
    Creato; nel suo appetito signorile
    Se dicerne il virille
    Animo ad sugiugar magiori regni,
Che non fu già più degni
    Cesare e gli altri chiari augusti divi
    Per valor, se fortuna al par s' estende.
    Chè s'el ciel destro intende
    Ad exaltar costui tra nostri vivi,
    Convien che anchor si scrivi
    Qual di Severo e di Antonin pregiato:
    'Questo ha l'imperio Roman propagato.'

The one in the sacred forum the highest ruler
has placed, so that to the ministry
which was conceded to Peter
may come back His bride in the Lateran seat;
so as to congregate again that scattered flock,
that, when it sees her living in adultery
without a true spouse,
will scatter to great Ocean's end.
    Now has He given the ministry into the hands
of Martin V, under whose holy guidance
the long-submerged Fisherman's ship,
together with those great keys
which were to him conceded with the papal mantle,
already have new vigor;
for he will so widely propagate the Christian faith
that the profane one will be totally submerged.
    The other Column in human temporal government
has already raised up its gentle offspring
who in his puerile age
gives rare indications of great valor.
Glorious, illustrious prince of Salerno
has he been created; in his lordly bent
is discernible the manly
courage to subjugate greater kingdoms;
    and of no greater worth than he were yet
Caesar and the other bright Augustan deities
for valor, should Fortune similarly exert herself.
For should the propitious heavens intend
to exalt him among our kind,
needs must it yet be said of him
as of Severus and of Antoninus the worthy:
"This one has enlarged the Roman Empire."

Questo fu al mondo dal buono Iove dato,
    Tanto benigno e sì pien di clementia
    Quanto la summa essentia
    Mostrasse in criatura al tempo nostro.
    Prudente, iusto, forte e temperato:
    Da diece stelle che gli dà influentia,
    Sotto la qual pollentia
    De tre che raggia Lui dal divin chiostro,
Sotto il cui splendido ostro
    Risponde in lui cossì viva speranza,
    Ardente carità e pura fede,
    Che d'aquistar mercede
    Più non ricercha la prima possanza,
    Perché quella billanza,
    Che aiusta quanto volgie l'universo,
    Non mai vedrà cambiar del biancho en perso.
Cantion, che speri anchor cantar perfecto
    Quel che preliba de l'alto mistero
    Del buon Romano Impero,
    Che per queste due aspeta el gran ristoro,
    Vatene lieta al prince jovaneto,
    Nepote al summo successor di Piero,
    E con parlar intiero
    Aprigli dil tuo ⟨cor⟩ ogni thesoro,
E se del tuo lavoro
    Volesse pur saper il novo auctore,
    Di' che un suo servitore
    A lui ti manda, che naque in Anchona,
    Amator del honor di sua corona.

            FINIS

This one was to the world given by kindly Jove,
filled with all the goodness and clemency
which the divine Essence
might have to show in a creature of our time.
Prudent, just, strong and temperate:
this, from the ten stars which influence him
under that power of the Three,
that He irradiates from the divine cloister;
    under whose splendid purple
quickens in this one such vigorous Hope,
burning Charity and uncontaminated Faith,
that to gain for him Mercy
the First Power no longer attempts;
because that scale
that adjusts itself as the universe moves,
will never see good become evil.
    O my song, you who yet hope to sing the fulfillment
of the high mystery of the goodly Roman Empire
of which this young man gives us such a foretaste,
the Empire that through these two Columns awaits renewal,
go happily to the youthful Prince,
nephew to Peter's great successor,
and with honest speech
open to him every treasure of your heart.
    And if of your creation
he should yet wish to know the unknown author,
tell him that a servant of his
born in Ancona, to him sends you
for he's a lover of the honor of his crown.
                    THE END

59   Praeterea ubi natalicia humanati Iovis solemnia Martinum per pontificem celebrata conspexerat, et faustum recentis anni principium ab anno salubri milleno quatricenteno quinto atque bis deno eiusdem humanati dei et theogoni Iesu indulgentissimo nomine antiquatae legis ritu circuncisi et antiquis a Latinis bicipitis Iani nomine cultum, Kalendarum Ianuariarum praeclarum diem, Andrea Constantinopolitano, ex praedicatorum ordine theologo insigni et sacri palacii magistro, pontifice coram egregie perorante, dedicatum viderat, exoptatam ad patriam remeavit.

60   Ex itinere Sutrium antiquissimum oppidum, turritum Viterbium eiusque mirificas thermarum aquas inspexit, et apud veterem Ervetum urbem Beatae Virginis aedem de marmore ornatissimam viderat, ex qua conspicuum arte frontespicium ligneumque orchestralem illum insignem atque pulcherrimum chorum maluit conspectare, et aeneas ante portas almae Virginis et angelorum imagines.

61   Sed postquam in patria consederat, cum nova per comitia sevir creatus una cum Paliaresio Pisanello aliisque collegis civibus rem publicam de more curasset, ex Venetiis interea a Zacharia Contareno consanguineo suo litteras accepit, per quas eum in Picenno vel Apulea in mercemonalibus exerceri quaeritabat. Ipse vero quom non ad pecuniae quaestus, sed ad nobiliora semper desiderium habuisset, et ut graecas quandoque litteras perdiscere Homerumve poetam facilius intelligere potest, orientales Graecas vel quascumque ad partes se potius quam in Latio exerceri maluisset, illico exacto magistratu ad Zachariam se Venetiis terrestri itinere contulit, qui cognito iuvenis animo, cum apud Cyprum res plerasque suas et diversa iam diu negotia exerceri habuisset, quibus Petrus praeerat, repetito Venetiis fratre, fratri in insula successorem suis in omnibus peragendis rebus Kiriacum misit; qui eam ob rem potius grate magis ea in parte negotium Kiriacus suscepit, ut quem iam diu celebri fama cognoverat, Ianum inclytum regem Ciprium

On Christmas Day, the feast of Jove incarnate, he saw Pope   59
Martin celebrate Mass and he was still in Rome on January 1, 1425,
the day when Jesus, the son of God made man, was circumcised
under the Old Law and given his most holy name, a day dedicated
by the ancient Romans to two-headed Janus, where he heard a
sermon delivered in the pope's presence by the eminent Domini-
can theologian, Andreas of Constantinople, the master of the papal palace. He then eagerly set off for home.

On his journey back he stopped at the ancient town of Sutri,   60
inspected the marvelous hot baths in the towered city of Viterbo,
and at the venerable city of Orvieto visited the richly adorned,
marble Church of the Blessed Virgin, where he admired its fine,
sculptured facade, its beautifully carved choir stalls, and the statues of the Virgin and angels above its bronze portals.

So he settled down once more in Ancona, where in the new   61
elections he was appointed one of the six *anziani* along with Pagliaresio Pisanello[54] and other colleagues and thus resumed his
active public life. Meanwhile, however, he had received a letter
from his kinsman, Zaccaria Contarini in Venice, begging him to
be his commercial representative in Piceno or Apulia, but since he
was always more interested in grander pursuits than simply financial gain, he preferred to do business in the East, in Greece or
elsewhere, which would give him an opportunity to learn Greek
and better to understand Homer. Accordingly, as soon as his term
of civic office was over, he at once went by overland route to see
Zaccaria in Venice. Zaccaria had long-standing commercial interests of various kinds in Cyprus; and when he heard what the
young man had in mind, he decided to recall his brother, Pietro,
then in charge of affairs in the island, to Venice, and sent Cyriac
with full authority to take his place. This commission Cyriac took
up all the more gladly, because it would allow him personally to
meet Janus, the king of Cyprus,[55] whom he had previously known

praesentia videre, et sua quandoque gratia regiaque benivolentia et consuetudine honeste quaesita potiri atque perfrui posset.

62   Itaque a Zacharia litteris ad fratrem Petrum acceptis, cum Anconem illico remeasset, paratam navim Nicolao Corseducio patrono conscendit et per Apuleam Monopolium Bariumque et Anterium collapsum vetustate oppidum vidit. Inde vero Bizantium venit, ubi navigium ad Cyprum Syriamve navigaturum expectans, primum Graeca litterarum principia modico ex tempore cognovit.

63   Sed enim interea quom Anconitanam quandam navim onerariam Benevenuto Scotigolo praefecto apud Chium insulam adventasse intelligeret, exinde Syriam petituram, Kiriacus ad eam se statim contulit; quem patronus ipse et negociatores in ea euntes Franciscusque Ferretri, viri Anconitani nobiles, quam laeto vultu animoque susceperant, et eo ipso curante iuvene Francisco erudito, Kiriacus honesta secum Andreolo Iustiniano, viro Maonensium praestantiae doctoque et dilligentissimo vetustatum cultori, benivolentia et consuetudine iunxerat, quo cum optumo viro pleraque vetustatis vestigia epigrammataque nobilia Graeca Latinaque collegerat; et ibidem eo potissimum intercedente, regium illum Graecum pulcherrimumque Novi Testamenti codicem viginti aureorum precio emit.

64   Expedita sed enim interea navi, et Kiriacus Nicolao Alpherio consanguineo suo curante suis confectis rebus, Syriam inde petentes per Aegaeum crebras inter insulas, Rhodum nobilem olim in Asia insulam applicuere. Et ex ea deinde haud mora concedentes Zephyro sufflante secundo Birutum venere, ubi exoneratis rebus Kiriacus se statim Damascum nobilissimam contulit mediterraneam Syriae atque vetustissimam civitatem, ubi Hermolao

only by reputation, and because it would give him a legitimate opportunity to seek and enjoy the king's gracious favor and company.

So carrying Zaccaria's letter to the latter's brother, Pietro, he at 62
once returned to Ancona and set sail in a ship owned by Niccolò
Corsedacio, which was ready to leave the port, going ashore in
Apulia at Monopoli, Bari, and the ancient ruined town of Anterium.[56] He thus arrived at Byzantium, where it did not take him
long to learn the rudiments of Greek while he was waiting for a
ship bound for Cyprus or Syria.

Before this vessel arrived, however, he heard that an Anconitan 63
ship, commanded by Benvenuto Scotigolo,[57] had put in at the island of Chios, intending to sail on to Syria. Cyriac, therefore, immediately sailed south to Chios, where he was very cheerfully
welcomed by the Anconitan nobles who were taking passage in the
ship—the owner himself, a number of merchants, and Francesco
Ferretti;[58] and it was through the introduction of the scholarly
young Francesco that he now began his close and intimate friendship with Andreolo Giustiniani,[59] a prominent and learned member of the Genoese Maonensian company on the island, along
with whom he recorded in his notebook many antique remains
and fine Greek and Latin inscriptions. On Chios, with the valu-
able help of Andreolo, he was able to buy for twenty gold pieces
his beautiful Greek codex of the New Testament.

When the ship was ready to sail and Cyriac had settled his own 64
affairs with the help of his kinsman, Niccolò Alfieri, they shaped
their course through the clustered Aegean islands for Syria, landing first at the once-renowned Asiatic island of Rhodes, and
thence continuing their voyage without delay before a favorable
west wind to Beirut, where the cargo was unloaded. Cyriac himself immediately struck inland to visit the ancient and renowned
Syrian city of Damascus, where, under the guidance of the

Donato Veneto patricio claro et inibi eo tempore negociatorum omnium praestantissimo nec non eruditissimo viro curante favitanteque, omnia tam amplissimae urbis egregia vetera novaque viderat.

65   Sed extra civitatis moenia sunt apostoli Pauli monumenta nostri, vicumque rectum, et dirruptam Annaniae prophetae casam, Ioannisque Damasceni doctoris beatissimi templum insigne, praeterea nobilem et turritam praecelsis moenibus arcem; sed omnia fere vetusta inter moenia aedificia Athemir begh potentissimo Persarum rege collapsa et solo aequata videntur. Viderat utique deinde nonnullas antiqua ab arce Sydonum reliquias, et aenea pulchra auro argentoque permista vasa mira et expolita fabrefactorum arte conspicua, e quibus ab eo empta quaedam sua inter eiusdem generis supellectilia vidimus. Vidit et ibi ingentem camelorum copiam advenisse, qui tum ex Arabica Felici Sabaeisque partibus et Gedrosiis multa plurigenum specierum aromata mercemonii causa Damascenum ad insigne emporium deferebant.

66   Erat ea in civitate praeterea vir quidam dives opum et negociator primarius nomine Musalach, qui filios saepe mercaturae causa ad Aethiopas et Indos mittere solitus. Kiriaco illas quandoque partes adire desideranti binos a Sabaeis nuper remeantes ostendit. Et cum expeteret ex his bonam sibi societatem dare, quam libere pollicitatus est.

67   Sed interea cum expeditus inde Byruthum remeasset navimque et socios revisisset, navis denique expedita Anconem repetit. Kiriacus vero per Tripolim Genuensi nave subvectus, Cypriam Amocestem venit, ubi Evangelistem de Imola physicum doctum et Zachariae nostri amicissimum convenit. Ex quo cum intelligeret Petrum paulo ante rebus sine ordine relictis Venetias navigasse,

Venetian patrician, Ermolao Donato, at that time the leading merchant there and a learned man in his own right, he viewed all the important ancient and modern monuments in that magnificent city.[60]

Outside the walls, also, there are the Street Called Straight and the ruined house of the prophet Ananias, both memorials of our St. Paul the Apostle, as well as the famous church of the blessed doctor, St. John Damascene; and he saw the fine, high-walled and towered citadel; but nearly all the buildings within the ancient walls had been destroyed by the powerful Persian king, Athemir Bey,[61] and leveled to the ground.[62] He also saw a number of antiquities from the ancient citadel of Sidon along with a beautiful collection of wonderfully wrought Damascene vases inlaid with gold and silver, some of which he purchased for his own collection of *objets d'art* at home, where I have seen them myself. Another sight was the enormous number of camels that had come from southern Arabia, Yemen and Baluchistan, laden with many kinds of spices to be marketed in that remarkable city.

In Damascus Cyriac met a rich and prominent merchant called Musalach who regularly sent his two sons to trade in Ethiopia and India. Since Cyriac very much wanted to visit these places, Musalach introduced him to his sons, who were just then back from Yemen. And when Cyriac asked that he be allowed to associate himself with them [when next they went], Musalach readily complied.

But meanwhile, when he had finished his business in Damascus and returned to Beirut, visiting his ship and companions there, the ship, its business completed, returned to Ancona. But Cyriac himself then boarded a Genoese ship bound for Tripoli and disembarked at Famagusta in Cyprus,[63] where he met the learned natural philosopher,[64] Evangelista de Imola, a great friend of Zaccaria Contarini, who told him that Pietro, Zaccaria's brother, had

65

66

67

ipso Evangelista suadente constituit ibidem manere dum a Zacharia litteras et suis in rebus ordinem haberet. Et interim ne tempus omni ex parte vacuum amitteret, praefecti urbis vicarius electus, cum ibi magistratum praetoria potestate gessisset binos fere per menses, Romanas sibi leges et omnia iuris consultorum egregia dicta tum primum videre lectitareque non sine incremento peritiae et oblectatione contigerat. Nam eo tempore causas, solum origine legum inspecta, laudatissime dixit, nec non civibus concordiam et quietem imponere operam solertissimam dedit.

68   Sed e Venetiis demum acceptis a Zacharia litteris, per quas rem suam agere Kiriacum vehementer angebat, licentia ab eo magistratu non sine difficultate impetrata, Leucosiam regiam civitatem pergit. Ubi primum serenissimam Iani regis maiestatem visere se contulit, quem posteaquam inclytum principem viderat atque praeclare loquentem audierat, perbella praesentia clarum suum et eximiae laudis nomen superatum cognovit. Qui splendidissimus rex cum Kiriacum vidisset et eleganter regiis suis de laudibus casibusque perorantem audierat, eum primum quam laeto vultu animoque perbenigne suscepit; et Bandino de Nores Hugoneque Soltaneo equitibus regiis et primariis in aula suis adstantibus Kiriacum ipsum honorifice statim sua regia familiaritate decoravit, ac optimatum suorum numero regio de more socium aggregavit.

69   Nec non Zachariae in rebus ex quibusque suis agendis regium omne suum auxilium obtulerat; Kiriacus vero, maiestati suae gratiae actae datis deinde ex Zacharia litteris, Lodovici Corarii Venetum vicebaioli auctoritate a Petro Berardino Leonelloque actore rebus Zachariae Petrique fratris omnibus acceptis, ita res ipsas per civitatem et extra diligentia solertiaque sua peregerat, ut nondum expleto anno negotium omne suum expleverat, debitores creditores in chalchulum et paucissimos numero redegit.

recently sailed back to Venice leaving things in great disorder. Cyriac, therefore, on Evangelista's advice, decided to stay in Famagusta until he received word from Zaccaria telling him what arrangements he wanted made. Meanwhile, to fill in the time, he got elected vicar of the Genoese *podestà* of the city, holding office for nearly two months, during which time he took pleasure in his first study of the rules and important opinions laid down in the Roman law books, thereby increasing his skill as a magistrate. He admirably pronounced judgments on the basis of the ancient legal texts alone and skillfully devoted himself to the task of creating concord and peace among the citizens.

But then Zaccaria's letter at length arrived from Venice, anxiously urging Cyriac to take his affairs in hand, so he proceeded on to Nicosia, having had some difficulty in getting leave to resign his office. His first visit in Nicosia was to King Janus, its serene ruler; and he had only to see and hear the king speak to recognize that his impressive personality outshone the renown of his name, while the king himself, attended in his hall by the royal knights, Badin de Nores[65] and Hugo Saltani and other notables, having listened to Cyriac's words of praise and his eloquent discussion of the king's recent misfortunes,[66] cheerfully and graciously welcomed him and regally admitted him to the company of his principal courtiers.

The king offered all his royal help with those of Zaccaria's affairs that needed settling; and Cyriac tendered to His Majesty Zaccaria's letter and thanked him for his gracious favor. Cyriac then, with the authorization of Lodovico Corario, the Vice-Bailie of the Venetians, took over all Zaccaria's and his brother Pietro's business from their agents, Pietro Berardino and Leonello, and administered it so diligently and skillfully, both inside and outside the city, that he completed the whole task within a year, having made an accurate list of debtors and creditors and having reduced them to a very small number.

70   Sed interim vero saepius inclyto cum rege ad venationes exercendas totam fere insulam exploravit. Et quod ad tam clari principis cumulum claritatis accedit, hoc loco praetereundum non duxi. Nam, ut e suis novimus litteris, dum rex ipse suo stipatus nobili comitatu aequos degens per campos perque colles et *invia lustra* varias inter feras aliferas exercens pardos, adeo se laetus in auro, arcu pharetrisque insignis gerebat, *qualis* olim pulcher *Apollo* per *hibernam Liciam aut per iuga Cynthi* suos *exercere choros* venabulis in armis splendidissimus conspectabatur.

71   Sed enim vero insuper pro bona Kiriaci fortuna, cum ex quadam felici pardorum venatione onustus praeda ad villam quandam se rex inclytus recepisset, et nobilem quendam ex Dacia iuvenem equestris ordinis insignibus decorasset, Kiriacus ad vetustum quoddam monasterium pergens, et libros de more perquirens, abiectos inter et longa squalentes vetustate codices antiquam Homeri Iliadem comperit, quam cum laetus cognovisset, non facile a monaco litterarum ignaro tetravangelico intercedente volumine comparavit. Liber enim ille primum et praedignum Kiriaco auxilium fuit Graecas non omnes litteras ignorare. Habuit et deinde alio a chalochiero in Leucosia Odissiam et Euripidis plerasque tragediasque ac Theodosii grammatici Alexandrini vetustatum codicem, quae omnia, dum aliquod dabatur ociolum, percurrere intelligereque operam diligentissimam dabat.

72   Etenim cum exactis rebus ab insula discedere decrevisset, pro digno de se munere regi optimo hoc sibi ponendae dicandaeque statuae inscribendum epigramma reliquit:

> .IANO.CLEMENTIS
> SIMO.PRINCI
> PI.OPTIMO
> NOBILISSQVE.HIER
> VSALEM CYPRI

During this period Cyriac often went hunting with the king   70
and was able to explore most of the island; nor should I omit to
mention what a brilliant spectacle this brilliant prince presented
on these occasions. For we have Cyriac's own description of how
the king, brightly dressed in gold, and armed with bow and quiver,
would ride with his company through fields and hills and trackless
glades, startling the birds as he chased his panther prey, just as
bright Apollo, armed with his hunting spear, dazzled the eye as he
was seen leading his singing band in wintry Lycia or through the
Cynthian uplands in days of old.[67]

In Cyprus too Cyriac made a particularly lucky find. After a   71
good day's hunting panthers, the king, laden with the kill, arrived
at a hunting lodge where he conferred knighthood on a Dacian
youth; and Cyriac, on his usual search for books, went to a certain
old monastery where, among its squalidly kept and long neglected
manuscripts, he was overjoyed to discover an ancient codex of Homer's *Iliad*, which he persuaded an illiterate monk, not without
difficulty, to let him have in exchange for a Gospel book. This
book afforded him his first great help in overcoming his ignorance
of Greek literature. Later on, in Nicosia, from another monk, he
also acquired an *Odyssey*, a number of the tragedies of Euripides,
and a book of antiquities by the Alexandrian grammarian, Theodosius;[68] and whenever he found a moment of leisure, he would
pore over the task of construing and reading them through.

At last, when he had finished his business, he decided to leave   72
the island, and as a worthy parting gift he composed the following
inscription for a proposed statue of the king:

The people
of Cyprus
dedicated [*this statue*]
to Janus,
the generous,

ARMENIAEQVE.
.REGI.
POPVLVS.CYPRIVS
QVOD SVA INSVPE
RABILI.VIRTVTE
PERENNI CONS
TANTIA.ET.LON
GANIMITATE RE
GNVM.PIENTISSI
MVM HOC PLVRI
FARIAM NEFAN
DORVM
IMMANITATE
INFESTISSIMISQVE
COLLAPSVM
PRAELIIS
BARBARICA
DENIQVE.
INCVRSIONE
SVBLATA
RESTI
TV
I
T

73   Postea vero concedens ab eo per Amacosten, navim quandam
Genuensium conscendens, suis Zachariaeque rebus abductis,
Rhodum venit, ubi posteaquam per dies consederat, invenit inter
primos et digniores homines Boetium Tollentinensem optimum
heremitani ordinis theologum et metropolitaneum Rhodianae ecclesiae pontificem, qui eum ut eadem ex provintia virum pergrate
vidit. Et eo duce Kiriachus aliam ibi cognoverat et honorificam
benivolentiam vendicarat Fantini Quirini, Rhodiana religione

excellent
and noble prince,
king of Jerusalem,
Cyprus and Armenia,
because by his invincible bravery,
his constant determination
and his magnanimity
he restored this devoted kingdom
[*which had*] collapsed
from a multiple enormity
of horrors and hostile battles
by finally destroying
the barbarian attack.[69]

Then he left Cyprus by way of Famagusta, where he loaded his   73
own and Zaccaria's goods and embarked on a Genoese ship that
brought him to Rhodes. After a few days there he met, among
other notables, the Augustinian theologian, Boezio of Tolentino,
metropolitan bishop of Rhodes, who was delighted to greet him as
a fellow countryman from the same part of Italy. Boezio in turn
introduced him to Fantino Quirini,[70] most reverend brother of the
religious order of the Knights of Rhodes; and under the guidance

equestris ordinis venerandissimi fratris, quibus iuvantibus multa
per civitatem et extra per insulam vidit vetustatum nobilia monumenta antiqua, moenia, columnas, statuas, bases et Doricis litteris
epigrammata, e quis plebis sacerdotis marmoreum caput, Vene-
ream statuam, et Liberi patris imaginem, quas a Graeco calohiero
tum forte defossas emerat et per Bartholomoeum sororium Anconem ad patriam misit, cum is navi quadam Anconitana Bonifacio
patrono Hierosolima petens Rhodum applicuisset. Viderat ibi
praeterea loci eiusdem amoena pleraque et dulcissima visui prata
virentia ac fructiferos regios paradiseos cedros et florentissimos
hortos, dignum quarti climatis in orbe specimen et oecumenicae
latitudinis medium.

74   Kyriacus vero Thraciam petens exinde per Aegaeum Chium
Andreolumque suum revisit, quocum suis compositis rebus, Calliepolim petens inde concessit, et non longe a portu Boreis obviantibus crebris ad Kardamilum eiusdem insulae se bona portum cum
navi recepit, ubi cum per dies secundas auras expectantes consiste-
rent, socii Genuenses nonnulli nobiles e navi ad terra desilientes,
alii per arbores visco pictas decipiunt aves, alii quidem escatis sub
unda hamis varigenos laqueare pisces amabant. Kiriacus vero, ut
non omnes diei horas omni ex parte vacuas amitteret, dum Graecos ⟨libros⟩ quos e Cypro nuper adduxerat perlegeret, in Euripidis
poetae vitam incidit, quae cum paucis litteris complecteretur Latinam fecit, et apud Chium Andreolo Iustiniano amico incomparabili misit.

75   Postridie vero Austro secundante Cardamilum reliquit Tene-
donque venit, et insulam olim nobilem suaeque antiquae civitatis
vestigia conspectare placuerat; et inde angustum per Hellespontum ad Threiciam in Cheroneso Calliepolim venit, ubi exoneratis rebus, Petro Simone Polidoro Anconitano negociatore curante,
camelis rebus suis onustis, Kiriacus regiam Andrianupolim

of the two men he saw the city and traveled about the island inspecting its ancient monuments, its walls, columns, statues, bases, and Doric-lettered inscriptions. From a Greek monk he bought for himself three recently excavated antiquities, a marble bust of a plebeian priest, a statue of Venus,[71] and another of Bacchus, which he dispatched home to Ancona in the hands of his brother-in-law, Bartolomeo, who had just arrived at Rhodes in an Anconitan ship belonging to Bonifazio, which was bound for Jerusalem. He also admired in Rhodes its lush and charming meadows, its regal parks of fruit-bearing juniper, and its flowery gardens — vegetation very characteristic of the fourth region and the middle of the inhabitable zone of the globe.

Making for Thrace, Cyriac then returned across the Aegean to 74 Chios and his friend, Andreolo, with whom he settled affairs before leaving for Gallipoli; but not far from the port a strong northern headwind forced them to put in to the port of Kardamyla on the island, where, while they lay at anchor for several days awaiting a favorable breeze, a party of Genoese noblemen went ashore, some to snare colorful birds in the trees, others preferring to catch fish of various kinds on baited hooks. Meanwhile, Cyriac did not want to waste every hour of the day in idleness, so he studied the Greek books he had brought with him from Cyprus, and while reading them came upon a life of Euripides that was brief enough for him to put it into Latin;[72] and he sent his translation to his good friend, Andreolo Giustiniani, at Chios.

Next day they left Kardamyla with a south wind behind them 75 and arrived at the island of Tenedos, where Cyriac had the pleasure of viewing the ancient remains of its once noble city, and then sailed through the narrow Hellespont to Gallipoli on the Thracian Chersonese. There Cyriac brought his goods ashore with the help of Pietro Simone Polidori, an Anconitan merchant, loaded them

mediterraneam Thraciae civitatem petit, ubi Iohanne Rimatres
Taraconesio negociatore regio intercedente, magni Theucri principis Murath Begh praesentiam regia sua in aula vidit, et magno
apparatu saepe equitantem, et spectacula sagitaeque certamina,
alto in malo phiala argentea in praemium posita, suos inter conspi-
cuos hippotoxotas lato campo ingenti splendore celebrantem
conspexerat. Sed cum ibidem per hyemem ad negotia expedienda
moram traxisset, dum aliquid dabatur ocii, Λίω Bolete Graeco
grammatico Iliadem Homeri et Hesiodi in re agraria principium
audivit, et eo curante ex Thessalonicea praeda Graecos nonnullos
codices emit, et praecipue Claudium Ptholomaeum Alexandrinum, geographum insignem sibi accomodatissimum, comparavit.
Praeterea Kiriacus ea in civitate cognoverat Nicolaum Ziba, Genuensem virum doctum et negociatorem praestantem, qui semper
inter Persas Hircanosque et Parthos versatus in mercemonialibus
erat, et cum eo illas quandoque partes visere composuit.

76   Sed inde cum exacta re concessisset, Calliepolim remeavit. Et
cum ea forte tempestate Anconitanam navim Thoma Blasii patrono per Hellespontum vellis transeuntem vidisset, ad eam se
statim perantere scapha devectus contulerat, et in ea, coriis tape-
tisque ad Zachariam transmittendis per Laelium oneratis, Cla-
raque ancilla Chaonia, praeclarae indolis puera, quam ex Theucrorum praeda apud Andrianupolim emerat, eandem per navim
Massiellae matri Ciucio[5] consobrino intercedente missa, Calliepolim iterum Nicolino nigro fidissimo liberto suo commitatus revisit,
quocum et Theucris comitantibus agogitis nobilissimas Macedoniae partes videre contendit, et per Ematheos Philippicosque campos ad Philipppos ipsam venit, civitatem praeclarissimam, ubi

on to camels, and set out for the inland Thracian city of Adrianople, where, through the good offices of the royal factor, Juan
Rimatres of Tarragona, he had a sight of the Turkish sultan, Murad Bey, not only holding court in his hall, but also riding on his
horse up and down the field in all his splendor, accompanied by
his magnificent, mounted bowmen, as he watched a great archery
competition for the prize of a silver bowl displayed on a tall standard. The business of selling his merchandise kept him in Adrianople for the winter, and in his leisure he listened to the Greek
grammarian, Lio Boles, expounding Homer's *Iliad* and the first
part of Hesiod's *Works and Days*; and it was thanks to Lio that
he was able to buy a number of Greek manuscripts plundered by
the Turks from Salonica,[73] among them being a text of the great
Alexandrian geographer, Ptolemy, which was particularly useful
to him. In Adrianople, furthermore, he met a well known and
learned Genoese merchant called Niccolò Ziba,[74] who regularly
traded with Persia, Parthia and the territory round the Caspian
Sea, and arranged with Ziba one day to visit these countries in his
company.

But now he had finished his business in Adrianople and re-   76
turned to Gallipoli. At this moment he happened to espy an Anconitan ship owned [or captained] by Tommaso di Biagio passing
under sail through the Hellespont, so he at once had himself
rowed out to her in a small boat[75] and put on board a consignment
of hides and carpets for Lelio to deliver to Zaccaria. On the Turkish slave market in Adrianople he had bought a very intelligent
servant girl from Epirus named Clara,[76] whom he wanted to send
home to his mother, Masiella, under the care of his cousin, Ciucio;[77] so he put her on board the ship too. Cyriac himself rowed
back with his faithful black manservant, Niccolino, and a number
of Turks as his guides, hastening away to visit Macedonia and its
important sights; and so, after traveling through the Emathian and
Philippian countryside, he arrived at the illustrious city of Philippi

multa veternitatis eximiae monumenta conspexit et temporis labe
collapsa de marmore moenia theatrumque et ingentia innume-
raque principum atque militum sepulchra, quae inter et ingens in
via spectaculum videtur:

C.VIBI.COR.^{nelii} MIL.^{iti}
V.^{quintae} LEG.^{ionis} MACE
DOCAE

unico de lapide monumentum, quod hodie Alexandri Bucephali
praesepium incertum Graeciae vulgus appellat, prope quod hinc
inde pleraque epigrammata comperit et digne suis adiecerat commentariis; quae potissimum loca visere nobilem iuvenis animum
incitasse cognovimus, quod apud Nasonem in Fastis de morte divi
Caesaris lectitarat:

Testes estote Phillipi
et quorum sparsis ossibus habet humus.

77   Exinde vero per seras se statim ad Thessalonicam contulit, antiquam Macedoniae atque nobilissimam ad mare urbem, in qua
primum egregia inter amplissimae civitatis monumenta vidit medio in foro Pauli Aemilii nostri mirificum arcum, et diruptum
Dianae templum, ex quo marmoreae in epistiliis statuae deorum
quam plurimae conspectantur; vidit et nostrae religionis sacras
plerasque ornatissimas aedes, in quis potissimum inspectare placuerat nobilissimum Demetrii trophaeafori martyris delubrum;
viderat enim insuper antiqua ex Lysimaco turritaque cocto de latere moenia, eiusque et aliorum heroum poetarumque epigrammata; et in tripode Musarum apud Heliconem olim posito de
Homeri Hesiodique tempore mentio non vulgaris habetur. Ibi etenim libros plerosque Graecos sacros gentilesque emit, et per
birremem apud Chium ad Andreolum suum transmisit.

itself, where he inspected many fine monuments of antiquity — the ruined marble walls, the theater, and a great number of large tombs of princes and soldiers; and what particularly attracted his attention was a huge monument on the road outside the city fashioned from a single block of stone, which the local Greek inhabitants dubiously call the Manger of Alexander's horse Bucephalus:

Gaius Vibius of the tribe Cornelia,
soldier of the fifth legion
Macedonica.[78]

And strewn in the neighborhood around this monument he found many inscriptions which he duly added to his *commentaria*. I know that what particularly inspired the young man to visit this region was the passage he had read in Ovid's *Fasti* about the death of Julius Caesar:

Be witnesses, Philippi
and those whose bones are scattered in her soil.[79]

Then, leaving in the evening, he went on to the ancient and noble coastal city of Salonica,[80] among whose excellent monuments he saw the marvelous arch of our own Aemilius Paulus in the main square, and the ruined temple of Diana with numerous marble statues of the gods on its architraves.[81] He also inspected many of the splendid Christian churches, delighting particularly in the big one dedicated to the warrior-martyr St. Demetrius; the turreted brick walls built by Lysimachus; and many inscriptions relating to heroes and poets,[82] including a rare inscription on a tripod of the Muses, which was brought to Salonica from Mount Helicon, and which refers to the age of Homer and Hesiod.[83] In Salonica, too, he bought many ecclesiastical and secular manuscripts, which he forwarded by galley to his friend, Andreolo, in Chios.

77

73

78 Exinde per Adrianopolim se iterum ad Calliepolim contulit, ubi acceptis ex Ancone litteris novit, Martino quinto maximo pontifice defuncto, Eugenium quartum optumum sibi successorem V. Nonas Martias creatum esse, quem cardinalem Senensem Gabrielem Condulmerium Picenni provintiae legatum apud Anconem per biennium fuisse memoravimus, qua de tam digni viri optimi electione laetum Kiriacum statim apud Adrianopolim Nicolao Ziba, et in Liburnia Iaderae Georgio Begnae, in Italia vero Iordano cardinali Ursino, Leonardo Aretino, mihique et aliis amicis plerisque dignis, haec talia scripsisse suis epistolis cognovimus eadem haec fere per verba:

Ego enim tam magni optumique principis mortem infelicem ecclesiae ac Italis fere omnibus perniciosissimam fore putabem; nunc vero perbeatam magis atque quodammodo opportunam arbitror accessisse, dum tam pium, humanum, clementem, sapientemque et religioni deditissimum hominem sibi delectum successorem intelligo.

Et subiecit:

Nam et si quando optumus ille *divum pater et hominum rex* Italiam religionemve nostram per sacerdotem quempiam restitutam fore annuerit, ego sub tam optimo pontifice auctam propagatamque videre putem, cum et eum semper se maximis in rebus ecclesiae provide, constanter, aeque, pie magnanimiterque gessisse recolimus.

79 Dixit. Et deinde Kiriacus, relicta Persarum quam cum Nicolao Ziba constituerat exploratione, expedire se et Italiam ad patriam remeare ac ipsum ad pontificem sanctissimum maturare decrevit,

He then proceeded, by way of Adrianople, back to Gallipoli,   78
where he found a letter from Ancona informing him that Martin
V had died and that Gabriele Condulmer, cardinal of Siena,
who — as we have seen — had served in Ancona for two years as
papal legate to the province of Piceno, had been elected on the
third of March to succeed him under the name of Eugenius IV.
This admirable election so pleased Cyriac that he at once, as I
came to know, sent letters to Niccolò Ziba[84] in Adrianople, to
Giorgio Begna in Zadar in Liburnia, and in Italy to Cardinal
Giordano Orsini, Leonardo of Arezzo, and many other influential
friends, as well as to myself, to this effect:[85]

> I reckoned that the death of so good a Pope as Martin would
> be unfortunate for the Church and disastrous for virtually
> everybody in Italy; but now in the event I see that it was,
> rather, in a sense quite fortunate and timely, in that so re-
> sponsible, humane, clement, wise and wholly devout a man,
> as I now learn, has been elected his successor.

And he added:

> For if the excellent "father of the gods and king of men"[86]
> wills that Italy and our religion shall be restored by any
> priest, I am convinced that so excellent a pope, Eugenius, is
> the very man to further this great task, because we have al-
> ready seen how prudently, firmly, justly, devotedly and large-
> mindedly he has always conducted the important affairs of
> the Church.

These were his own words. At this point Cyriac decided to give   79
up his idea of exploring Persia, as he had arranged with Niccolò
Ziba. His plan now was to get clear of his commercial business,
and then, having collected all the intelligence he could concerning

et sibi, de piissima Graecorum et totius orientalis ecclesiae unione et digna in Theucros expeditione expertior factus, quae pro re digna visa sunt litteris et ore detegere.

80 Et ut plenius rem ageret, Memnonem, Karoli olim Cephaloniae magnifici ducis filium, virum elegantem et perstrenuum armis, nuper ex amplissima magni Theucri aula adventantem convenit, a quo pergrate susceptus, multa et praedigna hac de re invicem conserendo, civitates et praecipua loca quae in Asia sub Theucri dictione manebant videre explorareque constituunt; et sic ex Calliepoli per Hellespontum ad Asiam transeuntes Prusam sub Olympo regiam Bythiniae civitatem venere, quam populosam et opulentissimam vidit vetustis novisque ornamentis conspicuam.

81 Sed ubi Babylano Palavisino Genuensi, viro nobili et negociatori egregio, curam mercemonalium rerum suarum dederat, ipse una cum Memnone ad Canuza Begh, pro Theucro in provintia satrapem ad Olympi montis diversoria praestolantem, se contulerant; qui ad finem suum Memnonem Kiriacumque, postquam cognoverat, perhumane suscepit. Nam et ille natione Graecus Graeceque perdoctus erat, et multa sibi de antiquis et nobilibus in ea provintia rebus et de insigni Cyzicenorum delubro egregie periteque commemorabat. Cui Kyriacus, cum ex eiusdem templi ruinis pleraque elaborata marmorea apud Montaneam, maritimum Prusiae civitatis emporium, ad nova in urbe aedificia instruenda deducta vidisset, ne tantae aedis vestigium posteris penitus aboleri videretur, persuasit ne deinceps permitteret ut aliquid ex parietibus, columnis et epistiliis extantibus tanti nostram ad diem spectaculi dirrueretur, cum ob venerandae antiquitatis pudorem tum et sui magnique Theucrorum principis honorem. Quae cum vir ille

a union with the Greeks and the whole Eastern Church and on an effective crusade against the Turks, to hasten home to Italy and to visit the pope in Rome in order, both orally and by written report, to lay before him whatever of importance in his view he had discovered on these matters.

To enable him to do this more expertly he visited Memnon,[87] 80 the son of Carlo, the late duke of Cephalonia, a man of parts with military experience, who had just arrived from the sultan's court. Memnon warmly welcomed him, and after a thorough discussion about eastern affairs, they decided to reconnoiter the principal cities and centers of Asia that were under Turkish domination; so they left Gallipoli, sailed through the Hellespont to Asia, and arrived at the royal city of Bursa in Bithynia under Mount Olympus, which Cyriac found to be a populous and very wealthy place embellished by remarkable ancient and modern buildings.

There he consigned all his own commercial business to the 81 trustworthy hands of the Genoese nobleman, Babilano Pallavicini,[88] an excellent merchant, while he himself went on with Memnon to visit the Turkish governor of the province, Canuza Bey,[89] who was staying at an inn on the slopes of Mount Olympus and who, on learning of their arrival, met them at his frontier and graciously received them. For Canuza Bey was a Greek by birth and education and thus able knowledgeably to discuss with Cyriac the antiquities of the province, especially the great temple at Cyzicus. Cyriac had observed at Mundanya, the port of Bursa, that many dressed marble stones from the Cyzican temple had been utilized in the erection of modern buildings; and on the score both of the respect due to antiquity and of the good reputation of the Sultan himself, lest all trace of the building be lost to posterity, he persuaded Canuza Bey to forbid any further destruction of the still-standing walls, columns, and architraves of this spectacular

doctus intellexisset dignissima verba, id se lubens facturum promisit.

82   Et Kyriacus magno eiusdem visendi operis incensus amore, cum exinde Prusam illico revisisset, agogite quodam ductore Theucro, Cyzicon nobilissimam Asiae civitatem venit, quae, ut aiebat, ad promuntorium Propontiaci littoris contra Praeconesiam insulam sita est, sed undique nobilia magnis undique lapidibus moenia ingentiaque civitatis aedificia immensis convulsa ruinis solo undique collapsa iacent.

83   Sed extant ⟨et⟩ praecelsa videntur excellentissimi templi vestigia Iovis altae de marmore parietes, in quis adhuc aurei fili signa conspectantur, quo de opere C. Plinius in suo de naturali historia libro inquit: Durat et Cyzici delubrum in quo filum aureum commissuris omnibus politi lapidi subiecit artifex, et reliqua. Stant et ornatissima in fronte aedis diversaque deorum simulachra, et ex longo ordine columnarum amplissimae bases, et quamvis maiori ex parte columnae solo collapsae sint tres et triginta numero adhuc suis cum epistiliis erectae videntur, ubi tale Kyriacus Graecum exceperat epigramma:

.ΕΚ.ΔΑΠΕΔΟΥ.

ΜΩΡΘΩΣΕΝ.

ΟΛΛΗΣ.ΑΕΙΑΣ.

ΑΦΘΟΗΙΗ.

ΧΕΙΡΩΝ.ΔΙΟΣ.

ΑΡΙΣΤΕΗΩΤΟΣ.

Et alia hic inde per urbem epigrammata comperit, ac ingentes de marmore portas amphiteatrique vestigia, et magnum terriquatientis Neptuni simulachrum, atque omnia conspectanda eum perbelle excitasse ferebat. Haec eadem quae apud Nasonem poetam ellegantissima lectitarat elegia:

monument. Canuza Bey had the learning to appreciate this argument and readily promised to do what Cyriac advised.

Cyriac then returned to Bursa and, all afire to see the temple, proceeded with a Turkish guide to the noble Asian city of Cyzicus which, as he says, stands on a peninsula on the southern shore of the Propontis opposite the island of Proconnesus and is everywhere strewn with the ruins of the huge stone walls and vast buildings of the ancient city.

Prominent among these are the towering remains of the superb temple of Jupiter with its lofty marble walls which still show the marks of the golden thread described by Pliny in his *Natural History*: "The temple at Cyzicus also survives, where the architect inserted a golden thread in all the joints of the polished stone, etc."[90] Still remaining are various statues of gods on the highly ornamented facade of the temple and the very wide bases of long rows of columns; and although the majority of the original columns have fallen to the ground, thirty-three of them with their architraves are still standing.[91] The building also bears this Greek inscription, which Cyriac recorded:

> The godlike
> Aristaeneus
> raised me from the ground up
> by the contributions
> of all Asia and
> the labor of many hands.[92]

He also found other inscriptions here and there in the city, as well as huge marble gates and remains of the amphitheater and a large statue of earth-shaking Neptune—sights, as he said, that all immensely excited him. Here he remembered the elegant verses he had read in Ovid:

Hinc et[6] Propontiacis haerentem Cyzicon oris
Cyzicon Aemoniae nobile gentis opus.

84   Exinde vero cum Prusam revisisset, relictis Babylano reliquiis,
Zachariae nomine rebus et compositis, cum Memnone pro expeditione in Theucros agendis cum pontifice conditionibus Italiam
per Bizantium remeare constituens, ut Nicaeam nobilem Bythiniae
civitatem videret, terrestri itinere agogite Theucro ducente Constantinopolim petit; et cum ad ipsam paulo extra iter Nycaeam
civitatem venisset, eam ad lacus Bythiniae ripas turritis cocto de
latere moenibus sitam invenit, et ad portam TI. CLAVDI GER-
MANICI, ad turrim vero Traiani epigrammata Graeca comperuit,
et talia per urbem egregia veterum monumenta conspexit, et magnam oecumenicae illius celleberimae synodi basilicam.

85   Exinde die noctuque iter adcellerans per silvas et difficilia loca,
ad Calcedoniam Bythiniae deletam vetustate maritimam urbem,
vicinum Bizantii emporium quod hodie Scutorion dicitur, venit, et
illico scapha Galatheam Peram magnamque Constantinopolim revisit, ubi Pascalinum Anconitanum consanguineum suum sua cum
navi post mensem Anchonem ad patriam navigaturum invenit; et
ne interim vacuum tempus amitteret, et ⟨ut⟩ dignum quid per
Asiam indagaret, se apud Chium insulam transeuntem per Aegaeum navim expectaturum composuit.

86   Exinde Tarraconensi bireme devectus, Lesbeam Mitilennum,
egregiam et olim potentissimam civitatem, adivit, ubi Georgio
Gathalusio praeside favitante plurima civitatis insignia vidit: theatra, columnas, statuas, basses, inscriptionesque Graecas atque La-
tinas et conspicuum de marmore arcum, quem Tetrastilon dicunt,
olim per praesidem insularum

On this side Cyzicus, clinging to the shore of the Propontis:
    Cyzicus, noble creation of the people of Thrace.[93]

He then went back to Bursa, left his unsold goods behind with 84
Babilano, settled Zaccaria's outstanding business, and decided to
return with Memnon by way of Byzantium to Italy in order to
discuss with the pope his proposals for an expedition against the
Turks. On his overland journey to Constantinople, still with a
Turkish guide, he made a detour in order to see the Bithynian city
of Nicaea — a towered, brick-walled city situated, as he found, on
the edge of a Bithynian lake. There he discovered Greek inscriptions on the gate of Tiberius Claudius Germanicus[94] and on the
tower of Trajan, and he inspected other ancient monuments of the
same quality as well as the great basilica where the celebrated ecumenical Council of Nicaea had met.[95]

Then he pressed on day and night through forests and difficult 85
country till he arrived at the ancient ruined Bithynian city of
Chalcedon, destroyed by age, which is today known as Scutari, a
trading port just opposite Byzantium.[96] Thence he took a boat
over to Galata in Pera and the great city of Constantinople, where
he found his kinsman, Pasqualino[97] of Ancona, who was propos-
ing to return home a month later in his ship. Meanwhile, so as to
lose no time, he decided to look around Asia Minor and to pick
up Pasqualino's ship at Chios on its way back through the Aegean.

So he took passage in an Aragonese galley to the fine and once- 86
powerful city of Mytilene on Lesbos, where, through the kind offices of Giorgio Gattilusio, the lord of the island,[98] he inspected
the city's many important sights: its theaters, columns, statues,
bases, Greek and Latin inscriptions, and its remarkable marble
arch known as the Tetrastyle, which was, by the ancient ruler of
the islands

.FL.VALERIO
DIOCLITIANO
CONSTANTIO
ET
MAXIMIANO
NOBILIS
SIMO
DEDICATVM.

87   Deinde vero acceptis a praeside ad Theucros in Asia correctores
litteris, visis et antea per insulam altis et antiquis de marmore
aquarum ductibus et urbium Pyrriae Methymnaeque disiectis vetustate muris, exiguam per cymbam ad Asiathicum proximum littus venit, et inde Pergameam ad nobilem et olim metropolitanam
Asiae civitatem adscendit et indigena ducente Theucro amplam
undique urbem perscrutavit et ingentes hinc inde vetustatum reliquias inspexit: immania templa, duo maxima amphiteatra, collos-
seaque nonnulla de marmore deorum heroumve simulachra, at
egregia inter sepulchra ingens et magnis editum lapidibus instar
altissimi montis tumulum. Quin et omnigenum denique nobilium
antiquitatum vestigia vidit et egregia pleraque Graecis Latinisque
litteris epigrammata.

88   Exinde se ad Aeoliam Cumem, antiquissimam Hesiodi patriam
et longi temporis labe collapsam civitatem, adierat. Hodie et ab
incolis Chrysopolim vocitatam audierat; et cum ibi nil notatione
dignum vidisset, Ioniam venit et Smyrnas antiquam eiusdem re-
gionis urbem et Homeri praeclari nominis insignem vidit. Nam et
ibi vetusto in lapide comperit epigramma quod illam Homeri patriam fuisse significabat, ubi pleraque suae vetustatis vestigia, portum insignem, et cocleam altissimam columnam inspexit.

89   Inde vero Phocaeas vetustam novamque venerat et ingentes
inibi aluminum mineras vidit, ubi Fredericum Iustinianum Andre-
oli sui socerum eiusdem loci patronum offendit, ac eo iuvante

Dedicated to
Flavius Valerius
Diocletian,
Constantius,
and
the most noble
Maximian.[99]

He also looked at the tall ancient stone aqueducts on the island   87
and the fallen stones of the walls of Pyrra and Methymna. Then,
armed with letters of introduction from Gattilusio to Turkish authorities in Asia Minor, he crossed the narrow strait in a little boat
to the nearest point on the Asiatic shore and took the steep road
up to the noble city of Pergamum, once the metropolis of Asia
Minor, where with a local Turkish guide he thoroughly investigated the city and the huge ancient remains scattered about it: vast
temples, two great amphitheaters,[100] a number of colossal marble
statues of gods and famous men and, among its fine tombs, an
enormous sepulcher made of great stones rising up like a high
mountain. He also saw what was left of all kinds of fine antique
structures and many good Greek and Latin inscriptions.

Next he came to the long-ruined city of Aeolian Cyme, the   88
birthplace of Hesiod,[101] which, as he learned, the local inhabitants
call Chrysopolis; but finding nothing worth recording there, he
proceeded to the ancient Ionian city of Smyrna, famous for its
connection with the illustrious name of Homer; and indeed he
found there on an ancient stone an inscription indicating that Homer was born there. Other evidences he saw of the antiquity of
Smyrna were its splendid harbor and a very tall spiral column.

Cyriac then went to old and new Phocaea and visited the big   89
alum mines, where he met their lessee, Federigo Giustiniani, the
father-in-law of his friend, Andreolo, who helped him to buy

aurea Philippi, Alexandri Lysimachique numismata insignia comparavit.

90   Exinde vero ad littus quod est in conspectu Chii insulae venerat, ubi perenteream scapham conscendens Chium urbem Andreolumque suum revisit ac Nicolinum nigrum libertum, qui ex Calliepoli reliquis rebus suis scriniisque adductis eum praevenerat [et] patronum expectaturus. Et ibi Kyriacus per dies apud ipsum Andreolum cum lectitando Graecos quos ad eum e Thessalonica libros miserat, aptando tum suas quascumque res expediendo, Pascalineam e Bizantio navim expectans, morabatur.

91   Interea cum magnam Venetum classem Chium hostiliter impetere crebra fama Aegaeum fere totum excitasset, Anconitana navis Paschalino quem supra memoravimus praefecto Chium applicuit. Cuiusce civitatis ordo, ne forte ab ea transeunte hostes de iis novi quid exploratum haberent, Pascalineam navim in portu firmari iussit. Sed cum quartum post diem, Andreolo Kiriaci gratia intercurante, Maonenses eam libere navigare permisissent, eadem in navi Kiriacus ipse suis impositis rebus concessit, et apud Cassiopeum Corcirae insulae portum in Venetianam classem incidit. Sed Andreae Mucenigo praefecto oblatis Genuensium litteris, expedita navis per Illyricum tandem Anconitanum ad portum applicuit.

92   Ubi postquam suos incolumes Kiriacus revisit, suis expeditis rebus, paucos post dies una cum Astorgio Anconitano pontifice ad urbem maximum ad pontificem Eugenium se contulerat, quem ad magnam Petri basilicae aulam, Aloisio optumo cubiculario suo curante, vidit et sibi primum duo hydrochoa Indica porcellanea auro elaborata speciosissima vasa dono dederat; et multa deinde

some remarkable gold coins of Philip, Alexander, and Lysima-chus.[102]

Next he came to the coast which is in sight of the island of   90
Chios, where he took a small passenger boat across to the island.
Here he once more visited his friend Andreolo and his black servant Niccolino, who had come from Gallipoli with Cyriac's remaining goods and book boxes and was awaiting the arrival of his
master. In Chios Cyriac stayed for several days at Andreolo's
house, both reading the Greek books he had forwarded from Salonica and sorting out and packing up all his goods and posses-
sions, while he awaited the arrival of Pasqualino's ship from Byzantium.

But the Anconitan ship, captained as we have said by Pasqua-   91
lino, arrived just at the time when pretty well the whole Aegean
was in a state of excitement over numerous reports that a large
Venetian fleet was on its way to attack Chios; so the city authorities, fearing that the Venetians might intercept the ship to get up-
to-date intelligence about the state of affairs in Chios, forbade
Pasqualino to leave the harbor.[103] After four days, however, Andreolo on Cyriac's behalf was able to persuade the Maonesi to allow the ship to leave port, so Cyriac loaded his goods on board.
When they arrived at the port of Cassiope on the island of Corfu,
they encountered the Venetian fleet; but when they showed their
papers from the Genoese to the Venetian commander, Andrea
Mocenigo, he allowed the ship to proceed, and so they at last arrived by way of Illyria at the port of Ancona.

There Cyriac found his family safe and sound. He stayed there   92
only a few days to settle his affairs and then hastened to Rome in
the company of Astorgio, the bishop of Ancona,[104] to see Pope
Eugenius. An audience was arranged by Aloysius, the papal chamberlain, in the nave of St. Peter's; and on this occasion Cyriac first
presented the pope with a pair of very beautiful Indian porcelain
ewers decorated with gold, and then clearly and fully put forward

sibi de excolendissima Graecorum unione, ac dignissima in Theucros expeditione, Memnonisque optuma hac in re compensatione,
ore litterisque perbellissime declaravit. Qui optumus et prudentis-
simus pater Kiriacum primo ut devotum filium perbenigne suscepit, et omnia ab se delata audierat et optima in mente reposita, ad
ea se pro tempore diligentem operam daturum promisit.

93   Interea Kiriacus, ut proximas extra urbem vetustates indagaret,
Tybur antiquissimam civitatem petierat; et per celebrem Tyburti-
nam viam hinc inde multa veternitatis monumenta conspexit, et
ad pontem Lucanum Marci Plauci insignia triumphalia ornamenta
regiosque Hadriani Caesaris hortos, quorum pleraque videntur
ornatissima scenarum spectacula.

P.PLAVTIVS
PVLCHER.TRIVM
PHALIS.AVGVR
III.VIR.A.A.A.F.F.
Q.TI.CAESARIS
AVG.V.CONSVLIS
TR.PL.PR.AED.AE
RAR.COMES.DR
VSI.FILI.GERMA
NICI.AVVNCVLVS
DRVSI.TI.CLAVDI
CAESARIS.AVGVS
TI.FILI.ET.AB.EO
CENSORES.INTER
PATRITIOS.LAET
VS.CVRATOR.VI
ARVM.STERNEN
DARVM.A VICINIS
LAETVS.EX.AVCTO

his views, both verbally and in written memoranda, concerning the fostering of union with the Greeks, an effective expedition against the Turks, and the payment due to Memnon for his part in this important work. The Holy Father benignly welcomed Cyriac as a son, and having very judiciously listened to everything he had to say, promised in due course to give it his fullest attention.

Cyriac in the meantime decided to investigate the antiquities in the environs of Rome, and set off for the very ancient city of Tivoli. Here and there along the famous *Via Tiburtina* he found many evidences of the ancient world, and near the Bridge of Lucanus he saw the splendid triumphal monument of Marcus Plautius and the royal gardens of the Emperor Hadrian, where many of its splendid porticoes are still to be seen. 93

Publius Plautius
Pulcher, whose father
celebrated a triumph,
Augur, member of the
Board of Three
for casting and striking
gold, silver and bronze [*coins*],
Quaestor of the Emperor
Tiberius Caesar
when he was consul for the fifth time [31 CE],
Tribune of the People,
Praetor in charge of the treasury,
Companion of Drusus
son of Germanicus,
uncle of Drusus,
son of the emperor
Tiberius Claudius Caesar
who, when he was censor [47–48 CE],
named [*Pulcher*] a patrician,

87

RITATE.TI.CLAV
DI.CAESARIS.AVG
GERMANICI.PRO
COS.PROVINTIAE
SICILIAE
VIBIA.MARCI.FIL
LAELIA.NATA
PVLCHRA

94 Et Tiburtinam ipsam denique civitatem altis in collibus emi-
nentem viderat, et eximia vetustatum vestigia et sacram Saxono
Herculi atque dirruptam aedem.

HERCVLI
SAXONO SACRVM
SEX.SVLPITIVS
TROPHIMVS AEDEM
ZOTHECAM CVLLI
NAM PECVNIA SVA
A SOLO
RESTITVIT.IDEMQ.
DEDICAVIT.K.DECEMBR
L.TVRPILIO DEXTRO
M.MOETIO RVPHO
COS.T.VTHYCVS
PERAGENDVM CVRAVIT.

95 Tiburtinaeque Sybillae colosseum de marmore caput vidit, et
ingentes Germanici Caesaris aquarum ductus per quos clarus ille
princeps caeruleos cursus amoenosque fontes in urbem aere suo
perducendos curavit. Viderat et Cymbricum pontem quem Salarium dicunt et nobilem unico ex lapide M. ANTONII ANTIL.
PR tumulum secus Tyberim ad quartum ab urbe lapidem situm,

chosen by his neighbors as
Superintendent of Road Construction
by the authority of the Emperor
Tiberius Claudius Caesar Germanicus,
proconsul of the province of Sicily;
[*his wife*] Vibia
daughter of Marsus;
Laelia, daughter of Pulcher.[105]

Finally he arrived at Tivoli high on its hill, where he viewed its   94
ancient remains and the ruined temple of Hercules Saxonus.[106]

Sacred to
Hercules Saxonus.
Servius Sulpicius
Trophimus restored the temple,
prayer niche and hearth
for burnt offerings
from the ground up
at his own expense
and dedicated them on
December 1 when
Lucius Turpilius Dexter and
Marcus Maecius Rufus
were consuls [*81 CE*].
The slave Eutychus
had the work completed.[107]

He saw the colossal marble bust of the Tiburtine Sibyl and the   95
tall aqueduct of Germanicus Caesar which that enlightened prince
built at his own expense to bring delicious streams of limpid water
into the city. He also viewed the Cimbrian — now called the Salarian — Bridge and the noble monolithic tomb of Marcus Antonius
Antyllus [?], prefect, situated by the Tiber at the fourth milestone

ac alia ex parte insignem illum quattuor e marmoribus integris turlum una cum Iordano Ursino venerandissimo cardinale prospexit, et Martini pontificis incuriam, qui opus egregium dirrui permiserat, accusavit.

96 Et inde Hostiensem ad portum se contulit et insignia antiquitatis suae vestigia conspexit et ab eo non longe Traiani optumi principis amplissimum navistatium.

97 At enim cum inde ad urbem remeasset, Sigismundum inclytum Pannoniae regem et designatum imperatorem Romam petiturum Italiam Senasque venisse perceperat. Cuius legati, Gaspar regius secretarius et Comus pontifex, ad Eugenium pontificem maximum venere; et ubi de adventu imperatoris ad urbem Cardinale de Comitibus et Berardo de Camerino, non absque Kiriaci persuasionibus, composuerat, Senis ad principem redeuntes Kiriacum comitem habentes aditum sibi ad Caesarem praebuere; a quo perhumane susceptus, multa et praedigna sibi Kiriacus de rebus gestis maiestati, honori dignitatique suae congruentibus et dignis in barbaros expeditionibus applicavit. Et sibi utique peregregium munus dederat aureum Traiani Caesaris numisma, ut optumi principis imitandi exemplar haberet, et Anconem potissime patriam eodem ab principe exornatam memoria quandoque recenseret. Qui munificus princeps, Brunoro della Scalla Veronensi Baptistaque Cygala Genuensi adstantibus, claris consiliariis suis, Kiriacum caesarea familiaritate donavit.

98 Et cum postea inde ad urbem ab Eugenio maximo pontifice aureo diademate insignitus maximis intentus negociis versaretur, et ex Liburnia illustres comites Stephanus Bartholusque Phrygipenates, Seniae civitatis principes, Romam ad eundem Sigismundum visendum venissent, cum his Kiriacus ad eum se iterum contulit;

out of the city; and, in the company of Cardinal Giordano Orsini, he inspected in another part of the neighborhood the splendid monument composed of four single marble blocks, which Pope Martin, as Cyriac complained, had allowed to fall into ruins.

Next he made an expedition to the port of Ostia, where he ex- 96 amined its principal antiquities and the great port[108] of the emperor Trajan nearby.

When he got back to the city, he learned that the Hungarian 97 king, Sigismund, emperor-elect, had arrived in Siena on his way to Rome.[109] Sigismund had already sent on his ambassadors, Gaspar, his royal secretary, and the Bishop of Como,[110] to see Pope Eugenius, and the pope, not uninfluenced by Cyriac, had made arrangements with the Cardinal Conti[111] and Bernardo of Camerino for the official reception of the emperor in the city. The ambassadors therefore returned to Siena with Cyriac in company, and they introduced him to the emperor, who graciously received him. Cyriac then laid before him many cogent arguments as to the deeds to be done only by an emperor of his sovereign authority, dignity, and worth, particularly with regard to a crusade to repel the barbarians; and to give Sigismund an exemplar of a good emperor worthy to be imitated, he presented him with a magnificent gold coin of the emperor Trajan, at the same time reminding him that Trajan had conferred a special luster on Cyriac's own native Ancona.[112] At this, the generous prince, attended by his illustrious councilors, Brunoro della Scala[113] of Verona and Battista Cicala of Genoa,[114] magnanimously admitted Cyriac into the circle of his imperial court.[115]

Later, when Sigismund had received from Pope Eugenius in 98 Rome his golden diadem and had begun his important diplomatic negotiations, two notables of Senj,[116] Counts Stefano and Bartolo Frankopan[117] arrived in Rome from Liburnia to have audience with him; and in their company Cyriac again came into the emperor's presence. He then resumed with Sigismund and his prefect,

et cum sibi et comiti Mathaeo claro praefecto suo coeptis de rebus recensendo multa saepius retulisset, ad ea se lubentissime optumo cum pontifice paratum respondit, sed antea ad perniciosam Basiliensium coniurationem dissolvendam operam dare oportere.

99   Praeterea dum tanto cum principe Kiriacus ingentes vetustatum reliquias undique per urbem disiectas aspexisset, ut gravi lacessitus iniuria, talibus denique dictis, Latinorum afflatus numine, principem excitarat:

> Equidem non parum putabam caesarei principis animum lacessere, quod qui nunc vitam agunt Romana inter moenia homines, marmorea ingentia atque ornatissima undique per urbem aedificia, statuas insignes, et columnas tantis olim sumptibus, tanta maiestate, tantaque fabrorum architectorumve arte conspicuas et nobilia in his magnarum epigrammata rerum, ita ignave, turpiter et obscene in dies ad albam tenuemque convertunt cinerem, ut eorum nullam brevi tempore speciem vestigiumve posteris apparebit. Proh scelus! et o, vos inclytae Romulae gentis manes, *aspicite[7] haec meritumque malis advertite numen.* Nam et ea praeclara sunt veterum monumenta, virorumque nobilis praesertim animos ad res maximas gerendas et ad gloriae et immortalitatis studium vehementer accendunt.

Qui optimus princeps ignavam hominum incuriam vituperans, nobilem iuvenis animum harum rerum curiosissimum laudavit.

100   Kiriacus vero deinde cum ceteras et praeclaras Italiae urbes videre indagareque maluisset, Pisas antiquam et olim insignem Tuscorum civitatem adivit, et eiusdem quaeque insignia vetusta novaque conspexit, et multa temporis labe hominumve incuria solo undique collapsa videntur; et quod magis adnotatione dignum considerasse aiebat, marmoream cathedralis ecclesiae domum et insigne illud et ornatissumum cimiterion, quod incolae Campum Sanctum appellant.

Count Matteo, the subject of their previous conversation, going into greater detail, to which the emperor replied that he and the pope were thoroughly agreed on their plans but that their first task was to get the dangerous Council of Basel dissolved.[118]

Cyriac also made a tour of the city with the emperor to view its   99
mighty ruins everywhere thrown to the ground; troubled by the terrible destruction and inspired by the divine presence of the Latins, he stirred the emperor's heart with these words:

I was sure you would be deeply shocked by the way the marble of these huge and elegant buildings throughout the city, these fine statues and columns, which the ancients erected so nobly at such cost, and with such craftsmanship and architectural skill, and these important historical inscriptions are continually being burned up into lime by the present inhabitants of the city in so lazy, barbarous, and indecent a fashion, that there will very soon be nothing left of them for posterity to see. What a crime! And O, you shades of the famous tribe of Romulus, "look upon these things and direct your righteous will to remedy these evils."[119] For these are the shining witnesses the ancients left behind them and they possess particular power to fire the minds of noble men to the greatest deeds and to the pursuit of undying glory.

The emperor, too, was disgusted at men's lazy indifference to the preservation of ancient monuments, and applauded the young Cyriac's close concern for them.

Desiring next to investigate other great Italian cities, Cyriac   100
now went to the ancient and once renowned Etruscan city of Pisa, where he examined all its principal ancient and modern monuments and found many places ruined by time and neglect. The two most noteworthy buildings in Pisa, as he said, were its marble-built cathedral and beautifully decorated cemetery, locally known as the Campo Santo.

101   Exinde vero Florentiam venit, Fluentinam olim clarissimam
Romanorum coloniam, nunc vero Tuscorum et omnium florentis-
simam Latinorum urbem, ubi praeclara multa et insignia rerum
ornamenta vidit, et primum amplissima vivo de lapide moenia,
portas deinde regias, et latissima strata viarum, sacra et superis
ingentiaque delubra, quae inter ad coelum alta testudine atto-
lentem vidit maximam illam et insignem beatae Reparatae Virginis
aedem, quod et mirificum opus Philippo ductante nobilissimo architecto omni ex parte perspexit, et marmoream ornatissimam
Cienceriam turrim; sed in conspectu conspicuum illud et marmoreum divi olim Martis, nunc vero Baptistae Ioannis sanctissimi
delubrum, tribus aeneis ornatissimis divinae historiae portis exor-
natum, partim eximium Nencii nobilis fabrifactoris opus, et intus
ab alto undique pendentibus aureis purpureisque civitatum victi-
galium donis completum; alta quoque magistratuum praetoria et
turritas arces, scenas publicas et privatas, civiumque palatia, et
conspicuas undique per urbem aedes, et denique ad Arni fluvii ripas lapideos quattuor et amplissimos pontes, Rubacontem, Veterem, Sanctae Trinitatis, et Carrareum, ac ingentia in foro Leonum
ferrea publicaeque libertati dedicata claustra.

102   Etenim exoptabilius quoque viderat amplissimos inter cives
Cosmam Medicem, Nicolaum Uzanum, Pallam Strocium, et inter
clariores Leonardum Arretinum illum Latinorum doctissimum,
Karolumque, et Philelphum Picennum nostrum, quos inter avidius vidisse memorabat Nicolaum Nicolum, illum aetate nostra
biblicultorem insignem et unicum Philadelphi illius studiosissimi
Ptholomaei Alexandrini diligentissimum consectatorem, quo
cum curiosissimo viro multa de antiquis dignissimis in orbe rebus compertis per nobilissimas Asiae et Europae per orientem
urbes, perque Ionicas insulas et Aegaeas, non absque iucunditate
invicem conferebantur; et potissimum de mirifico Cyzicenorum

Next he went to Florence,[120] once an illustrious Roman col- 101
ony, Fluentina, and now one of the most flourishing cities in Tuscany and all Italy. There he viewed many of its fine monuments
and works of art — its extensive solid stone walls, its regal gates,
its broad streets, and its large churches, including the fine great
Church of Santa Reparata lifting its dome to the sky, a marvelous
building which he thoroughly inspected under the guidance of the
most eminent architect, Filippo,[121] along with its highly decorated
marble campanile.[122] He also inspected the remarkable marble
baptistery in front of Santa Reparata, anciently dedicated to Mars
and now to St. John the Baptist,[123] the outside of which is adorned
by three very beautifully sculptured bronze doors[124] depicting sacred histories, partly the handiwork of the great artist, Nencio,[125]
while its interior is furnished with the gold and purple votive offerings of subject cities, suspended from on high. Nor did he fail
to view the lofty, towered palaces of the city magistrates,[126] the
public and private porticoes, the great houses of leading citizens,
the fine buildings all over the city, the four wide stone bridges —
Rubaconte, Vecchio, Trinità, and Carraia — spanning the Arno,
and finally the large iron cages of lions, symbols of popular liberty,
in the square.

But the experience in Florence he had looked forward to even 102
more was that of meeting, among its wealthiest citizens, Cosimo
de'Medici, Niccolò da Uzzano, and Palla Strozzi, and among
its most distinguished, Leonardo of Arezzo,[127] the most learned
man in Italy, Carlo of Arezzo,[128] and our Picene fellow countryman, Filelfo;[129] while the scholar he recalled having met with
special pleasure was the learned book collector, Niccolò Niccoli,
the unrivaled latter-day Ptolemy Philadelphus of Alexandria[130] — a
man of immense curiosity who relished discussing with Cyriac
all the antiquities he had discovered over the world, in the great
eastern cities of Asia and Europe, and in the islands of Ionia and
the Aegean. Niccolò particularly enjoyed Cyriac's report on the

delubro vir diligens audire gaudebat. Et interim una cum Karolo
Aretino, visa eximia bibliotheca sua, nummis imaginibusque antiquis, et insigni Pyrgotelis lupercalis sacerdotis simulachri cavata ex
Nicolo gemma, et talarati aeneo Mercurii agalmate, videre simul
et Kosmae viri opulentissimi preciosa multa eiusdem generis supellectilia.

103   Et apud Donatellum Nenciumque, statuarios nobiles, pleraque
vetusta novaque ab eis edita ex aere marmoreve simulachra, et demum, Leonardo Arretino amicissimo suo curante, regio in civitatis
praetorio apud amplissimum ordinem viderat antiqua illa e Pisis
deducta legalia Pandectarum volumina, et denique extra moenia
apud egregium Cartusiense monasterium viderat insignia sacro-
rum monumenta pleraque et Chrysostomi clarissimi doctoris caput et eximium Flavii Iosephi de Iudaica antiquitate librum.

104   Sed quod potissimum adnotari placuit, alto in colle adscendens
viderat Fesulanae antiquissimae civitatis moenia magnis undique
lapidibus condita, et collapsi amplissimi amphitheatri vestigia.

105   Postea vero Mediolanum petens per Bononiam Mutinam venit,
antiquam Togatae Galliae civitatem, ubi plerasque vetustatis suae
reliquias comperit et epigrammata pleraque nobilia, quae Scipionis
sui optimi pontificis gratia adnotanda et suis digne commentariis
reponenda curavit.

MEMORIAE
.L.PEDVCEAE
.IVLIANAE.
MORIB.NATAL.AC
PVD.PRISCIS INLV
STRIBQ.FOEMI.IN
COMPARAND.QVAE
VIXIT.ANNOS
.XIII.

wonderful temple at Cyzicus. Then, after inspecting Niccolò's splendid library, his antique coins and sculptures, the remarkable gem by Pyrgoteles, discovered[131] by Niccolò himself and representing a lupercalian priest, and his bronze statue of a wing-shod Mercury, he went with Carlo of Arezzo to view the similar precious collections which the wealthy Cosimo had acquired.

He also saw in the houses of Donatello and Ghiberti many 103 statues, both antique pieces and their own modern works in bronze and marble. Through the good offices of his friend Leonardo of Arezzo, he went to the Palazzo Vecchio where, in the presence of the Signoria, he inspected the ancient text of the Pandects brought to Florence from Pisa,[132] and finally he visited the famous Carthusian monastery[133] outside the walls of the city, where he saw many Christian antiquities, the head of the Eastern doctor, St. Chrysostom, and a copy of Flavius Josephus' *Jewish Antiquities*.

He also climbed the hill to the very ancient city of Fiesole, 104 where he took great pleasure in noting its large-stoned walls and the remains of its big ruined amphitheater.

He then set off for Milan[134] and arrived by way of Bologna at 105 Modena, an ancient city of Gallia Togata,[135] where he discovered many evidences of its antiquity, and by courtesy of Scipione its bishop[136] noted many of its important inscriptions which he recorded in his *commentaria*.

To the memory
of the honorable lady
Lucia Peducea Juliana,
comparable in her innate
character and modesty
to ancient and famous ladies.

.D.XLVII.CVM MA
RITO FECIT.ME.
.V.D.XX.
L.NONIVS.VER.

106   Ad marmoreum tumulum.

D.M
P.VETTIO
P.FIL.CAM.SABI
NO.EQ.P.IIII.VIR
AED.POT.ET MAG.
MVN.RAVEN.
CORNELIA MAX
IMINA.MARITO
INCOMPARAB.ET
SIBI.VIVA.POSVIT

107   Alio in tumulo in foro posito.

V.F
CLODIA
PLAVTILLA SIBI
ET.Q.VERCONIO
AGATHONI
MARITO OPTIMO
ET LVCIFERAE
.LIB.
IN.FR.P.XX.IN.AGR.P.XX.
.H.M.H.N.S.

She lived 47 years,
five months and twenty days.
Lucius Nonius Ver[us],
together with her husband
made this.[137]

On a marble tombstone: 106

To the spirits of the departed.
Cornelia Maximina while she was alive
dedicated this to her incomparable husband
Publius Vettius Sabinus
of the tribe Camilia,
son of Publius, Knight,
member of the Board of Four
with powers of an aedile, and
Magistrate of the city of Ravenna,
and to herself.[138]

On another tombstone set up in the marketplace: 107

Clodia
Plautilla [*built this*]
while she was alive for herself
and her excellent husband
Quintus Verconius
Agatho
and for her freedwoman
Lucifera.
It is twenty feet wide and twenty feet deep.
Heirs have no right to dispose of this monument.[139]

108   Ad sepulchrum alterum marmoreum.

BRVTT.AVRELIANAE
C.FILIAE MVSOLANAI
PATRON.ET ASTERI
AE.C.F.NEPTI MAR
CELLINAE
.X.COMIT.ET.MARI
NAE.ET.GALLIGANI
.COSS.
ORDINARI.QVAE.VIX.
ANN.XXXVII.MENS.
.X.DIES.XVIIII.
OB MERITA HO
NESTATIS ET CON
CORDIAE CONIVGA
LIS.FL.VITALIS.V.C.
.PROTEG.
ET NOTARIVS VXORI
AMANTISSIMAE.ET.SIBI

109   In fundamentis campanilis   cum quattuor figuris.

C.SALVIVS.C.L.	SALVIA.C.F.
AVCTVS APOLL	PRIMA FECIT
.V.	.V.
P.PLOTIVS.P.L.	SOSIA.S.L.
VRBANVS APOLL.	AMARYLLIS

110   In episcopatu in ornatissimo lapido.

D.M
C.MATERNIO
QVINTIANO
VETERANO

On another marble tomb: 108

The honorable
Protector and Notary
Flavius Vitalis [*built this*]
for himself and his dearest wife
Bruttia Aureliana
daughter of Musolamius,
the patron and of Asteria,
daughter of Gaius,
granddaughter of Marcellinus, ex-count
of Marina, and of Gallicanus,
the consul ordinarius [*317 or 330* CE]
to mark her respectability
and conjugal harmony.
She lived 37 years,
ten months and
eighteen days.[140]

In the foundations of the bell tower with four figures [in relief]:   109

Gaius Salvius Auctus,   Salvia Prima,
freedman of Gaius, and   daughter of Gaius, built it.
Publius Plotius Urbanus,   Sosia Amaryllis,
freedman of Publius,   freedwoman of Lucius,
paid their vows to Apollo.   paid her vows.[141]

On an ornate stone in the bishop's residence: 110

To the spirits of the departed.
Maternia
Benigna,
his daughter, and
Marcus Aurelius
Maximus,

EXPRAETOR
MATERNIA
BENIGNA
FILIA
.E.M.AVRELIVS
MAXIMVS
GENER
OB
MERITA EIVS

III   Inde vero per Regium Lepidi Parmam venit, egregiam civitatem, et apud cathedralem Beatae Virginis aedem sacra Largi, Cyriaci et Smaragdi monumenta conspexit, et ante templi postes
Macrobii nostri memorabile indigne neglecto epigrammate monumentum.

II2   Exinde itaque concedens, Placentia Ticinoque visis, et una cum
Antonio Panormita Augustini sanctissimi episcopi, Severinique
Boetii et paucis aliis vetustatum monumentis compertis, ad exoptatam denique Mediolanum nobilissimum Insubrium civitatem venit, quam amplissimis munitam suburbiis, copiosam rerumque
omnigenum opulentissimam vidit, vetustis tam et novis conspicuam ornamentis.

II3   Vidit praeterea Nicolaum Floro Flavianum, amicum antiquissimum suum et optumum ducalem ad aerarium quaestorem, qui
postquam eum perbenigne susceperat, cum eiusdem epistolares
orationes ad inclytum Philippum ducem illico detulisset, Urbano
Iacobo optimo suo intercurante secretario, Kiriaci annuente principe votis, nobilia multa vetustatum monumenta viderat, et insignia Latinis litteris epigrammata suis adiecerat commentariis, et
primum in quodam scalarum gradu aulae ducalis celeberrimae:

.O.V.F.
MAG.STATIAE
MAG.VXORI.ET

his son-in-law, [*dedicated this to*]
Gaius Maternius
Quintianus,
veteran and
former praetor,
because
of his merits.¹⁴²

Next he proceeded through Reggio Emilia to the fine city of   111
Parma and inspected the monument of SS. Largus, Cyriacus, and
Smaragdus in the cathedral church of the Blessed Virgin, outside
the doors of which he found a monument of Macrobius with a
sadly neglected inscription.¹⁴³

After leaving Parma he went to Piacenza and Pavia, where in   112
company with Antonio Panormita¹⁴⁴ he found memorials of the
holy bishop Augustine and of Severinus Boethius¹⁴⁵ and a few
other ancient monuments, and finally arrived at the noble Insub-
rian city of Milan, his destination.¹⁴⁶ There Cyriac admired the
extensive suburbs, the great and various wealth of the city, and its
remarkable ancient and modern buildings.

In Milan he met his old friend, Niccolò Fioroflaviano, an offi-   113
cial in the ducal treasury, who warmly welcomed him and at once
laid before the famous Duke Filippo¹⁴⁷ a letter that Cyriac had
addressed to him; and through the intercession of his secretary,
Urbano Iacobo, Filippo gave Cyriac permission to inspect the ancient monuments of the city. These included a fine series of Latin
inscriptions which Cyriac recorded in his *commentaria* beginning
with one on a staircase of the famous courtyard of the ducal palace:

[. . .] Mag[. . .] of the tribe Oufentina
[*built this for himself and*]
Statia Mag[. . .] his wife and

C.RVFIONI PATRI
ET
CASSIAE MATRI
TRIBONIAE HILA
RANE ET GINIO
MODE

114   Apud divae Theglae delubrum vetustissimum.

.V.F. . D.M.
MAGIVS
PARDION
SIBI ET
OPPIAE VALERIANAE
CONIVGI.ET.Q.OPPIO
CONSTITVTO

115   In aedium pariete Henrici Panigarolae.

PLVTIAE HERMIONI
ATILIA HERMIONE
ET
ATILIVS GALLICA
MATRI
DVLCISSIMAE

116   Apud sanctum Marcum.

FVFIA SYNORIS
CHRYSIPPO
CONIVGI
FEC
I
T

Gaius Rufio his father
and for Cassia
his mother and for
Trebonia Hilara and
[Ver]ginius
Mode[stus]¹⁴⁸

At the ancient shrine of St. Thecla: 114

To the spirits of the departed.
While he was alive,
Magius Pardion [*built this*]
for himself, his wife
Oppia Valeriana
and his son
Quintus Oppius Constutus.¹⁴⁹

On the wall of the house of Enrico Panigarola:¹⁵⁰   115

Atilia Hermione
and
Atilius Gallica
[*dedicated this*]
to their dearest mother
Plutia Hermione.¹⁵¹

At St. Mark's: 116

Fufia Synoris
made this
for her husband
Chrysippus¹⁵²

117   In ripa fossae urbanae.

L.VALERIO VIRILLI
ONI.VI.VIR.IVN.FRA
TRI PIISSIMO VRAD
SARIO.SACCONIS.F.
PATRI
TERTIAE TREXAE MAT.
SEPTVMIAE SECVND.SEP
TVMIAE EXORATAE.FILIAB.
VALERIAE TERTVLLAE VA
LERIAI VRBANAI SORO
RIB.LAETILIO BLANDO
VALERIAE SPICVLAE
VEGETO.LIBERT.AL
FRIMVS.CENS.
.T.F.I.

118   In urbanarum muro fossarum.

D.M
MARIAE.FESTIVAE
QVAE VIXIT.ANN.XX
XIIII.M.II.DIES.V.
MARIVS
MONTANVS.DOMINAE
ET CONIVG KARISSIMAE
OB EXIMIAM ERGA SE
PVDICITIAM
ET MARIA FESTA
ET MARIVS HIPPOLYTVS
MATRI KARISSIMAE

On a bank of the city's moat: 117

> In his will,
> Valerius Pudens
> ordered this built
> for his dutiful brother
> the junior *sevir*
> Lucius Valerius Virillio,
> his father Vradsarius [*Ursadarius?*],
> son of Sacco,
> his mother Tertia Trexa,
> his daughters Septumia Secunda and
> Septumia Exorata,
> and for his freed slaves
> Laetilius Blandus,
> Valeria Spicula and
> Vegetus.[153]

In a wall of the city's defenses: 118

> To the spirits of the departed.
> Marius Montanus
> [*dedicated this*]
> to his lady and dear wife
> Maria Festiva
> who lived 34 years,
> two months and five days,
> because of her extraordinary
> decency toward himself;
> and Maria Festa and
> Marius Hippolytus [*dedicated it*]
> to their dear mother.[154]

119   In fossae muro urbanae.

D.M
SEX TRVTTEDIO
SEX.F.POL.SABINO
INFANTI DVLCISSI
MO.SEX.TRVTTEDIVS
CLEMENS.PATER

120   Ad sanctum seraphicum.

VALERIVS.QVI
VIXIT.IN.SECVLO
.ANN.XL.
.M.X.D.V.IANVARIVS
EXORCISTA
SIBI ET CONIVGI FECIT

121   In aula post divi Nazarii phanum in hostii parte.

C.ALLIVS.PVD.
SIBI ET
NOVELLIAE FVSCAE
VXORI
.C.ALLIO MAXIMO
.C.ALLIO FVSCIANO
.C.ALLIONI GELLIONI
ET.NOVELLIVS VERVS

122   In urbanarum muro fossarum.

M.IVNIO PATRONO.P.M.
PIENTISSIMO.ET
.P.VARIO.EVTYCHO

In a wall of the city's defenses: 119

> To the spirits of the departed.
> Sextus Truttedius Clemens,
> father, [*dedicated this*] to his sweet infant
> Sextus Truttedius Sabinus
> son of Sextus,
> of the tribe Pollia.[155]

At the [church of] the seraphic saint [St. Francis]:   120

> Valerius Januarius
> the exorcist
> who lived in this world 40 years,
> ten months and five days,
> made this for himself
> and his wife.[156]

In a court behind the Church of St. Nazarius in a portion of   121
the entrance:

> Gaius Allius Pudens [*built this*]
> for himself and
> his wife
> Novellia Fusca;
> and Novellius Verus [*built it*]
> for Gaius Allius Maximus,
> Gaius Allius Fuscianus and
> Gaius Allius Nigellio.[157]

In a wall of the city's defenses: 122

> For the well-deserving and dutiful patron
> Marcus Junius [. . .] and for her dear husband
> Publius Varius Eutyches,

CONIVG.DVLCISS.LIBERTIS
LIBERTAB.IN.FR.P.XV.IN.AG.P.XV.

123   Alio in loco.

D.M
NOVELLIVS
AEQVALIS
SIBI ET EGNATIAE
L.F.PRIMIGENIAE
VXORI
CARISSIMAE
ET SECVNDO
MATVRO.MESSA
LAE SVCCESSORI
MODESTO
LIBERTIS SVIS
.T.F.I.

124   In urbanarum muro fossarum

MORTARIAE
P.F.PIISS.MASCEL
LIO FELIX.ET
LVTATIA.CHRI
STINA.FILIO
DVLCISSIMO
MEMORIAM
POSVERUNT
CONTRA
VOTVM

125   In aula divi Simpliciani.

M.VALERIVS
MAXIMVS

and for the freedmen and freedwomen.
Fifteen feet in front, twenty feet deep.[158]

In another location: 123

To the spirits of the departed.
In his will
Novellius Aequalis
ordered this built
for himself and
his dearest wife
Egnatia Primigenia
daughter of Lucius
and for his freedmen
Secundus, Maturus,
Messalla,
Successor and
Modestus.[159]

In a wall of the city's defenses: 124

Mascellio Felix and
Lutatia Crispina
erected this
monument most reverently
against their desires
to their dear [*daughter*]
Mortaria, daughter of Publius.[160]

In the court of [the Church of] St. Simplicianus: 125

Marcus Valerius
Maximus

SACERDOS
D.S.I.M.STV.
ASTROLOGIAE
SIBI.ET
SEVERIAE APR
VXORI
.H.M.H.N.S.

126   In divi Nazari delubro.

FAVSTVS.VI.VIR
ET.AVGVST.QVI
INTER.PRIMOS
AVGVSTALES.A
DECVRIONIBVS
AVGVSTALIS FAC
TVS.EST.VIRIAE
MAXIMAE VXORI
CARISS.ET.VRSO
LVPVLLONI LIBERTIS
FVTVRIS

127   In palatii fronte praetoriani.

C.ATILIVS
C.F
SECVNDVS
SIBI.ET
VALERIAE
P.L.CROCIN.
VXORI
SVAE.ET.IVVENI
VERNAE.SVAE.VIX.
A.X

priest
of the unconquered sun god Mithras,
learned in astrology, [*built this*]
for himself and
his wife
Severia Apr[. . .].
Heirs have no right to dispose of this monument.[161]

In the Church of St. Nazarius: 126

Faustus *sevir* and
augustalis, who was made
augustalis
among the first-ranking
augustales by
the members of the City Council
[*built this*] for his dear wife
Viria Maxima,
and for his slaves
Ursus, Lupus and Leo
who will be freed.[162]

In the facade of the governor's palace: 127

Gaius Atilius
Secundus
son of Gaius
[*built this*] for himself,
his wife
Valeria
Crocine, daughter of Lucius,
and for Juvenis
his home-born slave
who lived ten years.[163]

113

128   In vetustissimo basi sancti Dyonisi.

D.M
.I.O.M.IMMQ.
MAXIMI.ET.MAXIMAI
CALVINI MAXIMVS
MATRI
INCOMPARABILI

129   Ad sanctum Petrum.

D.M
Q.VITELLI
SATVRNINI
VITELLII
VERANIVS
ET CONSTANS
VI.VIR
IVNIORES
PATRI.OPTIMO

130   In aulae porticu post sancti Amabilis phanum.

.P.VRSIO
SEX.FIL
POLLIONI
PATRI VETTIAE
LEPIDAE MATRI
P.VRSIO.P.F.PAVLO
VI VIR IVN.FRATR.
CVR.AER
P.VRSIO ELAINO
.F.PIISS.
VRSIA.P.F.PRISCA

On an ancient statue base of St. Dionysius: 128

Calvinius Maximus
[*dedicated this*]
to the spirits of the departed
and to the immortal memory of
Maximia Maxima
his incomparable mother.[164]

At St. Peter's: 129

The Vitelli,
Veranius and
Constans,
junior *sevirs*
[*dedicated this*]
to the spirits of
Quintus Vitellius
Saturninus
their excellent father.[165]

In the cloister walk behind the Church of St. Amabilis: 130

Ursia Prisca daughter of Publius
[*dedicated this*]
to her father,
Publius Ursius Pollio
son of Sextus,
her mother Vettia Lepida,
her brother Publius Ursius Paullus
son of Publius,
junior *sevir* and treasury officer
and to the loyal freedman
Publius Ursius Elainus.[166]

131   Iuxta sancti Marci templum.

C.SATTIVS

.C.L.FELIX

SIBI ET

C.SATTIO

.C.F.

.O.V.F.

PATRO

NO

132   In sancti Georgii templo in basi quadam.

V.F

ATILIVS.MAC

RINVS.SECVNDVS

ATILIO.MACRINO

.PATRI.

ET.SVRAE.PVPAE

.MATRI.

ET.MACRINO

PRIMO.FRAT.

ET.MACRINAE

.SECVNDIN.

133   In pariete sancti Stephani.

P.VALERIO

.P.LIBERTO

.PALAT.

TACITO

VI.VIRO.SENI

ORI.ET.AVGVSTALI

Beside the Church of St. Mark: 131

> Gaius Sattius Felix
> freedman of Gaius
> [*built this*]
> for himself
> and his patron
> Gaius Sattius
> son of Gaius
> of the tribe Oufentina.[167]

In the Church of St. George on a base: 132

> While he was alive,
> Atilius Macrinus
> Secundus [*built this*]
> for Atilius Macrinus
> his father,
> Sura Pupa
> his mother,
> Macrinus Primus
> his brother and
> Macrina Secundina
> his daughter.[168]

On a wall of St. Stephen's: 133

> To Publius Valerius
> Tacitus,
> freedman of Publius,
> of the tribe Palatina,
> senior *sevir*
> and *augustalis*.[169]

134   Apud sanctae Mariae templum secretum in basi.

L.ARVLENVS
ANOPTES
APOLLINI

135   In divi Victoris templo.

D.M
AMANTIO
DVLCISSIMO
POSVERVNT
PARENTES
VERNA
PATER
ET LVPVLA MATER
.FILIO.
INNOCENTISSI
MO

136   Apud sanctum Nazarium in basi.

DIIS.MAN
L.REYNO PHI
LETO AMATORI

137   Ibi prope.

DIIS.MAN
L.GRAECINIO
POMPEIANO.ANIMVLAE
.IVCVNDISS.
QVI VIXIT ANNOS
XXIIII.MATER POSVIT
AEMILIA POMPEIA
SIBI

At the remote Church of St. Mary, on a base: 134

Lucius Arulenus
Anoptes
to Apollo.[170]

In the Church of St. Victor: 135

To the spirits of the departed.
His parents,
Verna
his father
and Lupula his mother,
set this up
for Amantius
the sweetest
and most innocent
child.[171]

At St. Nazarius, on a base: 136

To the spirits of the departed.
For his beloved friend,
Lucius Reynus Philetus.[172]

Nearby: 137

To the spirits of the departed.
Aemilia Pompeia
his mother erected this
for her happy little soul
Lucius Graecinus
Pompeianus
who lived 24 years,
and for herself.[173]

138   In basi quadam apud sancti Donini templum.

IOVI

IVNONI

MINERVAE

Q.VOCONIVS

EX

VOTO

139   Apud Brutianum rus agri Mediolanensis.

V.F

C.FABIVS

PLACENTINVS

SIBI.ET

COELIAE

OLYMPIADI

VXORI

AMANTISS.

ET.SVIS

140   In foribus sancti Bartholomoei templi.

.V.F.

M.SVLPICIVS

M.F.ACCEPTVS

SIBI.ET.M.SVLPICIO

.CASTO.

PATRONO

EROTI CENNAMO

CONLIBERTIS.PAT

RONI.ET.L.LVCILIO

FLORO AMICO

On a base at the Church of St. Donino: 138

Quintus Voconius
[*dedicated this*]
according to his promise
to Jupiter,
Juno and
Minerva.[174]

In the Brutian countryside of Milan: 139

While he was alive,
Gaius Fabius
Placentinus [*built this*]
for himself and
his beloved
wife
Coelia
Olympias
and for his [*family*][175]

On the doors of St. Bartholomew's: 140

While he was alive,
Marcus Sulpicius
Acceptus,
son of Marcus [*built this*]
for himself and for Marcus Sulpicius
Acastus his patron,
for his fellow freedmen,
Eros and Cinnamus,
and for his friend,
Lucius Lucilius Florus.[176]

141   In phani foribus sancti Bartholomoei.

V.F
Q.CAMPILIVS
Q.F
VIRILLIO VI.VIR
.IVN.SIBI.ET.
TATINIAE.M.F.
VERAE.VXORI
Q.CAMPILIO
PATRI
CASTRICIAE
CONDEXVAE
MATRI

142   In fossarum muro urbicarum.

CISALPINI
L.T
TRANSALPINI
.PATR.
COLL.NAVT.
COMENS
HERED.FAC.CVR.

143   Ad sanctum Marcum.

I.O.M
C.CASSIVS.C.F.
T^{H}YRSVS.VI.VIR
V.S.L.M.

On the doors of the shrine of San Bartolomeo: 141

> While he was alive
> Quintus Campilius
> Virillio,
> son of Quintus,
> junior *sevir* [*built this*]
> for himself and
> his wife Tatiana Vera,
> daughter of Marcus,
> his father
> Quintus Campilius,
> his mother
> Castricia Condexua.[177]

In a wall of the city's defenses: 142

> His heirs had this built
> for [. . .], trader
> in Cisalpine and
> Transalpine Gaul,
> patron of
> the guild of sailors
> of Comum.[178]

At St. Mark's: 143

> Gaius Cassius Thyrsus,
> son of Gaius, sevir
> willingly and justly fulfilled his vow
> to Jupiter, Best and Greatest.[179]

144   Derthonae ante postes monacorum sancti Martiani.

C.ORISCVS
ECNATI.FRON
TONIS
ET.IVLIAE.EVTYCHI
LIBERTI.FILIVS
ANN.XVI.HIC
ADQVIESCIT

145   In fossae muro urbanae.

D.M.
RAMMIAE
CALLITYCHE
FILIAE PIENTISS.

146   Apud Tradatem veterem Mediolanensem vicum.

VOTIS OMNIB.
CAELESTIB.CONSEN
TIENTIB.BENEVERTEN
TIBQ
L.PARIVS.HERMES

147   In silvis procul a Tradate litteris inscriptis videntur:

TREBVC.
CARPENTVM
BONA.NOCTE
VADE.DORMITVM

148   Mediolani extra portam Comensem in aede sancti Simpliciani
in ornatissimo tumulo.

At Dertona, before the gates of the monastery of St. Martia- 144
nus:

> Corsicus,
> aged sixteen,
> rests here;
> son of Egnatius
> Fronto
> and of the freedwoman
> Julia Eutychia.[180]

In a wall of the city's defenses: 145

> To the spirits of the departed.
> For Rammia
> Callityche,
> devoted daughter.[181]

At Tradate, an old suburb of Milan: 146

> Lucius Parius Hermes
> [dedicated this]
> since the Heavenly Powers
> agreed to and fulfilled
> all his vows.[182]

In the woods at some distance from Tradate is seen an inscrip- 147
tion:

> Six-foot long
> carriage
> on a good night
> go, having slept.[183]

In Milan outside the Como gate in the Church of S. Simplicia- 148
nus on a decorated tomb:

.Q.VIRI SEVERINI.
ATTIA SEVERINA.ET.Q.VIRIVS
ONESAS PARENTES

RAPTVS EGO SVPERIS PATRIBVSQVE ABLATVS
   INIQVE
CVM FRVI DEBVERAM AETATE FLORIDA LVCE
HIS REQVIESCO LOCIS VITAM CVI FATA
   NEGARVNT.
PRAECIPITEM MEMET SVPERI MERSERE SVB AVLAS
AC TVMVLO MERSERE GRAVI. VSVS ET ARSQVE
MIHI FVERAT; STVDIOSO CORDE REPERTA
MAXIMA QVADRIPEDVM CVRA, STVDIA QVOQVE
   PLVRA
FVERVNT. INGENIO SEMPER PLENVS, PROBITATE
   BEATVS
ET QVANDOQVE SIMVL PATRIBVS FINITO LIMINE
   VITAE
MANIBVS HIS QVIETI PARITER SOCIABIMVR VNA.
QVISQVE LEGIS, DOLEAS, DEVITES TALIA FATA.

QVI.VIXIT.ANNOS.XXVIIII
MENS.V.D.V
ET.ATTIO.EPICTETO.LIBERT.

149   In alio lapide.

V.F
AVE.ALCIME.BENE
TIBI.SIT
D.M.
C.IVLIO ALCIMO
RAVENNATI
COMPARATOR
MERCIS SVTORIAE

Attia Severina and Quintus Virius
Onesas, parents of
Quintus Virius Severinus

Snatched by the powers above and unfairly taken away from
my parents,
when I should have enjoyed the light in the bloom of youth,
I rest in these places, I to whom the fates have denied life.
The powers above sunk me headlong beneath their courts,
and they shut me in the heavy tomb. Practice and skill
Had I; and in my eager heart I found
The greatest concern for horses, and many other skills.
I was always filled with ability and blessed with honesty;
so that whenever they have crossed the threshhold of life,
we will associate together with the spirits of my parents,
peaceful like these.
You, whoever read this, feel sorry and avoid such a fate.

He lived 29 years,
five months and five days;
and for the freedman Attius Epictetus.[184]

On another stone: 149

Hail, Alcimus,
be happy.
To the spirits of the departed.
[*He built this*] while alive
for Gaius Julius Alcimus
of Ravenna,
purchaser

ET VIRIAE MARCELL
CONIVGI OPTIMAE
ET HERMIAE.LIB.ET
CAETERIS LIBERTIS
LIBERTABQ.MEIS
ET VIRIAE MARCELLAE
.H.M.H.N.S.

150   Derthonae in marmore ecclesiae maioris.

QVART.COMINIVS
.C.F.SIBI ET
TERTIAE PETRONIAE
M.F.VXORI ET
L.COMINIO.C.F.ET
C.COMINIO C.F.
FRATRIBVS ET
TERTIAE COMINIAE
SORORI ET
AMPLIATO ET FELICI
.LIB.

151   Et extra utique Ticinianae arcis ab antiquae gentis origine gestarum rerum insignes machinarum reliquias, preciosamque supellectilem, hortosque regios, et ingentia ferarum claustra, nobile sui magnificentissimi parentis opus, inspexerat, et Claraevallis Cartusiensiumque nobilia monasteria.

152   Deinde vero se Brixiam contulit, ubi plura veternitatis conspexit, videlicet:

L.CHAMVRIVS
L.L.PANDARVS

of shoemaker's wares,
and for Viria Marcella,
his excellent wife,
for the freedwoman Hermia and
for my other freedmen
and women
and Viria Marcella.
Heirs have no right to dispose of this monument.[185]

At Dertona, on a marble of the larger church: 150

Quartus Cominius
son of Gaius [*built this*] for himself
and for his wife,
Tertia Petronia, daughter of Marcus,
and for his brothers,
Lucius Cominius, son of Gaius and
Gaius Cominius, son of Gaius, and
for his sister,
Tertia Cominia, and
for his freedmen,
Ampliatus and Felix.[186]

And outside of Milan, in the castle of Pavia, Cyriac inspected   151
remains of the famous war engines going back to the beginnings of
the history of the Visconti family, the sumptuous furnishings, the
royal gardens, and the huge cages of the menagerie, which was
nobly built by the duke's magnificent father,[187] and he also visited
the abbey of Chiaravalle and the great Carthusian monastery in
Pavia.

He then proceeded to Brescia, where he saw many antiquities,   152
namely:

Lucius Camurius
Pandarus, freedman of Lucius,

129

IIIIII.VIR.AVG
SIBI ET
ZENONI.LIBERTO

.L.
.C.M.I.
IN.FR.P XX
IN AG P XX

153   In lapide aquae sanctae in aede sanctae Iuliae.

D.M
L.CAELI.ARRIAN.
MEDICO LEGIONIS
.II.ITALIC.QVI.VIX.
ANN.XXXXVIIII.MEN.
SIS.VII.SCRIBONIA
FAVSTINA
CONIVGI
KARISSIMO

154   Alio in loco.

M.NONIO.M.F.
FAB.ARRIO PAVLINO
APROCI XV.VIR.SACR.
FAC.CVLTORES.LAVDVM
EIVS

155   Alio in lapide.

CAECILIAE.L.F.
MACRINAE.P.
SENECIVS GARVLLVS
F.AB HEREDIBVS

sevir augustalis, [*built this*]
for himself and
his freedman Zeno.[188]

Site belonging to
C. M. I.
Twenty feet in front,
twenty feet deep.[189]

On the stone for the holy water in the Church of St. Julia: 153

To the spirits of the departed.
Scribonia
Faustina [*dedicated this*]
to her dearest
husband
Lucius Caelius Arrianus,
doctor of the Second Legion
Italica, who lived 49 years
and seven months.[190]

In another place:[191]   154

The priests of his household gods [*dedicated this*]
to the honorable Marcus Nonius
Arrius Paulinus Aper of the Fabian tribe,
son of Marcus, a distinguished youth,
member of the Board of Fifteen
for celebrating the sacred rites.[192]

On another stone: 155

Publius Senecius Garrulus,
her son, appointed by her heirs
according to her will, had this built
for Caecilia

TESTAMENT
F.I.

[no heading]:

L.VALERIVS
MARCELLINVS
.L.D.NEPOS.D.D.

156 Alio in marmore.

P.CLODIO.P.F.
FAB.SVRAE
Q.FLAMINI DIVI
TRAIANI PONTIF
II VIR.QVINQ.TRIB.
LEG.II.ADIVTRIC.
PIAE.FID.CVRAT
REI.P.BERGOM.
DATO.AB.IMP.TRA
IANO.CVRAT.REI
.P.COMENS.DAT AB
IMP.HADRIANO
COLLEGIA FABROR
.ET.CENT.

157 In aede sancti Bartholomei in monte.

ACCEPTO CHIAE
SERVO LANARI
PECTINARI
SODALES.POSVER

158 In aede sancti Sandri.

.B.M.IN PACE
FLANIGO SCVTA

Macrina
daughter of Lucius.[193]

[*no heading*]:

Lucius Valerius
Marcellinus his grandson [*built this*];
the land was given by a decree of the city council.[194]

On another marble:[195]   156

The guilds of firemen [*dedicated this*]
to Publius Clodius Sura,
son of Publius, of the Fabian tribe,
quaestor, priest of the deified Trajan,
member of the Board of Two
who took the five-yearly census,
tribune of Legion II
Adiutrix Pia Fidelis,
appointed Administrator
of the city of Bergomum
by Emperor Trajan,
appointed Administrator
of the city of Comum
by emperor Hadrian.[196]

In the Church of San Bartolomeo in Monte: 157

His fellow
wool carders set this up
for Acceptus,
slave of Chia.[197]

In the Church of Sant'Alessandro: 158

Good memory. In peace.
Flavius Higgo,

133

RIVS SCOLA TER
TIA QVI VIXIT.ANN.
.L.M.XXV.ET
MILITAVIT.AN.VI.CO
GNATVS DVLCISSIMVS
SORORIO AMANTISS.

159   Alio in marmore.

QVINTIA RESTITVTA
C.PETRONO FAB.FRON
TONI.VI.VIR AVG.BRIX.
OB MERITA VIRO PIEN
TISSIMO

160   Prope turrim de la Palata in pariete domus privatae.

· COLLEGIA.FABR.ET
CENT.L.CORNELIO
PROSODICO VI.VIR
AVG.BRIX.ET.VERON.
SACERD.COLLEG.IVVE
NVM BRIXIAN.PRI
MVM INSTITVTIS OB
MERITA EIVS HONORE
CONTENTVS IMPEN
DIVM REMIS.IN.TVT.
HS.N.D.

161   In pariete hospitalis extra aedem sancti Francisci.

L.POBLICIVS HEBE
NVS SIBI.ET.OPTATE
MVLVIAE CONTVB.
ET VELLIAE FIRMAE
PISAINAE

scutarius of the third *schola*,
who lived about 25 years
and served six years.
His dearest kinsman with his wife
[*erected this monument*]
to his beloved brother-in-law.[198]

On another marble:[199]   159

Quintia Restituta [*set this up*]
for her dutiful husband
Gaius Petronius Fronto of the Fabian tribe,
sevir augustalis of Brixia
because of his merits.[200]

Near the tower of Palata on the wall of a private house: 160

The guilds of firemen [*dedicated this*]
to Lucius Cornelius
Prosodicus *sevir*
augustalis of Brixia and Verona,
the first priest of the Young
Knights of Brixia,
appointed because of his merits.
Contented with this honor,
he reimbursed the expense,
leaving 500 sestertii
for its maintenance.[201]

In the wall of a hospital outside the Church of St. Francis: 161

Lucius Poblicius Hebenus
[*built this for*] himself, Optata
Mulvia, his companion,
and for Vellia Firma
Pisaina.[202]

162   In aede sanctae Agathae.

FL.LVPPIO EX
PRAEP.AVR.SEVE
RINAE MATR.DVL
CISS.QVAE.VIX.A.
LXXV.M.VII.VALE
MIHI MATER PIEN
TISS.

163   In eodem loco.

VICTOR.ARTHE
MIO.FRATRI.BE
NEMERENT.QVI
VIXIT.ANNOS
QVINQVEGINTA
ET MENSES QVAT
TVOR.AETERNVM
.SALVE.
QVI LEGERIS

164   Extra aedem sanctae Agathae in pariete.

.C.QVINTIVS.C.F.
FAB.CATVLLVS
DECVR.BRIXIAE
SIBI.ET
CORNELIAE.M.F.
MAGNAE VXORI
ET.Q.QVINTIO
.C.F.FRATRI
C.QVINTIO SECVN
DO.PATRI.ANTONIAE.
CATVLLAE

In the Church of Sant' Agata: 162

Flavius Luppio
ex-commander [*dedicated this*]
to his dear mother
Aurelia Severina
who lived 75 years,
seven months and nineteen days.
Goodbye from me, devoted mother.[203]

In the same place: 163

Victor
[*built this*]
for his well-deserving
brother
Artemius
who lived 50 years,
four months.
You who read this,
goodbye for ever.[204]

Outside the Church of St. Agatha, in the wall: 164

Gaius Quintius
Catullus, son of Gaius,
of the tribe Fabia,
councilman of Brixia,
in his will ordered this
[*to be built for*] himself and
his wife Cornelia Magna
daughter of Marcus,
his brother Quintus Quintius
son of Gaius,
his father Gaius Quintius Secundus and

137

MATRI
.T.F.I.

165 Et denique Veronam feracissimam et antiquam civitatem olim a Gallis conditam venit, ubi non exigua veterum monumenta comperit. Hanc praeterea urbem praeterfluit fluvius Athesis nomine, secundum quod dicit Papias, licet aliqui eum Athacem vocent, dicentes illum esse de quo meminit Lucanus; alii dicunt Athacem esse Ticinum, sed Papias dicit quod Athax est fluvius inter Laudnum et Remos iuxta Renum: sed Veronae fluvius est.

166 In hac urbe Ligurica vidit Kyriacus, ut in commentariis suis reposuit, laberinthum, qui harena nunc dicitur, et habetur quod constructum fuit anno Octaviani Augusti XXXIX, ante ortum Christi tertio, cuius pars exterior terrae motibus corruit, et nunc extat locus rotundus Harenae per totum magnis saxis undique constructus et perfilatus cum cubalis intus et multis antris multiformiter redimitus ⟨sit⟩. In huius autem rotunditate narrat Kiriacus ipse quod extant scalae magnis lapidibus appositae, quae quanto magis in altitudine protendebant, tanto plus in rotunditate videbantur ampliari; et secundum quod refertur, quinquaginta cubitis in altitudine extenditur, in cuius summitate quidam locus magnus et nobilis multiformis laboratus marmoreo de lapide circumquaque redimitus erat.

167 Vidit praeterea portam geminam triumphalem Bursariorum vivo de lapide constructam, quae duodecim numero exornata fenestris conspectari videtur, ubi tale Kiriacus Latinum exceperat epigramma.

COLONIA AVGVS
TA.VERONA.NO
VA GALLIENIANA
VALERIANO.II.
ET.LVCILLO.COSS.
MVRI VERONEN

for his mother
Antonia Catulla.[205]

Finally he came to the very fertile and ancient city of Verona,   165
founded by the Gauls, and he found there a considerable number
of ancient monuments.[206] The name of the river flowing through
Verona, according to Papias,[207] is the Athesis, although some call
it the Athax, asserting that it is the same as that mentioned by
Lucan;[208] others identify the Athax with the river Ticinus, although Papias says that it is a river between Laon and Rheims
near the Rhine; however, the river in question is in Verona.[209]

In this Ligurian[210] city Cyriac, as he recorded in his *commen-*   166
taria, saw the labyrinth known today as the Arena, which is believed to have been built in the thirty-ninth year of the reign of
Octavian Augustus, three years before Christ's birth. The outside
of the Arena has been shattered by earthquakes and its whole circuit is seen today to be constructed of large stones strung together,
while its interior is ringed about by many caverns and hollow
chambers of various shapes. Cyriac himself records that there are
stairways of large stones placed all round the circuit which seem
wider and more rotund as they rise in height; and report has it
that it is fifty cubits high and had a fine large area of multiform
shape, with a marble surround on the topmost level.

Another thing he viewed in Verona was the double triumphal   167
gate of the Borsari built of native stone and adorned with twelve
windows from which Cyriac transcribed this Latin inscription:[211]

The Augustan Colony
of Verona called
New Gallienian,
when Valerian
for the second time
and Lucilius were consuls [265 CE].
The walls of the Veronese

SIVM FABRICATI
EX DIE. III.NON.A
PRILIVM
DEDICATI.PR.NON.
DECEMBR.IVBENTE
SANCTISSIMO
GALLIENO AVG.N.
INSISTENTE.AVR.
MARCELLINO.V.P.
.DVC . DVC.
CVRANTE.IVL.
MARCELLINO

168   Alio in loco ibi prope.

DEO.MAGNO
AETERN
L.STATIVS DIODO
RVS.QVOT.SE PRE
CIBVS COMPOTEM
.FECISSET.
.V.S.L.M.

169   In civitacula.

CLAVDIAE.TI.F.
MARCELLINAE
BELLICI
SOLLERTIS
.CO.
M.ET.Q.HORTENSI
PAVLINVS.ET.FIRMVS

were constructed from April 3
and dedicated on December 4.
The revered Gallienus
our emperor
ordered them;
the illustrious Aurelius
Marcellinus,
commander
with a salary of 200,000 sesterces,
planned them;
Julius Marcellinus supervised [*the work*].²¹²

In another place nearby: 168

Lucius Statius Diodorus
willingly and justly
fufilled his vow
to God,
great [*and*] eternal,
because He granted
his prayers.²¹³

In a little city [*or* necropolis]:   169

Marcus Hortensius Paulinus and
Quintus Hortensius Firmus
[*dedicated this*]
to Claudia Marcellina
daughter of Tiberius,
[*wife*] of the consul
Bellicus Sollers [*ca. 108* CE].²¹⁴

170   Super flumen Athesis.

VETO RELIQVIAS.
PVPRONVS CALLISTVS
HOMO OPTIM
HIC IACET

171   In cimiterio sancti Nicolai.

LOCO PVBLIC.
DAT.D.D.
PARCIS . AVG
.SACR.
L.CASSIVS.VERVICI
.F.NIGRINVS.VI.VIR
.AVG.
.V.S.L.M.

172   In cimiterio sancti Firmi maioris.

P.GRAECINIO
.P.F.POB
LAGONI
ORNAMENTIS.CONSVLARIB.

173

OCTAVIA .. L.
.HILARA.
V.F.SIBI.ET
L.CAELIO.L.L.
STATVRAI. VIRO
SVO.ET.
L.CAELIO
L.F
FIRMO

Above the river Athesis: 170

> I forbid [*other*] remains [*to be buried here*].
> Publius Veronus Callistus,
> an excellent man,
> lies here.[215]

In the cemetery of St. Nicholas: 171

> Lucius Cassius Nigrinus
> son of Vervicus,
> *sevir augustalis*,
> willingly and justly
> fulfilled his vow.
> Sacred to the august Fates.
> Public land was given
> by decree of the city council.[216]

In the cemetery of St. Firmus the Greater: 172

> To Publius Graecinius
> Laco, son of Publius,
> of the tribe Publilia, [*honored with*]
> consular insignia.[217]

173

> While she was alive,
> Octavia Hilara,
> freedwoman of Gaius
> [*built this*] for herself,
> her husband
> Lucius Caelius Statura,
> freedman of Lucius,
> and her son,

FILIO
.H.M.H.N.S.

174   In curia pauperum.

MAGISTRI
M.LICINIVS.M.F.PVSILLIO
SEX.VIPSANIVS.M.F.CLEMENS
Q.CASSIVS.C.F.NIGER
MINISTRI.
BLANDVS.C.AFINI.ASCLAE.SER.
MVRRANVS.P.CLODI TVRPIONIS.SER
AVCTVS.M.FABRICI HILARI.SER.
COMPITVM REFECERVNT
TECTVM
PARIETES.ALLEVARVNT
VALVAS LIMEN DE SVA
PECVNIA
LARIBVS DANT COSSO
CORNELIO LENTVLO
.L.PISONE AVGVRE COS.

175   In tumulo marmoreo sito in maiori ecclesia.

P.IVLIVS.APOLI
ONIVS.SIBI.ET
ATTIAE VALERI
AE.CONIVG.OB
SEQVENTISS.
VIVVS.PARAVIT
ET EIVSQ.
DEI.COR.IN.ARC.
CONDIDIT
ET

Lucius Caelius Firmus, son of Lucius.
Heirs have no right to dispose of this monument.[218]

In the poorhouse: 174

Priests:
Marcus Licinius Pusillio son of Marcus;
Sextus Vipsanius Clemens son of Marcus;
Quintus Cassius Niger son of Gaius
Attendants:
Blandus, slave of Gaius Afinius Ascla;
Murranus slave of Publius Clodius Turpio;
Auctus slave of Marcus Fabricius Hilarus.
They rebuilt the crossroads shrine;
they raised the roof
and the walls;
they gave it to the household gods
at their own expense
when Cossus Cornelius Lentulus
and Lucius Piso the augur
were consuls [1 BCE].[219]

On a marble tomb located in the larger church: 175

Publius Julius
Apollonius
while he was alive
prepared [*this site*]
for himself and
his very devoted wife
Attia Valeria;
he put her deceased body
in the coffin;
and while alive

LOCVM SERVIO
DEDICAVIT

176   In aede divi prothomartyris.

D.M
C.CALVENTI
FIRMINI
CVRATORES
INSTRVMENTI
VERONAES
EX NVMERO
COLLEG.FABR.

177   In alio loco cum figuris.

EX TESTAMENTO
P.SACIDI.Q.F.
POB.PATRIS
P.SACIDI.P.F.AN.VI.
M.SACIDI.P.F.AN.IIII.

178   Et alibi.

CN.SERVILIVS
CN.L.
SYRVS
V.F

179   In phano divi Proculi.

PHOTINO
VESTIARIO
NICEPHORVS.LIB.
PATRON.OPTIM.
ET.SIBI.V.F.

dedicated
the site.[220]

In the Church of the Divine Protomartyr [San Stefano]: 176

The officers in charge
of the fire-fighting equipment
of Verona [*dedicated this to*]
the spirit of
Gaius Calventius
Firminus,
former member
of the guild of firemen.[221]

In another place, with sculpture: 177

In accordance with the will:
[*Tomb of*] Publius Sacidius son of Quintus,
of the tribe Publicia, father;
Publius Sacidius son of Publius, six years old;
Marcus Sacidius son of Publius, four years old.[222]

Elsewhere: 178

Gnaeus Servilius
Syrus
freedman of Gnaeus
made this while he was alive.[223]

In the shrine of St. Proculus: 179

While he was alive,
Nicephorus the freedman
made this for himself and
for his excellent patron Photinus,
the clothes dealer.[224]

147

180   Ibi prope in hortulo.

D.M
L.NOVELL.
RHODAN.
.T.F.I.

181   In domo ecclesiae antedictae.

D.LIVIAE.M
VENVSTAE
M.LIVIVS FORTV
NATVS
LIBERTAE.ET VXORI
BENE MERENTI
ANN.XXIII.M.VII.D
XVII

182   In vetustissimo sepulchro.

C.GAVI.C.F.QVINTAN
ANN.XLIII.M.X.C.GAVIVS
MENODORVS.FILIO PIISSIMO
D PATER.INFELIX M
AEQVIVS.ENIM.FVERAT
VOS HOC MIHI
FECISSE
ET.SIBI

183   In abbatia sancti Zenonis.

V.F
M.GAVIVS
SEVERVS SIBI ET
CORNELIAE
EPIMELIAE

Nearby in a garden: 180

> To the spirits of the departed.
> Lucius Novellius
> Rhodanus
> in his will ordered this to be made.²²⁵

Inside the aforementioned church: 181

> To the spirits of the departed.
> Marcus Livius Fortunatus
> [*dedicated this*]
> to Livia Venusta,
> his well-deserving
> freedwoman and wife
> [*who lived*] 23 years, seven months
> and seventeen days.²²⁶

On a very old tomb: 182

> To the spirits of the departed.
> The unhappy father
> Gaius Gavius Menodorus [*built this*]
> for Gaius Gavius Quintanus son of Gaius,
> who lived fourteen years and ten months,
> a most dutiful son, and for himself.
> It would have been fairer
> if you had done this for me.²²⁷

In the Abbey of San Zeno: 183

> While he was alive,
> Marcus Gavius
> Severus
> built [*this*] for himself
> and his excellent,

CONIVGI OPTIMAE
BENE MERENTI.ET.
M.GAVIO SERENO
ET CORNELIAE RESTI
TVTAE
LIBERTIS

184   In hortulo sancti Zenonis.

QVARTVA
HIC VIDVA VIXIT
ANN.LXXX
MARCELLINVS CARIS
SIMVS FRATER.CARIS
SIMAE SORORI ET
PIENTISSIMAE
MERITE
FECIT
QUEM OMNES ECLESIA
DILIGEBAT

185   In pila quadrata marmorea.

AVENIAE
BASSARIDIS
FILIAE.OPTIM.
M.GAVIVS
CORNELIVS
AGATHE.MER^{ite}
AVENIANVS
OMNI.INIVRIA
DEBILITATVS

well-deserving wife
Cornelia
Epimelia
and for his freed slaves
Marcus Gavius Serenus
and Cornelia Restituta[228]

In the garden of San Zeno: 184

Here lies the widow
Quartua;
she lived 80 years.
Her dear brother
Marcellinus
rightly
made this
for his dearest,
devout sister
whom the whole church
loved.[229]

On a square marble pillar: 185

Marcus Gavius
Cornelius
Agathemerus
Avenianus,
weakened
by much suffering,
[made this for]
Avenia Bassaris
his excellent daughter.[230]

186   Ab alio latere

VIXIT.ANN.
XXV.MEN.IIII.
DIEB.XIIII.
OMNI SENSV
VITA PIETATE
PERFECTISSIM

187   A tertio latere

ΘΕΑ
ΧΑΡΙΣ
ΒΑΣΣΑΡΙΣ

188   Ab alia parte lapidis

MANV MISS.
ALVMNA
ANN.IIII.DIER.
XVII.AMAVENA
MACRO
SPLEND^{ido} AEQ^{uiti} R.^{romano}
OMNI HONORE
FVNCTO

189   In alio lapide

CN.CORNELIVS
CVRVINI
.L.NERITVS
VI VIR
AVG.SIBI.ET
CLODIAE TONNI
ANAE.L.CHRESTAE
CONTVBERNAL.

On the other side: 186

She lived
25 years, four months
and fourteen days.
She was perfect
in every feeling,
in her life and in her devotion.[231]

On the third side: 187

Goddess.
Grace.
Bassaris.[232]

On the other part of the stone: 188

Foster daughter,
aged four years
and seventeen days,
manumitted by
Marcus Avena Macer,
the distinguished Roman knight
who enjoyed
every honor.[233]

On another stone: 189

Gnaeus Cornelius
Neritus,
freedman of Curvinus,
sevir augustalis [built this]
for himself and
for his companion
Clodia Chresta,
freedwoman of Tonniana.[234]

190   Exinde postquam diligenter omnia vetera perscruptasset, Mediolanum iterum reversus est, ubi per dies aliquot magno cum principe moratus est.

191   Deinde vero Mantuam petiit, civitatem vetustissimam Italiae in provintia, quae quondam Venetia, quae et Gallia Cisalpina nuncupatur, prout egomet in suis commentariis repperi; mentionem dignissimam, ni fallor, hoc loco praestantiae tuae destinandam curavi.

192   Haec enim civitas sita fuit, secundum quod refert Isidorus et Paulus Longobardus, a Mantho: '⟨Manto⟩[8] Tiresiae filia post interitum Thebanorum in Italiam delata ⟨Mantuam⟩' condidisse dicitur' . . . et dicta Mantua quod manes tueatur, ut scribit Isidorus: ab ipsa etiam Mantho dicta est Mantua civitas. Virgilius vero, qui ex hac urbe traxit originem, non minimum civitati decus, dicit quod filius eiusdem Manthos, Ogus nomine, eandem civitatem a matris nomine Mantuam appellavit. Ipsa autem dicta est Mantho sive Manthos quia denominaretur a manes et tueor, quia manes, id est deorum mortuorum, tueretur. Haec, alii ut dicunt, de quodam viro nomine Tibere filium habuit, qui dictus est Obius sive Obnus, et idem dictus est Bianor a bis fortis, scilicet corpore et animo. Unde Virgilius: *sepulchrum incipit apparere Bianoris.* Hic, ut quidam volunt, condidit Mantuam, quam ex Manthois matris nomine Mantuani nominaverunt. Fuit autem Tiresias huius Manthois genitor, magnus Thebanorum vates, de quo meminit Statius in Thebanorum historia. Haec de exordio urbis huius patent ex auctoribus memoratis.

193   Tempus autem fundationis eius expressum inde habetur; antiquissimum enim opinari potest ex quo vel a Mantho Tiresiae vatis filia vel a filio ipsius Manthois constat conditam. Nam interitus Thebanorum, sive Thebarum expugnatio, facta per Graecos post diutinam obsidionem pro certamine regni inter Ethioclem et Polinicem, Edipi Thebanorum regis filios, Troianum praecessit excidium per annos circiter sexaginta hoc modo. Edipus enim tempore

After he had carefully investigated all the antiquities of Verona,   190
he returned to Milan and stayed there for several days as a guest of
the duke.

He then made for Mantua, a most ancient city in the Italian   191
province of Venetia, which the Romans also called Cisalpine Gaul,
as I have found recorded in Cyriac's own *commentaria*; and I cite
them here because I am sure they will particularly interest you.[235]

Mantua was founded, according to Isidore[236] and Paul the Dea-   192
con, by Manto, the daughter of Tiresias; she is said to have come
to Italy and to have founded it after the destruction of Thebes.
Isidore says that it is called Mantua because it protects its *manes*; it
is also named after Manto. But Vergil, who shed great luster on
the city by being born there, says that Ocnus, the son of Manto,
called the city Mantua after the name of his mother. She was
called Manto, or Mantos, because her name was derived from
manes and *tueor*, since she guarded the *manes*, that is to say, the
shades of the deified dead. Other writers say that she had a son by
a certain man called Tiberis, who was called Obius or Obnus, and
also had the name of Bianor, meaning doubly strong, that is to say,
in body and mind; hence Vergil says, "the tomb of Bianor begins to
appear."[237] It was this man, as some believe, who founded Mantua,
which the Mantuans named after his mother, Manto. Manto's father was the great Theban seer, Tiresias, of whom Statius speaks
in his *Thebaid*. So much, then, for what we find in the ancient
authors about the origin of the city.[238]

From these texts we can deduce the date of its foundation;   193
for the fact that it was founded either by Manto, the daughter of
the seer Tiresias, or by her son, means that it is very ancient. For
the fall of Thebes and the destruction of its inhabitants was the
result of a long siege in which the Greeks, Eteocles and Polynices,
the sons of the Theban king, Oedipus, contended for the rule of
the city; and that this event preceded the fall of Troy by about
sixty years is calculated as follows: Oedipus lived in the time of

Abimelech iudicis Israel erat. Troia vero excisa fuit anno tertio
Abdon iudicis Israel. Ab ultimo vero anno Abimelech usque ad
tertium Abdon fuerunt anni sexaginta. Troiae vero excidium praecessit conditionem urbis Romae per annos CDXXXI secundum
Hieronymum. Condita fuit autem Roma anno ante Christi adventum per annos DCCLII secundum Orosium; et sic, etiam non
computatis annis qui praecesserunt ab interitu Thebanorum, post
quem, ut dictum est, fuit Mantua haedeficata, usque ad excidium
Troianum, si recte calchulabitur, invenientur MCLXXXIII anni
praeteriti a Mantua condita usque ad Salvatoris adventum. In cronicis autem Mileti sive Eusebii habetur quod condita fuit Mantua
anno nativitatis Abraam DXXX, qui fiunt annis ante urbem conditam DCLXX. Nam Abraae nativitas praecessit urbem conditam, secundum Augustinum, circiter MCC annos, quod testatur
libro XVIII de civitate Dei, de quibus si detrahantur anni DXXX,
qui fuerunt a nativitate Abraam usque ad haedificationem Mantuae, ut dictum est, restat fuisse ab haedificatione Mantuae usque
ad conditionem Romae annos DCLXX, quibus si addantur anni
DCCLII qui fuerunt ab urbe condita usque ad Christi adventum,
recte calchulando anni MCCCCXXII.

194   Hanc civitatem praeterfluit amnis Mincius Padum influens,
quam etiam munitissimam et inexpugnabilem reddit lacus eam
ambiens. In suburbano quoque pago super ripam ipsius lacus sito,
qui et Pietolis dicitur, natus fuisse fertur Virgilius, urbis Man-
tuanae decus eximium, in quo enim loco Kiriacus ipse prudenter
perscruptatus est si aliquid dignum invenisset veternitatis, praesertim de Marone Virgilio; qui apud ripam fluvii Tartari hoc vetustissimum repperit epigramma:

M.VERGILIO.M.F.
ANTHIOCO.VNIGENITO
SIBI ET PAMPHILO.

Abimelech, the judge of Israel. Troy fell in the third year of Abdon, the judge of Israel. Sixty years elapsed from the last year of
Abimelech to the third of Abdon. The fall of Troy, according to
St. Jerome, occurred 431 years before the foundation of Rome,
and according to Orosius, Rome was founded 752 years before
the birth of Christ. Thus, not even counting the sixty years that
elapsed between the fall of Thebes (after which, as we have said,
Mantua was founded) and the fall of Troy, an accurate calculation
will show that 1183 years intervened between the foundation of
Mantua and the birth of our Savior. In the chronicles of Miletus
or Eusebius, however, we find that Mantua was founded 530
years after the birth of Abraham, which makes 670 years before
the foundation of Rome. For St. Augustine, in Book 18 of his
City of God, says that the birth of Abraham occurred about twelve
hundred years before the foundation of Rome, and if we subtract
from these the 530 years that elapsed, as we have said, between the
birth of Abraham and the building of Mantua, we are left with
670 years between the building of Mantua and the foundation of
Rome; and if to these we add the 752 years between the foundation of Rome and the birth of Christ, our accurate calculation
gives us 1422 BCE [as the date of Mantua's foundation].[239]

The river Mincio, a tributary of the Po, flows past Mantua and 194
a surrounding lake strongly protects it and makes it unassailable.
In a place outside the city called Pietoli on the shore of the lake it
is said that Vergil, the crowning glory of Mantua, was born; and
Cyriac himself carefully searched it to see if he could find any important ancient remains, particularly regarding Vergil. On the
banks of the river Tartarus he found this very ancient inscription:

> [. . . *made this tomb*] for Marcus Vergilius
> Antiochus the only-born son of Marcus,
>   for himself and for Pamphilus.[240]

195   Mantuae ad puteum in lapide.

L.ANNIO.L.L.DIPHILO
MAIORI
L.ANNIO.L.L.DIPHILO
MINORI
L.ANNIVS.DIOMEDES.
LIBERTEIS

196   Alio in loco.

CASSIAE.L.F.
TERTIAI.MATRI

197   In parietibus ecclesiae sancti Silvestri.

V.F
FVRIA.SEX.F.PRIMA
SIBI.ET.M.ACILIO.LF
VIRO.ET.P.FVRIO
P.F.VIRO.ET.
.Q.CAESIO.M.F.
VIRO

198   Et deinde vero se Januam contulit, insignem maritimarum Ly-
gustiae civitatem, quae secundum Plinium ⟨in⟩ libro de naturali
historia in provintia est Liguriae, quae nunc Longobardia dicitur.
Scribit enim quod haec civitas protenditur a Vintimilio et fluvio
Merula usque ad Sigestrum et flumen Macrae, in qua provintia est
Janua et fluvius Pulcivere. Paulus vero Longobardorum scriptor
historiae scribit quod est in quinta Italiae provintia, quae Alpes
Cociae dicitur, et quod ipsa provintia a Liguria usque ad mare
extensa ab occiduo Gallorum finibus copulatur; in qua Terdona,
monasterium Bobii, Janua et Saona civitates habentur.

199   Scribitur in cronicis quod Janus, quidam princeps Moisi
contemporaneus, de orientis partibus in Italiam veniens, ibi primus

In Mantua, on a stone by a well: 195

> Lucius Annius Diomedes
> for his freedmen
> Lucius Annius Diphilus,
> senior freedman of Lucius
> and Lucius Annius Diphilus,
> junior freedman of Lucius.[241]

In another place: 196

> For my mother Cassia Tertia
> freedwoman of Lucius.[242]

On the walls of the Church of S. Sylvester: 197

> While she was alive,
> Furia Prima daughter of Sextus
> built this for herself
> and her husbands
> Marcus Acilius son of Lucius,
> Publius Furius son of Publius and
> Quintus Caesius son of Marcus.[243]

Next he went to Genoa, chief city of the Ligurian coast, which   198
Pliny in his *Natural History* locates in the province of Liguria, now
called Lombardy. He writes that this state extends from Ventimi-
glia and the river Merula as far as Sestri Levante and the river
Magra, and Genoa and the river Polcevera are in the same territory.[244] Paul [the Deacon], author of the *Lombard History*, says that
it is in the fifth province of Italy, called the Cottian Alps, and that,
extending as it does from Liguria to the sea and adjoining the
frontier of Gaul in the west, it contains Dertona, the monastery of
Bobbio, and the cities of Genoa and Savona.[245]

It is written in the chronicles that Prince Janus, a contemporary   199
of Moses, came to Italy from the East and was the chief ruler

omnium regnavit, quamvis ab aliis historiis dicatur quod Abraae
tempore regnaverit. Hic Januam civitatem construxit et de suo nomine Janiculam appellavit, et ibi ad hoc probandum adducuntur
Solini verba dicentis: Quis ignorat vel editam vel conditam a Jano
Janiculam, a Saturno Saturniam?

200   Alius Janus Troianus origine post Troiae excidium in Italiam
venit. Dicit etiam quod cum idem Janus navigaret et ventum pro-
sperum haberet loco qui Albarium dicitur, obscuritas grandis in
aere apparuit quae vulgo Albasia dicitur, apud alios Cigaria, quae
loco nomen dedit Albanum. Procedens vero loco, qui Galiganum
dicitur, cum terrae situs illi placuisset vela calavit; unde et locus sic
dictus est. Loco vero, qui Serzanum dicitur, saltans in terram descendit, et ex illo saltus Serzanum vulgo, quasi saltus Jani, locus
ille nomen accepit. Veniens autem ad ipsam civitatem Ianiculam,
castrum ibi haedificavit loco qui nunc Castellum vocatur, fecitque
turres et fortilicia ubi nunc est archiepiscopale palatium, et muris
fortissimis communivit, et sic eam ampliavit Ianus secundus.
Convenientibus etiam ibidem diversis habitatoribus, civitas magni-
ficari coepit. Quod autem de Iano cive Troiae refert, dicit tantum
se per famam publicam et antiquam novisse.

201   Subiungit quoque quod Ianua fuit haedificata per annos CVII
ante urbis Romae conditionem, et ante adventum Christi per annos MVcXLVI,[9] et in tertia mundi aetate. Hoc autem constare
dicitur et per supradicta verba Solini, scilicet quod Ianus Ianiculam quae modo Ianua dicitur haedificavit, et per cronicas autenti-
cas; sed auctorem sive scriptorem non nominat. Quod Ianus Moisi
temporibus regnabat quando populi in deserto tenebat ducatum et
quod Roma condita fuit, ⟨si⟩ computabuntur, invenientur anni
fluxisse VIIc.VII.[10] quibus Ianuae haedificatio praecessit urbis Romae conditionem. Si autem a Moise usque ad Christi tempora
computabuntur, invenientur, ut dictum est, anni qui fluxerunt
MDXLVI. Istam autem computationem annorum dicit se fecisse
secundum assignationem Hieronymi, qui minorem numerum

there, although other histories assert that he reigned in the time of Abraham. Janus built the city of Genoa and named it Janicula after himself, as is proved by the words of Solinus: "Who does not know that Janicula was built and founded by Janus and Saturnia by Saturn?"²⁴⁶

Another Janus, of Trojan birth, came to Italy after the fall of Troy. Cyriac says that when this same Janus was sailing with a favorable wind to a place called Albarium, a thick fog appeared of a kind commonly called Albasia (though others call it Cigaria), thus giving Albarium its name. He then proceeded to a place called Galiganum, which he found so pleasantly situated that he called for sails to be lowered, hence the place's name. At a place called Serzanum he jumped ashore and from that leap, or *saltus*, of Janus it got its vernacular name. ²⁴⁷ Arriving in Janicula, Janus built a fortress on the site now called the Castello and erected towers and redoubts on the site of the present archiepiscopal palace, which he fortified with very strong walls; and Janus II similarly added to the city. With the influx of people from various places the city began to grow large. [Cyriac] says that his remarks about Janus the Trojan citizen were based on popular and ancient oral report alone.

He adds also that Genoa was built 107 years before the foundation of Rome and 1546 years before the birth of Christ, in the third age of the world. This statement, he says, depends on the already quoted assertion of Solinus that Janus built Janicula, which is called Genoa, and on authentic chronicles, but he does not name any author or writer. Reckoning from the fact that Janus ruled in the time when Moses was leading his people in the desert and from the date of the foundation of Rome, it will be found that 707 years elapsed between the building of Genoa and the foundation of Rome. Moreover, if one calculates the period between the time of Moses and the time of Christ, one finds, as already said, that 1546 years elapsed. Cyriac says that he made this calculation on the evidence of St. Jerome, who gives the smaller number. But

200

201

ponit. Beda enim et Methodius maiorem numerum ponunt, dicentes quod Galli, quorum dux fuit Bellovesius, eam haedifica-
verunt.

202   Titus Livius praeterea non nominat eam Ianuam sed Genuam;
dicitque ipsam anno ab urbe condita DXXXIIII a Magone Poe-
norum duce cum triginta navibus rostratis et multis onerariis in
quibus erant duodecim milia peditum et ferme duo milia equitum
nullis munitam praesidiis cepit et paene destruxit. Circa quae tempora Mediolanum fuit expugnatum etiam a Marcello, per quod
patet quod saltem per annos CCXXX fuit Ianua ante Christi adventum. Alibi dicit quod Scipio, frater puber Scipionis, navibus
Genuam venit in occursum Hannibalis Alpes transgressuri. Refert
etiam Titus idem quod Lucretio prorogatum est imperium a Romanis, ut Genuam oppidum a Magone Poeno diruptum rehaedifi-
caret anno ab urbe condita DXLV.

203   Et ut ad propositum revertar, in hac autem civitate Kyriacus
ipse repperit, Francisco Barbavara ducalibus intercedentibus litteris curante, et praeclara omnia civitatis ornamenta; vidit et insignem illum preciosissima de smyragdo crathera atque C. Marii
marmoreum caput. Etenim ibi primarios et inter cives viderat
Ioannem Grillum, opulentissimum civem, Franciscum Spinolam,
Benedictum Necronem, Paulum Imperialem, nec non doctissimos
homines Iacobum Bracellum, Nicolaum Camulium, egregios publicae rei secretarios, quibus a claris viris praedigne in urbe et extra
per eximia et ornatissima hortorum diversoria splendida conviva
atque perlaute fuerat, et sibi omnia tantae urbis insignia ostenta-
runt, et amplissimam navistatii portusque murorum molem, naves
longas et onerarias ingentes.

204   Sed postquam hic omnia viderat, Romam se rursus ad pontificem contulit. Et cum per dies in urbe versaretur, audivit Anconi-
tanos cives, adversus quosdam patriae rebelles concives piraticam
exercentes, naves Paliaresio Pisanello praefecto in expeditione

Bede and Methodius give a larger number, asserting that the
Gauls built Genoa when Bellovasius was their leader.²⁴⁸

Livy, however, names the city not *Janua*, but *Genua*, asserting   202
that 534 years after the foundation of Rome the Carthaginian general, Mago, captured and almost destroyed the totally unguarded
city with thirty triremes and many cargo ships, with twelve thousand infantry and nearly two thousand cavalry on board.²⁴⁹ About
this time, too, Milan was captured by Marcellus, which clearly
shows that Genoa existed at least 230 years before the birth of
Christ. Elsewhere he says that [Publius Cornelius] Scipio, the
younger brother of [Gnaeus Cornelius] Scipio [Calvus], came
with a fleet to Genoa to resist Hannibal, who was about to cross
the Alps.²⁵⁰ Livy also reports that in the year 545 after the foundation of the city the command of Lucretius [Spurius] was extended
by the Romans so that he could rebuild the town of Genoa, which
had been ravaged by Mago the Carthaginian.²⁵¹

But to return to our story: Provided with ducal letters of in-   203
troduction with the help of Francesco Barbavara,²⁵² Cyriac acquainted himself with all the principal sights of the city and he
saw the famous bowl made of most precious green stone and a
marble bust of Gaius Marius. Among the leading citizens he met
in Genoa were the wealthy Giovanni Grillo, Francesco Spinola,
Benedetto Negrone,²⁵³ and Paolo Imperiale, as well as Giacomo
Bracelli and Niccolò Camulio, learned secretaries in the service of
the city, who elegantly and sumptuously received him as their
guest both within the city and at their beautiful rustic retreats
outside its walls, and showed him all the sights of that remarkable
city, the massive walls of its shipyard and port, the great galleys
and huge merchantmen lying there.²⁵⁴

After he had seen everything in Genoa, Cyriac then returned to   204
Rome to pay another visit to the pope. Some days after Cyriac had
arrived in Rome he heard that the civic authorities of Ancona were
preparing a naval expedition under the command of Pagliaresio

parare; et Thomam Blasii filium antiquum, qui suam ex Balearibus insulis onerariam navim Caetanum ad portum duxerat, illam hoc in apparatu conducto milite ducere et Paliaresium praefectum ad Illyrici sinus oras expectare, et simul una rebelles impetere cives et in potestatem redactos extremo supplicio afficere debere iussisse.

205   Quibus auditis Kyriacus haec omnia moleste ferens, nam potissime verebatur ne quando illa perniciosa coepta civilium discordiarum in civitate tam diu intemeratae unionis integra seminarium denique pestilentissimum essent, quoad licuisset remedia in posterum, una cum Nicolao Petrelli scribae fratre ex urbe se ad Thomam patronum apud Caietam contulit. Qui cum Kyriacum audisset, iuvenis ille generosus non parum laetatus omnia sibi suo de consilio se facturum spopondit.

206   Et cum expedita e Caieta navis Neapolim ventura esset, ut interim quid dignum vetustatis inspiceret, Neapolim terrestri itinere petit. Et cum primum per iter Terrecinas, maritimam et antiquam Latinorum urbem, vidisset, Divi Augusti marmoreum templum, portumque eximium, et ab urbe Roma ingentia silicum strata viarum conspectare maluerat.

207   Sed ex Caieta per Neapolitanum iter Linterneas memorabiles magni Scipionis villas, eiusque marmoream statuam, et ingentia cocto de latere amphiteatra conspexit.

208   Inde vero per Suessam turritam Capuam venit, insignem olim Campaneae civitatem, ubi non parva veterum monumenta comperit. Et extra potissime ad tertium ab urbe lapidem inculta inter et silvestria loca maximi amphiteatri reliquias maximorum lapidum vidit, et procul inde antiquas magnae civitatis portas et pleraque subterranea ingentia mirificaque domorum aedificia.

209   Exinde per Aversam oppidum Parthenopaeam illam nobilem Neapolitanam regiam civitatem adivit, Ioanna serenissima Karoli regis filia regnante [. . .].[11]

Pisanello²⁵⁵ against certain rebellious citizens who were operating as pirates. They had ordered Tommaso, the eldest son of Biagio, who had arrived with his merchant ship from the Balearic Islands at the port of Gaeta, to join in the expedition when he had taken troops on board and to wait for Pagliaresio at the Illyrian Gulf; and together they were to attack, defeat, and destroy the rebels.

This news much disturbed Cyriac, because he greatly feared 205 that these dangerous beginnings of discord in a city that had so long been inviolately united would before long engender worse troubles, requiring future remedies; he therefore, in the company of Niccolò, the brother of the clerk Petrelli, left Rome to see Tommaso at Gaeta; and that noble young man was very pleased to hear what Cyriac had to say and promised to follow his advice in everything.

Since Tommaso's ship would be leaving Gaeta for Naples, Cyr- 206 iac meanwhile set off for Naples by land in order to see what he could find in the way of antiquities. The first place he stopped at on his way was the ancient Latin coastal city of Terracina, where he was delighted to see the marble temple of Divus Augustus, the fine harbor, and the wide, hard-paved road leading from Rome.

At Liternum on the way from Gaeta to Naples he viewed the 207 famous country seat of the great Scipio, his marble statue, and the huge brick amphitheater.

Thence by way of Sessa he came to the splendid towered Cam- 208 panian city of Capua, where he discovered not a few ancient monuments; and three miles outside the city in a wild, woody setting, he particularly examined what was left of the huge stones of the great amphitheater, and at some distance away, the ancient gates of the great city and the many huge and remarkable subterranean remains of ancient houses.

Then, passing through the town of Aversa, he arrived at the 209 royal Parthenopean city of Naples, which was governed by Joan, the illustrious daughter of King Charles [. . .].²⁵⁶

TIBEPIOC IOΤΛIOC

TAPCOC.OCΛIOP

OΤPOIC ΛITHΠOΛEI

TON NAONN KAI.TΛE

HTΩINAΩI ΠEΛAΓ

ΩN ΣEBACTO ΓO

.EPOC.

KΛIEΠITI POΠOC.

CΤNTECACACEPTΩNI

ΛIΩNPAOIE

PΩCEN

210   Exinde, Hercule Puteolano praetore ducente, posteaquam ad Caesareum cavum Virgilii divi poetae monumenta viderat, Puteolos venit, et ibi praeclara multa vetustatum Sybillae vidit, templa, Averni lacus; et adusque Misenum celeberrimum montem omnia Cumarum Baiarumque monumenta conspexit, in quis Neroniana Lucullianaque insignia pleraque aedificia nostram ad diem mirifica conspectantur.

211   Inde vero per Neapolim Beneventanam ad insignem Sannitum urbem venerat, ubi ingentia utique multa vetustatum vidit, et maximi sui amphiteatri vestigia, nobilemque Traiani Caesaris arcum praeclarum suo cum epigrammate conspectare maluerat, quod inclytus olim ille S.P.Q.R. fortissimo illi principi ornatissimum dederat.

212   Sub statua marmorea.

T.NONIO MARCEL

LINO.V.C.COS.CAP.[umo]

PATRONO

DIGNISSIMO

OB INSIGNIA BENE

FICIA QVIB.LONGA

POPVLI

Tiberius Julius
Tarsos [*dedicated*]
the temple
and its contents
to the Dioscuri
and to the city.
Pelagon,
imperial freedman
and administrator,
completed it
at his own expense.²⁵⁷

Next, with Ercole, the *podestà* of Pozzuoli as his guide, Cyriac   210
viewed the landmarks of the revered poet Vergil near the imperial
cavern and then arrived at Pozzuoli, where he saw many renowned
Sibylline antiquities and temples and the lake of Avernus; and all
the monuments of Cumae and Baiae down to the famous promontory of Miseno, including many splendid buildings built by Nero
and Lucullus still to be admired to this day.

Then he went back through Naples to the famous Samnite city   211
of Benevento, where he saw its huge and numerous antiquities,
particularly the remains of its large amphitheater and the fine and
noble arch of the Emperor Trajan with its inscription,²⁵⁸ a highly
ornate monument that the ancient Senate and People of Rome
dedicated to that powerful emperor.

Beneath a marble statue: 212

The entire people of
Beneventum
decreed that this should be erected
for the distinguished man
Titus Antonius [*or* Nonius] Marcellinus,
governor of Campania
and worthiest of patrons

TABEDIA SEDAVIT
VNIVERSA PLEBS
BENEVEN
TANA
CENSVIT PONENENDAM

213   [*no heading*]

D. M
Q.PLOTIVS.Q.F.
QVIR
ROMANVS

214   De hac urbe reperitur in cronicis antiquis. Beneventum et Arpi
Italiae civitates a Diomede constitutae, ut dicit Solinus. Fuit autem Diomedes unus ex principibus Graecorum qui fuerunt in obsidione Troiana, qui ab Illyricis interemptus est, ut scribit Papias,
addens quod Diomedis urbs in Apulia, quam Diomedes sub Gargano monte condidit. Ibi tamen non exprimit quod fuit dicta Beneventum, alio autem loco dicit: Beneventum civitas est quae prius
dicta est Sanium, et alibi dicit: Sannis civitas est in Apulia et Sanium est Beneventum, et Sanitae gens est quae in CXXX miliario
distat a Roma media inter Picenum et Campaniam. Ex historia
quoque Longobardorum habetur quod Sannium est quattuor-
decima Italiae provintia, et in ea Sanium civitas, a qua et tota
provintia nomen accepit. In Sanio provintia est civitas ipsa Beneventana; metropolis habetur. Nobilis in Apulia archiepiscopus eius
duo et viginti sub se suffraganeos habet. Miletus et Hieronymus
scribunt quod Beneventum in Sannio a Romanis conditur anno ab
urbe condita CDLXX. Et credo quod illa conditio fuerit recondi-
tio sive reparatio quia sicut dictum est secundum Solinum, Beneventum fuit a Diomede constitutum, qui fuit ante Romam longis-
simo tempore, et cetera.

because of the outstanding benefits
by which he calmed
the long vexations
of the population.[259]

[no heading]   213

To the spirits of the departed.
Quintus Plotius son of Quintus,
and a Roman
citizen.[260]

This is what we find written about the city in ancient chroni-   214
cles.[261] Solinus says that Beneventum and Arpi were cities founded
by Diomedes.[262] Diomedes was one of the Greek princes at the
siege of Troy who was killed by the Illyrians, as Papias records,
adding that there is a city called Diomedis in Apulia, founded by
Diomedes at the foot of Mount Gargano. Papias does not mention here that the city was called Beneventum, but elsewhere he
says that Beneventum is a city previously called Samnium, while
in another place he says that Samnis is a city in Apulia and that
Samnium is Beneventum and the Samnite people lived 130 miles
from Rome between Picenum and Campania.[263] In the *Lombard
History* we read that Samnium is the fourteenth province of Italy
and that Samnium is a city in it from which the whole province
took its name. In the Samnium province is the city Benevento itself and it is the metropolitan see.[264] The noble archbishop [of
Benevento] has in Apulia twenty-two suffragan bishops under
him.[265] Miletus and Jerome record that Beneventum in Samnium
was built by the Romans 170 years after the foundation of Rome;[266]
but I believe that this was really a refounding or rebuilding of the
city, because Solinus, among other things, says that Benevento was
founded by Diomedes who lived a very long time indeed before
Rome was founded.

215   Sed postquam Kiriacus ipse omnia ibi digna litteris commenda-
rat, Neapolim iterum revisit, ubi cum paucos post dies, expedita et
completa milite navi, Daniele Parentino episcopo et Ioanne Bosculo Florentino ab Eugenio pontifice ad Alphonsum regem oratoribus Siciliam petentibus acceptis, navigasset, Kiriacus notus et
amicissimus illis digna plurima ab iis audierat de rebus inclyto
cum rege agendis qui adversus Tuniseum regem Iarbeam tum forte
insulam ingenti classe premebat.

216   Et cum tandem navis in Siciliam Messanam ad urbem praeclaram applicuisset, legati illico Syracusas terrestri itinere petiere; et
Thomas, Petro Caietano egregio Anconitanorum consule curante,
additis expeditioni suae militibus, ut Anconitanae classi obviaret,
ad Illyrici sinus fauces navigavit. Ibi die postero non longe ab
Otranti promuntorio nobili Baleariam navim unamque biremem
omnifariam machinis munitam, Paliaresio viro quidem praestante
et imperatoria potestate praefecto, adventantes videre, et cum se
invicem iunxissent, Tarentinum ad sinum, ubi Calliepolitano in
portu piraticam illam navim considere intellexerant, advenere.

217   Sed enim cum inclyta olim regina Maria, Tarentini principis
mater, navim illam suo in portu salvam fore se permisisse suos per
oratores praefecto nuntiasset, non nullas post hinc inde per litteras
legatosque contentiones, tandem infecta re classis Anconitanam ad
patriam remenso aequore remeavit.

218   Vale, decus saeculi nostri et patriae ornamentum.

Having recorded all the important sights of Benevento in his 215
notebook, Cyriac then returned once more to Naples. A few days
later, when the ship was ready for sea and the troops were embarked, and when Daniele, the bishop of Parenzo, and the Florentine Giovanni Bosculo, Pope Eugenius' ambassadors to King Alfonso, had come on board on their way to Sicily, they set sail; and
the two emissaries, who were already old friends of Cyriac's, told
him a great deal about what they were to discuss with King Alfonso who, with a large fleet, was at that moment attacking the
Tunisian sultan on the island of Djerba.[267]

When at last the ship arrived in Sicily at the famous city of 216
Messina, the ambassadors immediately left for Syracuse by land.
Meanwhile, Tommaso, with the assistance of Pietro Gaetani, the
Anconitan consul, enlisted further troops and set sail for the
mouth of the Illyrian Gulf to join with the Anconitan fleet. The
next day, not far off the promontory of Otranto, they sighted a
Balearic ship in company with a galley loaded with all kinds of
armament, under the general command of Pagliaresio. They then
joined forces and arrived at the Gulf of Taranto, where, as they
had learned, the pirate ship was at anchor in the harbor of Gallipoli.

However, the former queen Maria, the prince of Taranto's 217
mother,[268] sent her representatives to Pagliaresio to inform him
that she had given permission for the pirate ship to take safe refuge in the port and so, after many arguments back and forth by
letters and messengers, Pagliaresio at length had to abandon his
plan; and the fleet sailed back home to Ancona.[269]

Farewell, Lauro. You adorn our age and are a credit to your city. 218

CYRIAC OF ANCONA

CORRESPONDENCE

1   Kiriacus de Picenicollibus Anchonitanus viro clarissimo P⟨etro⟩ de Bon⟨ar⟩el⟨lis⟩ Liberii filio Anchonitano salutem plurimam dicit.

2   Cum Venetiarum ad urbem profecturus iter haberem et ad ve-tustissima Fauni moenia ventum consisterem, huc ubi *iam dies coelo concesserat alma*, occeano cadente Phoebo, *placidum per membra so-porem* tacitae *sub noctis curriculo* carpere placuit. Sed paulo ante-quam cristatus ales vigili ore tepidum provocaret diem, necdum in *luteis Aurora fulgente bigis astra fugarat Olympo*, et ecce iamque in ipsa, ut videbatur, aula Fauni obtulit se mihi *in sonnis ante oculos insignis forma* et maiestate puer pluribus undique comitatus claris equestris iurisve consulti ordinum viris spectatissimis aliisque civibus orna-tissimis. Hic ea forte tempestate adolescentulus, amisso genitore, huiusce praesul urbis considebat. At ego itaque dum tantorum coetum diu admirans hominum *perlegerem oculis*, vir ex his quidam eques ad me magna se gerens gravitate conversus, talibus me vehe-menter obiurgando dictis visus est:

3   'Unde haec tam caeca tamque obscena, Kiriace, obumbraris ca-ligine, qui Cristiano indutus habitu, sacris almae fidei nostrae amissis codicibus, tanta cum tui frequentia et curiositate diu gen-tiles lectitare poetas insudando magno cum labore contendis, cum praesertim, ut sane intelligis, tam a nostra penitus religione alieni sint, ut Iovem ipsum Cretensem multum pollutum vitiis hominem et mortalem deum esse omnipotentem variis undique carminibus cecinere; quin etiam innumeros e fide devios infandosve errores in suis ut patet operibus inseruere.

4   'Sed quid plura? Quaerendo tempus in verbis, deducemus quod ut de totius summa rei sententiam dicam. Quis neget maximus

: I :

Cyriac to Pietro de' Bonarelli
Rimini, March 15, 1423[1]

Greetings from Ciriaco de' Pizzicolli of Ancona to the illustrious 1
Pietro di Liborio de' Bonarelli of Ancona.

On my way to the city of Venice, I broke my journey at the 2
ancient walls of Fano. *The fostering day had already withdrawn from
the sky* and the sun was setting into the sea when I decided to
snatch *peaceful sleep in my body's members beneath the chariot of the si-*
lent night.[2] But shortly before *the crested cock aroused the warming day
with its waking cry, when Dawn in her saffron-colored car had not yet put
the stars to flight from the shining heavens,* behold a boy, *distinguished in
beauty and dignity,* appeared to me *in a dream,* in Fano's very palace,
it seemed, surrounded by a numerous company of notable knights,
esteemed lawyers and other prominent citizens.[3] This mere lad
chanced to be presiding at the time as head of this city in the ab-
sence of his father.[4] *As my eyes swept in wonder*[5] over this gathering
of great men, one of the knights turned to me, quite serious in his
demeanor, and delivered the following strong rebuke:

"Why are you overshadowed by this dark and dreadful cloud, 3
Cyriac? Why, though dressed in Christian attire, do you abandon
the sacred books of our fostering faith to spend so much of your
time struggling with eager attention, sweat, and toil, to read pagan
poets, especially since, as you know well, they are so utterly foreign
to our religion? For instance, they proclaimed in poems of all different kinds that the Cretan Jove, himself a mortal man much de-
filed by vices, is Almighty God; and furthermore, as is obvious,
they inserted numerous unspeakable errors divergent from the
faith in their works.

"Need I say more? In the interest of brevity, I shall lay out what 4
I intend to say as my opinion on the whole matter. Who will deny

Latinorum ille poetarum, quem tu tam grandibus excellere facis
laudibus, Maro, in suo posuisse nobiliori volumine alios inter errores humanas corpore iam solutas animas iterum nova ad corpora
redituras? Ut Lethaei ad fluminis undam per Anchisem filio scisci-
tante canit: "*animae quibus altera fato corpora debentur.*" Quantisque
utique in locis Iovem ipsum vocet "*omnipotentem divum patrem ac
hominum regem*" praetereo.'

5   Vix haec ubi tandem dicta conticuerat, cum omnes ei simul ore
frementes annuere. Ast ego ubi verba haec tam temere a rei quid-
ditate dissentire accepi, moleste ferens, dumque multa in pectore
volvens pluribus munire suasionibus vocem, magno tuendi mei
vatis amore summopere animi vires excitare cogor. Sed cum tam
maxima responsurus tantorum in conspectu virorum ingenii dif-
fidens vis et eloquentiae subnubilus formidarem, Elyconeas ubi ad
auxilium proposcere coepi deas, ecce iamque adventare mihi ex
alto vidi, Urania concitante, Caliopem et perdulcissime suam pul-
santem liram. Meam ocius in cantu rapuit mentem et coelum alte
petens ad magni Iovis solium se supplicem contulerat, quem lacteo
sic ore coepit obsecrare: 'O divum pater optime aeterneque rerum
opifex, *namque omnia potes*, ne, pater, absiste petenti auxilium praestare tuum. Disice telo nephas. Nam vides in ipsa cornigeri aede
indignos nostros ab omnibus lacerari vates.'

6   Dixerat. At ille genitor alte syderea in sede obnixus, oculos per
omnia lustrans, qui nutu vibrante coelum annuerat precanti divae,
protinus ad accitum sic alloquitur Cilleneum: 'Vade, nate, cape
virgam et optimos nostri numinis auxiliare praecones, Calliope
monstrante viam.'

that Vergil, the greatest of the Latin poets, whom you exalt with great praise, wrote in his most important work,[6] among other errors, that human souls, once they have been set free from the body, will come back again to new bodies? For instance, in answer to his son's inquiry at the bank of the river Lethe, (the poet) sings through Anchises: '*the souls to whom fate owes other bodies.*'[7] I pass over the numerous passages in which he calls Jupiter himself '*the almighty father of gods and king of men.*'"[8]

Barely had he lapsed into silence, when all expressed noisily   5
their agreement with him. But when I perceived that these words differed radically from the truth, taking it ill and all the while pondering in my heart the many ways to buttress my speech with persuasive arguments, greatly desirous as I was to defend my poet, I was strongly compelled to stir the powers of my mind. But now that I was about to make such an important reply in the presence of these gifted men, I was afraid. Lacking confidence in my innate powers and somewhat overshadowed in eloquence, I began to pray to the goddesses of Helicon for help. At that very moment I beheld Calliope coming to my aid from on high at the urging of Urania and plucking sweetly on her lyre. Swiftly she caught up my petition in song and, making for the heavens on high, betook herself as a suppliant to the throne of mighty Jove, whom she began to implore with milk-white countenance: "O good father of the gods and eternal craftsman of the universe, *you have power over everything:*[9] do not, father, fail to grant my petition. Destroy injustice with your shaft. For you see our poets being attacked by everyone in the very temple of the horned god."[10]

When she was finished, the father, steadfast on his starry   6
throne, scanned everything with his eyes. He nodded to the praying goddess with the nod that causes heaven to shake, and summoning the Cyllenian,[11] addressed him as follows: "Go, son, take your wand and help the excellent heralds of our divinity. Calliope will show you the way."

7   Dixit. Tum ille, *magni parentis imperio parante, aurea munitis thala-ria pedibus* et baculum gerente manu, aethereumque tonante cur-sum et littora radente Piceni, Musa duce, in praefata consedit au-lea Fauni. Huc vero Mercurius ubi me ex abdito cava occulerat nube, suisque exuens divinis ornamentis mira ope vultu et habitu induerat se meo. Hic autem primum meae responsionis officium summens et ad praelibatos conversus viros, divino afflante spiritu *placido sic pectore coepit:*

8   'Magnam quidem, o viri, ut accipio, tantorum oppinare vatum dementiam temere praesumpsistis. *Aspicite ergo namque omnem, quae nunc obducta tuentibus vobis mortales hebetat visus, nubem eripiam.* Vi-debitis autem, viri boni, optimus ille magni numinis poeta Man-tuanus suis nonnullis in divinis carminibus, quamquam sub Iovis nomine, veram aeternam ac omnium causarum causam deitatem divina cum mente intuendo, sublimare. Videtur autem multis in locis peroptime se nostrae conformare religioni vetustaeque pri-mordialis Pentatheuci legi, ut in sexto inquit per Anchisem:

> *Principio coelum ac terras camposque liquentes*
> *lucentemque globum lunae thitaniaque astra*
> *spiritus intus alit, totamque infusa per artus*
> *mens agitat molem et magno se corpore miscet.*

et continuo subdit:

> *Inde hominum pecudumque genus, vitaeque volantum,*
> *et quae marmoreo fert monstra sub aequore pontus.*

Patet ergo sane divinus ille vates verum intellexisse deum, quem a principio universarum opificem rerum omnem a se nutu condide-rat mundum, quamvis ille pluries id nomen poetice Ioviali nomine cecinisset.

He spoke. Then Mercury, *as the power of his mighty father prepared*   7
the way, donned his golden winged sandals and, wand in hand, thun-
dered his way through the sky along the shores of Piceno with the
Muse as his guide, and took a seat in the aforesaid palace of
Fano.[12] Here Mercury secretly concealed me in a sheltering cloud,
doffed his divine trappings, and, by virtue of his wondrous power,
assumed my features and garb. He took over my function of re-
sponding, turned to the men, inspected them, then, divinely inspired, *began calmly as follows:*[13]

"Gentlemen, as I see it, you have rashly taken it on yourselves to   8
assume that highly accomplished bards are quite mad. *Well, look,*
for I shall remove all of the cloud that is now drawn over your gaze, blunt-
ing your mortal vision.[14] You will see, good men, that the excellent
Mantuan poet of great inspiration, in some of his divine poems,
though he calls the godhead 'Jove,' still, gazing at it with prophetic
vision, exalts it as the true and eternal cause of all causes. Moreover, he is seen in many passages to conform perfectly to our religion and to the primordial Law of the Pentateuch. For example, in
the sixth book [of the *Aeneid*], he speaks through Anchises:

> *First, the spirit within nourishes heaven and earth and the flowing*
> *plains and the bright sphere of the moon and Titan stars;*[15] *and*
> *mind, spreading through the limbs [of the universe], sets in motion*
> *the entire mass and mingles with the vast frame;*

and he adds immediately:

> *From this comes the race of men and beasts and the lives of birds and*
> *the curious creatures that the sea bears beneath its bright surface.*[16]

Thus it is quite clear that the inspired poet meant the true God,
the craftsman of the universe, who constructed the whole world by
himself with a nod, although he frequently sang that name poeti-
cally under the name of Jove.

9 'Quin etiam ut de varietate dei nominum diceret, ostendendo quem praedominaretur deum in loco ubi rerum inclita Roma condenda fuerat, per Evandrum ait in octavo:

> Hoc nemus, hunc, inquit, frondoso vertice collem,
> quis deus incertum est, habitat deus; Arcades ipsum
> credunt se vidisse Iovem, cum saepe tonantem
> aegida concuteret dextra nymbosque cieret.

10 'Sed cur tantis percurramus in verbis, cum sacer maximus ille fidei catholicae princeps Augustinus ad nostram maxime tuendam religionem suos codices huiusce nostri vatis carminibus roborare summopere laboravit? Idem Hieronymus Lactantiusque fecere.

11 'Videtur an vobis satis manifestum perpulcre nostrae fidei inhaerere poetam, quando ad beatos Elysii posuerat sedes felices optimorum animas omni cum gaudio aeternis frui amoenissimo in loco bonis?

12 'Et primo, ut martirum defingeretur paritas, inquit in sexto praefati:

> Hic manus ob patriam pugnando vulnera passi,
> quique sacerdotes casti dum vita manebat,
> quique pii vates et Phoebo digna locuti,
> inventas aut qui vitam excoluere per artes,

viros ut activarum rerum optimos repertores cultoresque simularet.

13 'Alia vero ex parte ad impia posuit Tartara monstra inter immania Thesiphonem sceleratas acerrime ferro lacerare animas, necessariamque adiecit, ut nostrae magis conveniret se legi, iudice sub aequo scelerum confessionem. Nam inquit subinde per Sibillam Phoebi vatem canens:

"Nay more, so that he can speak of the variety of the names of 9
God, when showing what god prevailed in the place where world-
famous Rome was to be founded, he says in Book 8 through
Evander,

> A god—what god we do not know—dwells in this grove, this hill
> with its leafy crest; the Arcadians believe they have seen Jove himself
> whenever he shakes with his right hand the booming aegis and sum-
> mons the clouds.[17]

"But why should we run through passage after passage when 10
the foremost churchman of the Catholic faith, Augustine, to defend our religion most effectively, took great pains to reinforce his
works with the poetry of this our bard? Jerome and Lactantius did
the same.

"Is it not sufficiently clear to you that the poet adheres magnifi- 11
cently to our faith, since at the blessed dwellings of Elysium he
maintained that the fortunate souls of the just enjoy eternal goodness in a most delightful place?

"And first, to give equal status to the martyrs, he says in the 12
sixth book of the aforesaid work:

> This group is those who were wounded fighting for their country and
> priests who were unstained throughout their lives and the poets who
> were upright and spoke worthy of Phoebus, or those who enhanced
> life by discovering new skills,[18]

so as to equate the great practitioners of practical skills with the
great inventors of those skills.

"From another standpoint, he wrote that Tisiphone afflicts the 13
souls of sinners most harshly in wicked Tartarus, among savage
monsters; and, to be more consistent with our Law, he added a
required confession of sins before a fair judge. For he says right
after, singing through Phoebus' prophet, the Sibyl:

Gnoscius haec Radamantus habet durissima regna
castigatque auditque dolos subigitque fateri
quae quis apud superos, furto laetatus inani,
distulit in seram commissa piacula mortem.

Et hic, ut severissimas ad moerentem culpam poenas religiose tribuerat, immediate subdiderat:

Continuo sontes ultrix accincta flagello
Thelsiphone quatit insultans, torvosque sinistra
distentans angues vocat agmina saeva sororum.

14 'Sed quid enim divinus iste vates de divino ignoverat misterio, cum de adventu sacratissimi humanae pientissimae culpae redemptoris mirifice suum per fatidicum carmen vaticinatur canens suo in pastorali libello:

Ultima Cumaei venit iam carminis aetas.
Iam redit et virgo, redeunt Saturnia regna
iam nova progenies coelo demittitur alto.

15 'Praeterea vos dum obiicitis illi posuisse animas corporibus iterum redituras, hoc autem potissime videtur se nostrae conformare legis opinioni, cum firmiter habetis in fide coelicolum animae novissimo in die inire corporibus glorificatis uniri. Quid enim aliud infert cum cecinerit inde:

Has omnes, ubi mille rotam volvere per annos,
Lethaeum ad fluvium deus evocat agmine magno,
scilicet inmemores supera ut convexa revisant,
rursus et incipiant in corpora velle reverti?

16 'Quas ob res optimus ille vetustarum conmentator rerum Macrobius ad huiusce altissimi poetae de deorum religione peritiam

Cnossian Rhadamanthus rules this harsh realm and reproves and hears about their falsehoods and forces each person to confess to what he did in the world above, gloating over some vain deceit, while he put off making atonement for his sins until death, too late.

And here, when he has scrupulously assigned the harshest penalties to the sinner who is grieving for his sin, he immediately adds:

Without delay, vengeful Tisiphone, armed with a whip, makes them writhe as she leaps upon them and, holding the grim snakes in her left hand, summons her savage company of sisters.[19]

"But what did that divinely inspired bard not know about the divine mystery, since, remarkably, he predicted in prophetic song the coming of the most holy redeemer of mankind's fortunate fault? For he sings in his book of pastoral poetry:

14

The last age of Cumaean prophecy has come. Now returns the virgin, the reign of Saturn returns; now a new offspring is being sent down from high heaven![20]

"Moreover, although you fault him for writing that souls will return again to bodies, this especially seems to conform to the opinion of our Law, since you firmly believe that the souls of the heaven dwellers begin to be united with their glorified bodies on the last day. What other inference can be drawn from the following lines?

15

A god summons all these in a great company to the river Lethe when they have rolled the wheel for a thousand years, so that, forgetful of course, they may revisit the vault of heaven and begin to wish to return to bodies.[21]

"For these reasons that excellent interpreter of antiquity, Macrobius, to prove this most exalted poet's knowledge and experience

16

comprobandam, haec suis in Saturnalibus verba conseruit dicens: "Videturne vobis probatum sine divini ac humani iuris scientia non posse profunditatem Maronis intelligi?"

17 'Sed ut ne per talia omne datum duceremus tempus, finem faciam et solum pro rei summa dicam quod ille utique noster Catholicus Maronisque imperator et materni eloquii poeta Dantes in suo christianissimo volumine exclamavit summum Iovem ut verum humani generis redemptorem in terra crucifixum esse secunda in parte carminis:

> Et se licito m'è, o summo Jove,
> che fusti in terra per noi crucifixo,
> son li justi occhi tuoi revolti altrove?

18 'Patet namque nescia mens hominum veri, cum sacratissima divinarum rerum archana misteria honestissimo sub velamine fictionis ab excellentissimis operta poetis insane variis incusando calumniis elaborare. Proh scelus! Hii quidam fuere qui, suis divinis momentis atque optimis institutis, hominibus, ad bene beateque vivendum lumen, doctrinam, et honestissimis moribus disciplinam dedere.'

19 Nam haec ubi caducifer dicta dedit, me aperta nube ad locum referente meum, divinam resummens formam, et magno corruscante lumine, ubi mille Dei volantum vitae gloriam almae Trinitati cecinerant, *in tenuem auram nostris ex oculis* evolavit. Exim ego *excutior e sonno* membra; tibique optimo Pieridum cultori portentuosam hanc scribere visionem ut dignum amicitiae nostrae munus existimavi.

20 Tuque iam vale. Ex itinere apud Ariminum Idus Martias MCCCCXXIIIº.

regarding the worship of the gods, composed these words in his *Saturnalia*, 'Does it seem proved to you that without a knowledge of divine and human law Maro's depth cannot be understood?'[22]

"But lest I use up all my allotted time on such matters, I shall 17
end my speech and say only by way of summary that our Catholic expert on Maro and poet of our mother tongue, Dante, in the second part of his most Christian work, cried out that supreme Jove was crucified as true redeemer of the human race on earth:

> And if I may be allowed, supreme Jove,
> who were crucified on earth for us,
> are your just eyes turned elsewhere?[23]

"For it is a mind clearly ignorant of the truth about humanity 18
that strives in its madness to attack with varied calumnies the best poets when they conceal the sacred, secret mysteries of the godhead beneath the legitimate veil of fiction. How criminal! These are the ones whose inspired influence and excellent moral teachings, a light to a good and happy life, have instructed and trained humanity in honorable behavior."

When the wand bearer finished speaking, the cloud opened and 19
restored me to my place, while he resumed his divine shape; and, as a multitude of God's flying creatures sang the glory of life to the fostering Trinity, he flew with a great flash of light *from our sight into thin air*.[24] Thereupon *I shook off sleep*[25] from my limbs and decided to write down this portentous vision for you, excellent devotee of the Pierides, as a gift worthy of our friendship.

And now, farewell. On the road at Rimini, March 15, 1423. 20

: II :

1 Ciriacus Anconitanus Leonardo Aretino sal. p. d.

2 Cum hisce diebus ad Urbem, Leonarde praecelentissime, litteras quasdam ab inclito Pannoniae rege sive imperatore Sigismundo
cardinali cuidam missas e Senis legerem, in iis Romanum se regem
inscribere animadverti, ut forte minorem imperatoris titulum
capescere videretur. Ego sed enim vero maius longe ambitiosiusve
nomen regium in Romanos sumpsisse videbar quam imperatorium
Caesaremve aut augustale, quamquam etenim magis errore et im-
peritia rerum Romanarum a suis iam diu praecessoribus hoc in
consuetudinem ductum putarim, quam animi nova aliqua elatione
aut insolentia. Qua quidem in re tuam velim hac in parte sententiam habere.

3 Vale ex Fluentinis scenis Idibus Decembribus Olympiadis autem DLII anno tertio.

: III :

1 Leonardus Kyriaco salutem.

2 Melius erat, o Kyriace, non tantum sapere quantum sapis, si-
quidem te scientem aliorum errata conturbant, quae ab ignorante
nulla molestia praeterirentur. Habet enim ignorantia multis in

: II :

Cyriac to Leonardo Bruni
Florence, December 13, [1432][1]

Cyriac of Ancona to Leonardo of Arezzo, greetings.   1

Recently, most excellent Leonardo, I read a letter sent to Rome   2
from Siena by the illustrious king of Hungary, or "emperor," Sigismund, to a certain cardinal. In it, I noticed that he described
himself as king, perhaps so that he might seem to be taking a title
less than that of emperor.[2] But it would seem to me that among
the Romans, taking the royal title was far more ambitious than the
imperial, the Caesarean, or the Augustan, though I would think
him led into this habit more by the error or inexperience of Roman affairs on the part of his long past predecessors than by any
new pride or arrogance of the spirit. Therefore, I would like to
have your opinion on this matter.

Farewell from Florence.[3] December 13 in the third year of the   3
552nd Olympiad.

: III :

Leonardo Bruni to Cyriac
Florence, after May 31, 1433[1]

Leonardo to Cyriac, greetings   1

It would have been better, Cyriac, not to know as much as you   2
do know, since the errors of others, which are passed over by the
ignorant without any loss, upset you as a man of learning. For

malis quiddam boni, quod minus angitur quia minus sentit. Atque, ut ad postulata veniam tua, admiratum te dicis in hoc novo Sigismundi principis adventu quod, qui ante coronationem se regem scriberet Romanorum, post coronationem vero, quasi maius quiddam et dignius exprimere volens, imperatorem se nuncupabat, non regem, quod tu perperam factum arbitraris. Itaque te id reprehendisse ais et quaeris a me num idem sentiam quod tu, an contra putem.

3   Ego vero et in his et in aliis permultis plurima quotidie mihi videor errata cognoscere. Sed utor Democriti regula: rideo enim illa, non fleo. Quid enim mea refert quemadmodum barbari loquantur, quos neque corrigere possim, si velim, neque magnopere velim si possim? De rege tam et imperatore idem sentio quod tu, et iam pridem ridens barbariem istam, hoc ipsum notavi atque redargui.

4   Tres enim gradus maiorum dignitatum apud Romanos, de quorum principe loquimur fuere: rex, dictator, imperator. Ex his suprema omnium potestas rex est. Post regem vero secundum tenuit dignitatis locum dictatura. Post dictaturam imperium tertio gradu consequitur. Huiusce rei probatio est quod Octaviano imperatori, optime se gerenti, volens senatus populusque Romanus dignitatem augere, pro imperatore dictatorem eum facere decrevit; quod ille non recepit, sed flexo genu recusavit quasi maioris fastus maiorisque invidiae dignitatem, existimans imperatoris nomen modicum ac populare, si ad dictatoris fastigium compararetur. Inferioris ergo dignitatis imperator est quam dictator, ut patet ex hoc. Maiorem vero esse regiam potestatem quam dictaturam ex eo potest intelligi quod Iulius Caesar, dictator quum esset, affectavit regem fieri, cuius gratia interfectus est, non ferentibus civibus ut regiam

among its many evils, ignorance has something good, namely, that it suffers less distress because it feels less. And so, to come to your question, you say you were astonished, during this recent coming of the Emperor[2] Sigismund [to Italy], because before his coronation he described himself as King of the Romans, but after his coronation, as if wishing to express something grander and more dignified, he called himself *imperator* rather than king, which you consider to have been done incorrectly.[3] And so, you say, you found fault with this and ask me whether I share your opinion, or think the contrary.

In fact, I seem to recognize a great many errors in this and many other matters every day. But I follow the rule of Democritus: I laugh, not weep, at them.[4] What difference does it make to me how the barbarians speak, whom I could not correct if I wanted to, nor especially want to if I could? As for the king, or "emperor," I think the same as you. I laughed at this barbarism long ago, and I have censured it as incorrect usage.

The Romans, whom we are discussing in particular, had three levels in high offices of leadership. These were king, dictator and general (*imperator*). Among these the king was the most powerful of all. After the king, the dictator held the next level of authority. *Imperium* [the power of command] followed in the third rank after the dictator. The proof of this is that when the senate and people of Rome wished to increase the authority of the *imperator* Octavian, who was conducting himself extremely well, they voted to make him dictator instead of *imperator*; he did not accept this, but refused it on bended knee, as a rank of greater splendor and greater envy, believing that the title of *imperator* was modest and popular when compared with the exalted rank of dictator.[5] So it is obvious from this that the *imperator* was of lower rank than the dictator. And it can be understood that the royal power was greater than the dictatorial because Julius Caesar, when he was dictator, desired to become king, for which he was killed, since the

assumeret potestatem, sed dictaturam, utpote minorem, aequis animis in eo patientibus.

5   Haec igitur quae adhuc dixi, etsi nulla penitus alia super adderentur, ipsa per se vel sola probant abunde regium nomen quam imperatorium esse praestantius, nisi forte aut senatum dum pro imperatore dictatorem facere volebat, aut Caesarem dum ex dictatura rex fieri cupiebat, non intellexisse vim istarum dignitatum existimemus. Sed nolo his esse contentus, praesertim ad te scribens, cuius aures, novi, quam avidissimae sint vetustatis simul ac veritatis. Explicemus ergo singulorum naturam, qua cognita et inter se comparata, differentiam sui dilucide nobis ostendent. Regem omnes sic accipiunt quasi suprema quaedam et absoluta sit potestas, supra quem in suo regno nemo sit, sed ipse praesit omnibus; ex quo fit ut rex nisi unus dumtaxat esse non possit. Plures enim reges simul eidem regno praesidentes sese mutuo impedirent naturamque perimerent regis, quae non omnibus praeesset, sed haberet paritatem.

6   Patet hoc in antiquis modernisque regibus. Neque enim Numa neque Hostilius neque Ancus neque alii deinceps Romani reges consortem aut socium regni habuere. De Romulo et Tatio ferunt, sed alter Sabinorum, alter Romanorum rex erat, et in propinquo collati repugnante natura sese passi non sunt. In modernis quoque regibus hoc idem apparet; neque enim Francorum neque Anglorum plures simul reges regnum gubernant, sed unus et solus, cui fratres, cui patrui, cui propinqui omnes genua submittunt. Cessit iam quandoque apud hos filio pater, ac regiam potestatem se vivo transferre in filium voluit, ipse dimisit, quoniam duos simul regiam potestatem habere contra naturam est huius dignitatis. At

citizens would not tolerate him assuming the royal power, though they calmly allowed him the dictatorship as being lesser.[6]

Therefore what I have said until now, even if nothing else be added to it, by itself alone proves abundantly that the name of king was more distinguished than that of *imperator*, unless we think that the senate, when it wished to make a dictator out of an emperor, or when Caesar wanted to become king out of his dictatorship, did not understand the force of these ranks. But I do not want to be content with this, especially writing to you, whose ears, I know, are all agog for antiquity as well as for the truth. Let us therefore explain the nature of each of them, which when understood and compared among themselves, will present their differences clearly to us. Everyone accepts the king as some supreme and absolute power, above whom there is no one in his kingdom, while he is superior to all. From this it follows that there can only be one king at a time. If many kings preside over the kingdom at one time, they would interfere with each other and destroy the nature of kingship, which would not be superior to everyone, but would have parity. 5

This is obvious in ancient and modern kings. For neither Numa nor Hostilius nor Ancus nor any of the Roman kings after them had a consort or associate in his kingdom. They say that Romulus and Tatius did, but one was king of the Sabines, the other of the Romans, and when they were put together — which nature opposed — they could not tolerate each other. The same thing appears also in modern kingdoms, for several kings at a time do not rule the French or the English kingdom, but one alone, to whom brothers, uncles and relatives all drop to their knees. Among them, when sometimes the father has yielded to the son and wished while alive to transfer the royal power to the son, he himself renounces this, since it is against the nature of this office for two to have the royal power at the same time. But there have very often been plural *imperatores*, for the imperial power is not supreme, but 6

imperatores simul plures saepissime fuerunt. Non est enim suprema potestas imperium, sed salva re publica, salva auctoritate
senatus, et populi salva libertate, imperator creabatur. Est enim
imperium armorum exercituumque ad tutandam augendamque
rem publicam commissa auctoritas. Itaque imperatore existente,
nihilominus consules praetoresque ac ceteri magistratus in re publica manebant, rege autem existente manere non poterant, quod
patet ex dictatura. Illa enim, quod vim quandam regiae potestatis
habere videbatur, simul atque inducta fuerat in rem publicam, ceteri magistratus interibant, et abrogati per creationem dictatoris
censebantur praeter tribunos plebis. Et in hoc differebat dictator a
rege, quod dictatore existente plebs plebeique magistratus vim
auctoritatemque suam retinebant; rege autem existente, tribunicia
potestas plebisque auctoritas omnis omnino solvebatur. At enim
cum imperatore cuncti simul magistratus in re publica perstabant,
et auctoritas vigebat senatus, et populi libertas servabatur. Ex quo
apparet imperatorem non esse dominum sed legitimam potestatem, nisi forsan Crispum Sallustium ignorasse vim dignitatem-
que imperatorii nominis arbitremur, qui inquit: nam cum tute per
mollitiem agas exercitum supplicio cogere, id est[1] dominum non
imperatorem esse.

7   Volo insuper unam vel alteram rationem inducere, quo maioris
dignitatis regium nomen esse ostendam. Imperium enim quibus-
dam magistratibus recte tribuimus. Nam omnes, qui iurisdictio-
nem exercent ac punire et coercere possunt, imperium habere dicimus. At regnum habere illos nunquam diceremus, quoniam nomen
imperii legitimam potestatem significat; regnum autem habere supra leges esset.

8   Praeterea quae Deo tribuimus vocabula, ea praestantissima sunt
existimanda. Cum enim Deus ineffabiliter excellat, nec ulla humana reperiri digna possint eius maiestate, illa Deo tribuimus,

an *imperator* was chosen or elected when the republic, the authority of the senate, and the freedom of the people was still safe. For the *imperium* is an authority of weapons and armies created for preserving and expanding the state. And so, when an *imperator* existed, the consuls, praetors and other magistracies nevertheless continued their role in public affairs, but when there was a king, they could not continue, as is clear from the dictatorship. As soon as that office, which seems to have possessed quasi-royal powers, had been introduced into public affairs, the other officials would disappear, their office (except for the tribune of the plebs) being considered in abeyance through the creation of a dictatorship. The dictator differed from the king in this, that when there was a dictator, the people and the people's magistrates [i.e., the tribunes] retained their authority, but when there was a king, the power of the tribune and the authority of the plebs was entirely and in every way dissolved. From which it appears that the emperor was not a master, but a legitimate [or legal] power, unless we suppose that Sallust misunderstood the power and authority of the *imperator*'s title when he said: "for when you yourself live softly and subject your army to punishment, that is [the action] of a master, not an *imperator*."[7]

In addition, I want to adduce one other reason to show that the 7
title of king was of higher authority. We rightly attribute *imperium* to various officials, for we say that all those who exercise jurisdiction and are able to punish and use force have *imperium*. But we will never say that they have royal power, since the name of *imperium* signifies legitimate [or legal] power; the royal power, however, is above the laws.

Furthermore, the words we use regarding God should be reck- 8
oned the most preeminent [that we have]. For since God is inexpressibly superior to everything, and nothing can be found that is worthy of his majesty, we bestow on Him the titles that are

quae apud nos sunt maxima, quoniam maiora tribuere non habemus. Dum autem regem nuncupamus ac regnum caelorum dicimus, ut sacrae litterae poetaeque testantur. Imperatorem vero qui deum vocaret, vix quisquam reperiretur, propterea quod rex potestatem supremam absolutamque significat; imperator vero longe inferior est. Ex his omnibus luce clarius apparet, qui imperatorium nomen regio nomini anteferunt, eos in maxima ignoratione versari.

9   Sed heus! Tu qui hunc errorem notasti, cur alium huic annexum tacitus praeteristi? Coronari enim imperatorem ubinam gentium mos fuit? Quis imperatorem Romanum antiquis illis temporibus coronatum fuisse unquam audivit aut legit? Non Augustum, non Tiberium, non Caligulam, non Neronem (cum praesertim hi duo extremi intolerandae superbiae ac luxuriae forent): non Traianum, non Hadrianum, non Antoninum; nemo, inquam, istorum coronam imperii unquam suscepit aut habuit aut usus est, nisi forte lauream, quum triumphasset aut rostratam quod classem hostium cepisset, quae duae coronae non imperatorum erant magis quam quorumcunque triumphantium aut vincentium. An ergo, quod illi tantam imperii magnitudinem habentes non faciebant, hi quatuor iugerum possessores coronabuntur? Enim vero, non ut imperatores, sed ut reges, Romani coronantur. Cur ergo se post coronationem imperatores scribunt, non reges? Deinde totum hoc ignorantiae est, cum ne reges quidem Romanos unquam coronari mos fuerit. Romulus enim et hi qui post eum fuerunt reges numquam coronam receperunt aut gestarunt aut usi sunt. Idem quoque observatum est a Tuscorum regibus, ut numquam corona uterentur, sed trabea dumtaxat et palmata tunica. Quare hanc barbariem, quaeso, cum sua ignorantia valere sinamus, et nos

greatest among us, since we have nothing greater to bestow. We thus call him king and we speak of the kingdom of heaven, as the Scriptures and poets witness. Hardly anyone could be found who calls God *imperator*, because "king" signifies supreme and absolute power; *imperator* is far inferior. From all this, it is clearer than light that those who give the imperial title precedence over the royal are sunk in the deepest ignorance.

But look! You who noticed this mistake, why did you pass over 9 in silence another one associated with it? Among what people was it ever the custom for emperors to be crowned? Who ever heard or read that the Roman emperor in those ancient times was crowned? Not Augustus, nor Tiberius nor Caligula nor Nero (especially since these last two were the extremes of arrogance and extravagance); nor Trajan nor Hadrian nor Antoninus; not one of them, I say, assumed or possessed or used an imperial crown, unless perhaps a laurel wreath when he had triumphed, or a rostral crown when he had captured an enemy fleet — those two crowns did not belong to emperors as such but to whoever triumphed or was victorious. Therefore, since those who had such great imperial power did not do it, will these owners of a few acres be crowned? In fact they are crowned, not as Roman emperors but as kings. So why do they describe themselves as emperors rather than as kings after their coronation? This is completely ignorant, since it never was the custom to crown even the Roman kings; Romulus and the kings who came after him never received or wore or used a crown. The same was observed by the Etruscan kings, never to use a crown but only a robe of state and a tunic embroidered with palms. So, I submit, let us bid farewell to this ignorant barbarism, and let us enjoy the ancient writings of the most learned

antiquis doctissimorum virorum scriptis, quod unicum est refugium, oblectemur, non curiosi quid agant isti aut quemadmodum loquantur. Vale.

: IV :

1 Kyriacus Anconitanus ad Leonardum Arretinum in Caesaream laudem.

2 O quam hodie bellissime tuam illam sententiam probare cogor, Leonarde Latinorum doctissime, qua dixisti nostra in hac aetate inertissima melius nobis quandoque esse non tantum, id quod paucissimum est, sapere quantum sapimus; eo quod longe minus de ea Poggii nostri, quae nova divinum nostrum in Caesarem audivimus, insana nuper et iniquissima oppinione torquerier, quamvis eum in te, quem usque gerere non didici morem commendem, hominum scilicet errata ridere magis, ut Democritus ille docet, quam flere. Ego quidem saepius eruditorum litteris barbariem permoleste ferebam.

3 Dicam enim quid hac in re mihi contigerat, paulo altius amicitiae tuae repetens. Nam dum exactis diebus ex Ancone Peloponensiacas oras petens nostrum per Adriacum navigarem, crebris obsistentibus euris flatibus et eois, tandem Melidea, quaedam in Illyrico insula *tuto placidissima portu*, nos diutina atque procellis aegra navigatione *fessos excaeperat*. Ex qua denique per cymbam, ut ego, quod magis optabam, Illyrica litora percurrerem, ad V Iduum Novembrium diem Iaderam, nobilissimam Liburnorum urbem,

men, which are our one refuge, setting aside any curiosity about what those sort of people are doing or how they are talking. Farewell.

: IV :

Cyriac to Leonardo Bruni
Zadar, January 30, 1436

Cyriac of Ancona to Leonardo of Arezzo, in praise of Caesar. 1

Leonardo, most learned of the Latins, how fully must I agree 2
today with your sentiment that, in this torpid age of ours, I would
be better off sometimes knowing less than I do, though that is
little enough, because, were that so, I would be far less tormented
about our friend Poggio's mad and highly unfair opinion, which I
heard recently, regarding our divine Caesar. Rather, I would suppose in you behavior that I myself have not yet learned: to follow
the teaching of Democritus, who said it is better to laugh at people's errors than to weep over them. Too often have I taken great
offense at the barbarism of learned men of letters.[1]

In connection with that, I am going to tell you, presuming 3
upon your friendship, what happened to me. A few days into
our voyage from Ancona through our Adriatic on the way to the
shores of the Peloponnesus, when frequent headwinds arose from
the east and southeast,[2] Molat, an island in Illyricum, *with its safe
and calm harbor*, had received us, exhausted as we were by our long
and gale-ridden sea voyage.[3] Finally, as I set out from there in a
small boat to pass along the Illyrian coast — something I especially
wanted to do — we came on the ninth of November to the famous
Liburnian city of Zadar, where the first person I saw running

adivimus. In qua primum mihi obviam occurrentem vidi Georgium Begnam, virum quidem humanae rei doctum et quem semper claritati et benivolentiae tuae deditissimum cognovi. Quo cum suavissimo viro multa conserebamus verba vicissim honestissimis nostris periocunda curis, tuum et in his saepe recensendo excolendissimum nomen.

4   Et enim eo duce, alia inter civitatis egregia et memoratu dignissima vidi, maritima prope moenia insignem Meliae nobilissimae mulieris arcum, ubi tubicen ille aequorei numinis Τρίτων mira fabrefactoris arte conspicitur, et consculptum quod habet epigramma ut nostrae dignum spectationis, quom nec vidisse semel satis esset sed et pluries utique lectitare iuvasset, primorum in conspectu Liburnorum hominum de altissimis maiorum nostrorum meritis ad inextimabilem comparationem incidimus.

5   Et quom ad summos Romuleae gentis viros verbis transvolaremur, et Georgius ille noster multa de Caesare, alii vero de Scipione non pauca egregie disseruisssent, tandem Marinus quidam, Soloneus Palatinus, vir haud inter vulgares, quom ex Fluentina urbe, immo potius nova, ut ita loquar, achademia, nuper advenisset, particulam quandam novi cuiusdam ex Poggio coepti libelli obtulit in medium. Quoiusce postquam nefanda audivimus verba, ni potius morbo animi quam iudicio ob coeptam nuper in Guarinum simultuariam contemptionem[1] talia evomere cognovissem, longe minus et peritiam hominis amicitiam ve kari pendendam, immo penitus aspernendam esse censerem. Ea quidem ob tantae maiestatis viri pudorem ac veluti summam Latini nominis iacturam audire scire referre ve ut et proximum sacrilegio crimen, nefas putandum est. Ea igitur summo omnium silentio praetereunda opprimendaque fore concernimus.

6   Sed expleta iam ipsa cum concione die, occeano cadente Phoebo, suam quisque domum petientes, ego et Georgius noster

toward me was Giorgio Begna,[4] a man learned in humane affairs whom I have always found to be dedicated to your fame and goodwill. With this very pleasant gentleman we had many enjoyable conversations related to our most honorable concerns, and in these we often recalled your highly venerable name.

Giorgio took me on a tour of Zadar's important and memorable sights, including a remarkable arch belonging to the noblewoman Melia near the harbor wall, on which one sees a marvelously sculpted image of that well-known trumpeter of the sea god, Triton.[5] On this arch is also carved an inscription[6] that proved worthy of our inspection: it was not enough to see it only once, but we took pleasure in reading it over and over again; and, in the company of the leading men of Liburnia, we fell to comparing the inestimably lofty merits of our ancestors.

When our conversation turned to the greatest men of the nation of Romulus and my distinguished friend Giorgio had with distinction discoursed much about Caesar, while others spoke not a little about Scipio, an official of Spalato named Marino,[7] — hardly undistinguished, since he had recently come from the city of Florence or, as I might say, from the new academy — brought into the discussion a passage from a new little work by Poggio.[8] When we heard Poggio's unspeakable remarks, had I not recognized in them the ventings, not of good judgment, but of a mind recently diseased by quarrelsome scorn for Guarino, I would have concluded that, far from valuing his expertise or his friendship, we should completely spurn them. Indeed, to hear, to know, even to refer to Poggio's remarks must be thought of as a crime close to sacrilege, because they offend shamefully so majestic a person and they utterly disregard the reputation of the Latins. We decided, therefore, that they should be passed over in total silence and suppressed by everyone.

When together with our conversation the day came to its end, as Phoebus set into the Ocean, we retired, each to his own place, I

4

5

6

suos revisimus solitos Lares, ubi exiguo refecti cibo parum de auditis laeti. Nam potissime nostrum substernabat animum amicissimi nominis oratoris temerarium indignissimae orationis exordium. Tum demum nos inter luce clarius putantes talia divo
Caesari nihil, sed sibi ipsi scriptori quam plurimum nocitum iri,
omnem cogitationem nostram membra somnulo persolvimus.

7   Sed enim antea paulo quam cristatus ales vigili ore tepidum
provocaret diem, ex alto obtulit se mihi in sompnis ante oculos
securissimus ille deus et curarum omnium pacator Ὄνειρος et
continue mihi talia peregrina voce locutus est: εὔδεις, Ἀνκώνος
υἱὲ δαίφρονε παλαιόφιλε; οὐ χρὴ παννύχιον εὔδειν βουλη-
φόρον ἄνδρα. Et haec ubi dicta, meorum effugit oculorum ob-
tuitu ac se statim nubibus confundit et occulit.

8   Ego quidem caput erigens conspexi amicissimum Georgium
nostrum mea me qua pridie fuimus concione deducere. Hic primum ex abdito lato atque virenti campo serenissimo sub caelo di-
versas video magnarum gestarum² rerum imagines, quarum forma
eminentior una, vertice galeata ac pectoris fulgida, nymbo aureo
devecta curru, quem candidissimus Pegasus alis agebat aureis, alias
omnes egregie videbatur praestare; pedibus calcando solum, *caput
inter nubila* mittens, sydera videbatur hippureo pulsare galero.
Quam cum propius conspexissem, oculos et ipsa in me vibravit
ardentes, quorum territus fulgore avidusque tantae celsitudinis
nomen audire, ubi ad auxilium heliconeas poposci deas, ecce
adventare mihi ex alto vidi binas e Pieridum choro pulcherrimas
habitu nymphas quarumque prima, Polymnia, ad me conversa,
placido sic pectore coepit:

9   'Tu qui res divas hominum meditare velis, aspice, nanque illam
vides insignem ante te conspicuamque iconam. Inclita atque rerum

and my friend Giorgio returning to our usual abode, where we had a light supper, little cheered by what we had heard. For what most underlay our mood was the ill-considered exordium of the unworthy composition of the orator whom we called our very dear friend.[9] Finally, agreeing among ourselves that it was clearer than light that through such views no harm would be done to the divine Caesar but very much harm to their author himself, we put aside all thought and dissolved our limbs in sleep.

But a little before the crested bird was to call forth the warm day with his watchful call,[10] the reassuring god, Dream, subduer of all anxieties, appeared to me from on high as I slept and straightway spoke to me in a foreign tongue the following words: "Do you sleep, prudent son of Ancona, lover of antiquity? A counselor should not be sleeping the whole night through."[11] This said, he departed from my sight, and immediately mingled with the clouds, and hid.

Raising my head, I saw my good friend Giorgio, leading me from the place where we had our discussion the previous day. Here, in a remote field, broad and green, beneath a very calm sky I saw various images of great historical deeds. One of them,[12] towering in stature over the rest, head helmeted, breast bright, with a golden halo, conveyed in a chariot drawn by brilliant white Pegasus with his golden wings, seemed outstandingly to surpass the others. Treading the ground with her feet, but *with head in the clouds*,[13] she appeared to strike the stars with her equestrian helmet. When I beheld her from closer range, she herself aimed her burning eyes at me. Frightened by their brightness and eager to hear the name of such an exalted being, I asked the Heliconian goddesses for assistance; and behold I saw coming toward me from on high two nymphs from the chorus of the Pierides, in most beautiful garments. The first of them, Polyhymnia,[14] turned to me and *began from her calm heart thus to speak:*[15]

"You who wish to contemplate godlike human achievements, behold, for you see before you an outstanding visible procession.

maxima Roma fuit. Vides ne illam suam primaevam generosissimam gentem, Tarpeias olim rupes coronatis equis scandentem, Phebeamque comis virginem ferentem, Torquatum Camillum Fabios Marcellos Scipiones ad divos usque Iuleae generosissimae gentis viros?'

10 Et quom *haec ubi dicta recessisset in auras*, ego iam attonitus tantorum praesentia heroum admirans, hac de habita pridie contentione memor, desiderans quisnam e duobus praestantior esset intelligere, qui ante alios omnes ad armisonae deae dexteram incedentes purpureis aequatis cristibus suis niveis equare crinibus videbantur, ecce et altera nympharum praestantissima, Caliope, ad me tam ardue rei avidum accedens *roseo sic ore locuta est*: 'Quisquis es inermis qui omnibus exutus plumis profunda nostrae arcis culmina scandere praesumpsisti, sed age, loquere! Iam te quidem amice iuvabo.'

11 Ego sic demum posita formidine coepi: 'O diva et facundissima Musarum, Caliope, Latinus homo sum et Anconigena, quippe Latinorum gloriam vetustorum non modo codicibus admirator, sed quicquid ab iis dignum ere et marmore posteris nobis relictum est. Et sic, dum per Illiriacum hac in tempestate navigarem, apud Liburneam Iaderam indignissima nostro de Cesare verba audivi ex particula quadam a Poggio, quondam amicissimo nostro, nuper editae orationis. Sed cum ex ea indignatione ad insignem hanc spectationem me profundae mentis idea contulisset ac tua mihi Polymnia soror deam Romam Romulidamque nobilissimam gentem videre me quam brevissimo ordine detexisset, ut a te, diva, nunc ea quae diu scire tam avido pectore cupiebam, ex ore sanctissimo discam, non domestico quidem sermone, sed tuo numini digniore et vatis tui Meonidis more, te supplex oraturus advenio,

Rome was famous, the greatest of all things in nature. Do you not see her, first and most noble of peoples, as they once ascended the Tarpeian Rock on crowned horses, escorting Phoebus' long-tressed virgin?[16] Do you not see Torquatus, Camillus, the Fabii, the Marcelli, the Scipios — right down to the godlike men of the most noble Julian family?"

This said, she withdrew into the air.[17] Surprised and awed by the   10 presence of such great heroes, and mindful of yesterday's discussion, I longed to learn which was the more eminent of the two figures who strode at the right hand of the armor-clanging goddess, ahead of all the others, and who, judging from their equally purpled plumes and snow-white hair, seemed of equal status. And behold, Calliope,[18] the other most excellent of nymphs, approached me in my eagerness for so lofty an object and spoke with her rosy-red lips:[19] "Whoever you are who, unarmed and unadorned by any plumes, presume to climb the lofty heights of our citadel, come, speak. I will certainly give you friendly assistance."

Finally, putting aside my fear, I began: "O Calliope, goddess,   11 most eloquent of the Muses, I am a Latin man, born in Ancona, an admirer of the ancient Latins' glory, not only for their books, but also for whatever else worthwhile in bronze and marble they left behind to us,[20] their descendants. Thus it was that, when in the course of my storm-tossed voyage along Illyria, I heard in Liburnian Zadar utterly shameful words about our Caesar, from a small part of a speech recently given by Poggio, once my very good friend, I was indignant. But now that an idea from deep within Mind[21] has granted me this spectacular vision, and now that your sister, Polyhymnia, has revealed to me the goddess Roma and the noble race of Romulus in rapid overview, that I might now learn from your sacred lips, goddess, what I have long been craving greedily to know, I come as a suppliant asking you, not in my native tongue, but in a one worthier of your divine presence — that of

τίς δ' ἄρα τῶν ἄριστος ἔην σύ μοι ἔννεπε, Μοῦσα, Λατίνων
μεγαθύμων ἠδ' ἀρηιφίλων Ῥωμαίων; τίς δὲ μάλιστα μέ-
γιστος ἔην ἐκ μεγίστοιν δυοῖν λαμπροτάτοιν προπορευόν-
τοιν ἡρώων ἁπάντον;'

12   Illa quidem me primum paulo suspensa admirans, exinde dulcissima atque peregrina voce cecinerat: χαῖρε, φίλε ἀγαθὲ, et
suavissime suam pulsando lyram meam ocius in cantu rapuit mentem et caelum alte petens ad magni Iovis solium se supplicem
meque contulerat, quem lacteo sic ore coepit obsecrare: 'O divum
pater optime aeterneque rerum opifex, *namque omnia potes*, ne, pater, absiste praecanti auxilium praestare tuum. Audivimus nuper
inter Italos divinum Caesarem verbis indignissime lacessiri ac Romanos inter primarios et nobilissimos heroes sibi Affricanum su-
periorem praeferre clarissima rerum gloria contendunt.'

13   Ille quidem haec postquam audierat verba, statim alte *syderea in
sede* obnixus, *oculos per omnia volvens* et *nutu vibrando caelum annuerat
poscenti divae*. Et magna deorum habita concione, tandem Paphiae
Deliaeque contemplationibus[3] expretis,[4] maturato diu arcano cum
Marte conloquio, protinus ad accitum sic *alloquitur Cylleneum*:
'*Vade, nate, cape virgam*, nebulas dissipare, vera detegere, et optimum nostri numinis auxiliare collegam.' Dixerat. Ille *primum ad-
nexa talaria pedibus* et baculum gerente manu, musa duce, postquam aethereum transnaverat iter, insignem petierat Liburneam
civitatem ac praefata se medio obtulit concione. Hic enim primum
ubi *cava nube* Caliopen circunfudit, vultu et habitu induerat se
musae, et nos undique postquam paululum conspectarat, ad me
tandem conversus, sic breviter *ab imo pectore coepit*:

14   'Magna si Romulidum nomina excellentiora ve ab ore sanctissimo scire tam avido pectore flagitasti, hanc, ὦ παλαιόφιλε,

your prophet Homer: 'Do thou tell me, Muse, who was the best of the greathearted Latins and the warlike Romans? Which of the two great, brilliant men who passed by was the best of all heroes?'"[22]

She kept me in wondering suspense for a little while, then sang   12
in her delicious, foreign voice: "Hail, good friend"; and strumming her lyre sweetly, swiftly swept me up in song and, making for the high heavens, brought herself and me as suppliants before the throne of mighty Jupiter, whom she implored with milk-white countenance: "O great father of the gods and eternal fashioner of all things — *for you are all-powerful*[23] — do not withhold your aid from one who prays to you. We have heard recently that in Italy divine Caesar is the subject of undeserved verbal attacks; and that the Romans were preferring for themselves Africanus as superior among their principal and noblest heroes; they are competing for supreme glory."

When he heard this, he leaned heavily on his *starry throne, cast-*   13
ing his gaze over the whole of creation, and shook heaven with his nod as he assented to the goddess's prayer.[24] He convened a grand council of the gods, and when the opinions of the Paphian and Delian goddesses[25] had been expressed,[26] he hastened to hold a long, private conference with Mars, then forthwith summoned Mercury to his presence and *instructed him as follows: "Go, my son, take your staff,*[27] part the clouds, uncover the truth; and help this excellent colleague of our divine power." Thus he spoke. Mercury *first fastened winged sandals to his ankles,*[28] took up his staff, and, guided by the muse, journeyed through the air to the Liburnian city to join our discussion. He enveloped Calliope in a *hollow cloud,*[29] took on the features and dress of the muse, then, looking us all over, he turned at length to me and began a brief but heartfelt speech:[30]

"O lover of antiquity, since you have asked with eager heart to   14
learn from the most holy of lips if there are more excellent great

summam e nobis aeterni Iovis iussu sententiam habeto, et in eadem qua nobis exorsus peregrina voce fuisti: ἡρώων τῶν δ' ἁπάντων Ῥωμαίων χαλκοχιτόνων πρῶτος μετ' ὄπισθεν νικηφόρον Καίσαρα δῖον, μέγ' ἄριστος ἔην Π. Κωρνήλιος Σκιπίων Ἀφφρικήνος, ὁ δὲ μοναρχοποιὸς πολυφέρτερος ἦεν, ἔμπης τὼ δύο προπορευόντε εἰς μεγ' ἄστεως εἴδολον ἐγγυτέρω Καίσαρ' αὐτὸν καὶ Σκιπίονα ὁρᾶς.' Exinde se ad alios vertens, Latinis magis domestico more⁵ dixit: 'Vos, qui de summis Latinorum viris et de duobus iis maxime ad armisonae deae simulacrum primis contemptionem vestris imparem viribus habere quam temere praesumpsistis, haec tamen vestri palaeophili gratia ex Iove optimo maximoque audite:

15 'Quamquam innumeri sint Romuleae gentis gloriosissimi virtute viri, tamen omnibus laude praestaret inclytus Affricanus, ni Caesarem semper excipiendum esset ob eam et potissime ipsam a se conditam, quam vos ignare cotidie improperare sibi conati estis, divinam et caelo similem monarchiam. Ea sed enim abmota, ita paribus gloriosi laudibus pariter ambularent, ut vix decernendum foret an Scipioni Caesarem Caesari ve Scipionem gloria militiae atque virtutis antecelleret.

16 'Sed ut clarius rem aperiam, *aspicite, namque omnes quae nunc obductae tuentibus vobis mortales hebetant visus, nubes eripiam.* Et primum optimo de principatu pauca dicam, exinde quam breviter aliqua eo de ipso conditore principe recensebo et errorem corripiam quantuluncumque vestrum. Nam ut a principio et in omne deinceps et perpetuum tempus splendidissima illa caelicolum regna ab uno, optimo maximo Iove, principe pulchro atque perpetuo ordine

names among the sons of Romulus, here is eternal Jove's highest judgment, delivered through me at his command and in the same exotic tongue in which you phrased your request. 'Of all the bronze-clad Roman heroes, the first and quite the best—after the divine, victorious Caesar—was Publius Cornelius Scipio Africanus. But the founder of the monarchy was by far the better man. In other respects, Caesar himself and Scipio, the two men you see marching before you, came closest to embodying the ideal of the City.'" Then, turning to the others, he addressed them in their native Latin tongue: "Those of you who have so rashly presumed to engage in a debate unequal to your powers as to which of the two best Latin heroes most embodied the image of the goddess with the loud-clanging armor,[31] hear this message from great and mighty Jove, by way of a courtesy to your antiquity-loving friend:

"Though the men of Romulus' race most glorious in valor are   15
too numerous to count, still, the celebrated Africanus would surpass them all in praise were it not for the single exception of Caesar, precisely because Caesar founded the very monarchy that you ignorantly try to denigrate, though it was divinely inspired and modeled on heaven itself. Except for that achievement, Caesar and Scipio would walk in equal glory and praise, and it would be hard to decide whether Scipio surpassed Caesar in military genius and virtue, or Caesar Scipio.

"But to make this clearer, *behold, I shall remove the clouds that,*   16
drawn across your eyes, now obscure your mortal vision.[32] First, I shall say a little about the best form of government, then review as quickly as I can something about its founder, the prince himself, correcting your erroneous views, however slight they may be. For you do not yet understand how, from the beginning and forever afterward, the realms of the heaven-dwelling gods have been ruled with beautiful, everlasting order by the one prince, Best and Greatest Jove. But those of you who, ignorant of all that is divine and

gubernantur non usque intelligere potuistis; sed qui servilem igna-
vamque libertatem effingere moliti estis, meliorem quam caelo
mundum diversis e capitibus constituere, divinarum omnium rerum atque humanarum ignari, tam temere et inconsulte sperasti.
Nam frustra vobis delata sunt quae tantum per aevum de universae naturae principiis, de increato demogorgone et omnium opifice
deo per tot Graeciae gymnasia φυσιολόγοι, illi viri doctissimi,
diversis in didascalibus indagarunt.

17   'Sed ad rem nostram ut veniam, non et inter politicas didicisti,
posthabitis olygarchia atque tyrannide, quantum democratiae
praestat aristocratia tantum vel longe dignius aristocratiae ordini
divinam ipsam antecellere monarchiam? Quam demum ab eo ipso
C. Caesare nostro summa animi virtute conditam, tantum summo
ipsi placitam Iovi fuerat, ut Caesaris imperante filio divo Augusto,
ex quo tum clauso Iano, sevis reconditis armis et toto iam orbe
pacato, aurea recensita saecula, ab altissima caelorum arce descen-
dens in solum miro et inusitato ordine humano se generi immisceri dignatus est.

18   'Et sic dum ipse divum pater et hominum homines inter huma-
natus versaret, sub divi Augusti filio et Caesareo tertio loco principe Tiberio, caesareum hunc ita placuit principatum probare, ut
hac et si cum eo caeli terraeque orbis imperium divisum haberet,
sanctissimo ore annuit reddendum fore Caesari quae sunt Caesaris
et quae Dei sunt Deo, ut haec et vos inter, divis et e praeconibus
homo leo bosque sacratissimis testantur litteris.

19   'Cognoverat haec enim vates ille vester, deorum numine quodam afflante, dum Civile in Bello cecinerat victricem causam pla-
cuisse diis, victam sed tantum homini. Tum vero ad urbem inter
prodigia ad sublime Tarpeiae rupis culmen Caesarei loco numinis

human, strive to fashion a servile and craven freedom, to establish
a world better than heaven from different and conflicting heads,
indulge in a hope that is rash and ill-advised. In vain have the
learned men of science handed down to you through many ages
their various teachings about the first principles of the universe,
about the uncreated demiurge,[33] the God who is creator of all
things, discoveries they made in so many schools of Greece.

"But to come to the matter in hand, did you not learn that, 17
among political systems (setting aside oligarchy and tyranny as less
esteemed), to the degree that aristocracy surpasses democracy in
dignity, to the same degree, or indeed to a far greater degree, does
godlike monarchy surpass aristocracy?[34] And the monarchy
founded by our own Gaius Caesar with supreme courage and intellect was so pleasing to Jove that, when Caesar's divine son Augustus was ruling in what was accounted a golden age—by whom
the doors of the temple of Janus were closed, savage weapons were
put away, and the whole world was at peace[35]—he came down to
earth from his high heavenly citadel and, in a wondrous, unprecedented dispensation, deigned to mingle with the human race.[36]

"And thus, when the father of gods and men, himself incarnate, 18
moved among men in the reign of Emperor Tiberius, Augustus'
son and the third in the line of Caesars, he was so pleased to approve this Cesarean principate that, just as though he held joint
command with Caesar over heaven and earth, he agreed in a sacred pronouncement that what is Caesar's should be given to
Caesar, and what is God's, to God,[37] as, among the four divinely
inspired heralds, the man, the lion, and the ox bear witness among
you in their most holy writings.[38]

"Your famous poet realized this when, under a kind of divine 19
inspiration, he sang in his poem on the *Civil War* that the victorious cause pleased the gods, the vanquished only a man.[39] It
was then that, among the prodigies on the lofty summit of the
Tarpeian Rock, in place of Caesar's divine spirit, Jove's bird[40]-

alta et peregrina voce talia *Iovis ales* locuta est: γᾶν ὑπ᾽ ἐμοὶ
τίθεμαι, Ζεῦ, σὺ δὲ Ὄλυμπον ἔχε. Quae, postquam magnus
audierat Iuppiter, *annuit et totum nutu tremefecit Olympum.'*

20   Ad haec ubi conticuerat deus, dum attonitus admirabatur coe-
tus, ego ad eum tandem haec subiectissima hominis voce reddide-
ram: πᾶν ἐδάνεις, θεόφραδε Ἑρμῆς, Διὸς παῖς μοναρχό-
φιλε. Et omnia nostris auribus consona luculentissime cecinisti.
Nam et ego saepius egregias per Italiae urbes viros haud inter
vulgares cum hac de re pluries verba fecissem, hanc eandem sententiam, quam tu nuper, sanctissime vates, altius recensueras, deli-
bavi.

21   Et inter doctissimos paucos post Aretinos illos Latinorum
primarios L⟨eonardum⟩ et K⟨arolum⟩, quos ab aliis semper excipiendos putavi, alterum apud Anconem, civitatem nostram,
mecumque sentientem habeo Franciscum Scalamontium, equitem
praestantem et amicissimum mihi virum ac Picenos inter doctissimum. Habui et Aretinum alterum reique nostrae optimum scribam Bartholomaeon, qui peste indigna nuper solutum corpore, ad
vos magno sub axe per Aelisium remeantem vidisti. Habeo et
alium unicum tertio loco amicissimum, quem hac in concione
cernis, Georgium Begnam Iadertinum. Quibus cum vero vicissim
dum multa pluries magnis de caesareis meritis verba conserebamus, alia inter de adversa sentientibus mirabamur quod qui reges, in quibus absoluta urbis potestas fuerat, praeter Tarquinos
probant, imperium vero, quo cum S.P.Q.R. libertas semper vigebat in urbe suis omnibus moderata magistratibus, detestare conantur. Sed quod non usque nostrum cognoscere potuit intellectum,
hoc unum intelligere magnopere praecii curabamus quo enim
pacto quae sub regimine consulum Romana inclyta res diu poten-
tissima steterat, sub principibus tandem penitus ad ima corrueret.

22   Ad haec ille *subridens, altius caput* extollens divinumque aspirans
ambrosiae odorem, talia coeperat verba dare: 'ὦ *rerum nescia hominum*

proclaimed in a loud, foreign voice: 'I place the earth under my rule, Zeus; you hold Olympus.'[41] And when great Jupiter heard this, *he assented, causing all Olympus to shake.*"[42]

When the god had finished and the gathering stood in wonder and amazement, I replied in a subdued human voice, "Prophetic Hermes, son of Zeus, lover of monarchy, you know everything."[43] All of your splendid song rang agreeably in our ears. For in frequent conversations with men of distinction in the important cities of Italy I myself have often touched on the same opinion that you expressed more profoundly just now, most holy prophet.

Among these few most learned scholars — after those two leading men of Arezzo, Leonardo and Carlo,[44] whom I have always put in a special category — I count another, a man of my own city-state Ancona, Francesco Scalamonti, a distinguished knight and my close friend, the most learned man in Piceno, who agrees with me. I included also another man of Arezzo, Bartolomeo, the excellent secretary of my republic, who died undeservedly in the recent plague.[45] You saw him as he made his way to Elysium beneath the great vault of heaven.[46] I have in the third place another special friend whom you see in this discussion, Giorgio Begna of Zadar.[47] In the course of my frequent and lengthy struggles with these men on the subject of Caesar's great merits, we marveled that, among other matters of disagreement, those who approve the kings, whose power over the city was absolute (the Tarquins excepted), try to disparage the empire,[48] in which the freedom of the Senate and People of Rome always flourished in a city governed entirely by its own magistrates. But there was one thing that we could not understand, one thing we strove mightily to comprehend: how was it that the famous Roman state, which had long remained powerful under the governance of consuls, finally suffered utter collapse under the emperors?[49]

Smiling at this, the god raised his divine *head higher*, breathing *the scent of ambrosia*,[50] and began to speak: "*O ignorant mind of man*,[51]

20

21

22

mens, non adhuc intelligere valuit omnia esse hominum tenui
pendentia filo et quae diu potissimum valuere subito corruere
casu? Nam et quid homines a caelicolis nisi locorum intercapedine
distarent, si perpetuo Caesare eiusque filio Augusto Traiano ve
optimo principe stabilem et perpetuum mundi ordinem pater ille
divum mortalibus conservaret? Ast enim quom rem humanam
superi diu stare et nimium potentem videre, Parcas iusserant quin
verso rerum cardine magnam et orbivagam *volvere molem.* Sic et post
longum urbis senium et inconsultam hinc inde regiae principatus
sedis translationem, miserabilem rei calamitatem vidistis.

23   'Et enim ab eo si constitutus non esset optimus principatus,
antea longe deteriorem in modum sub consulibus quassatam illi-
sam dirutam substernatamque urbem, rem et publicam[6] conspice-
retis. Quid Graccorum memorem factiones? Quid C. Marii Sullae
ve seditiones et infandas ab iis optimorum civium caedes? Quid L.
Catelinae nesciat perniciosissimam coniurationem? Non et inrepa-
rabiles alias innumeras putandum a posteris et inferioribus virtute
viris factiosas insurgere conspirationes? Nec unquam sine Caesare
tantum urbis imperium a consulibus Senatu ve P.Q.R. collatum
propagatumve esse noveritis, neve tot in optimam formam provincias coloniasque deductas civitates ve constitutas municipales, tot
rogatas[7] honestissimas leges, tot aequissimos praetores, aediles,
praefectos, ac alios plerosque optimos in urbe magistratus additos
cognoveritis. Sed demum sub Flavio Constantino principe sic rerum ordine verso, vidimus egregiam illam Iovis avem, praeclarissimam olim rerum imaginem, nescio quo pacto ignava[8] quadam
cavea sacerdotum ordini permixtam, eam tandem squallentem in-
feram et silvestrem belluam deductam, ac velut ingens et ⟨h⟩orri-
bile monstrum Celeno simile omnia aduncis pedibus substernare.
Sic enim mortalibus vobis *omnipotens* rerum *fortuna* atque *ineluctabilia fata* tulere.'

are you still unable to understand that all things human hang upon a slender thread, that once-mighty states can come crashing down? For if the Father of the Gods were to preserve in perpetuity for mortals the world order of Caesar and his son Augustus or that excellent emperor Trajan as a thing stable and lasting, what would distance mankind from the gods except a spatial interval? For whenever the gods have seen an overly powerful human state survive for a long time, they have commanded the Fates *to turn the pivot of the world*[52] and send the unsteady mass tumbling down.[53] Thus in the city's old age, after the ill-advised transfer of the imperial capital,[54] you beheld her piteous downfall.

"Actually, if the best form of government[55] had not been established by Caesar, you would have seen the city and the state deteriorate much sooner, shaken, crushed, demolished, and prostrate, under the rule of consuls.[56] No need to mention the cabals of the Gracchi, the mutinies of Marius and Sulla, their unspeakable massacre of the nobility. Who does not know about Lucius Catiline's deadly conspiracy? One can imagine countless other conspiracies arising, hatched by later, lesser individuals, causing irreparable divisions. Nor would you ever know of the City's great empire, gathered and enlarged by the consuls and the Senate and People of Rome, without Caesar. Never would you know of provinces and colonies brought into optimal form, of so many self-governing communities established, so many honorable laws passed, so many irreproachable praetors, aediles, prefects, and other excellent magistrates in the city of Rome. Finally, however, under the emperor Flavius Constantine, the natural order was reversed[57] and we saw Jove's noble bird, once the majestic symbol of the Roman state, somehow led captive along with the priestly order in a demeaning cage, as if it were some filthy, wild beast of hell like that huge, frightening monster Celaeno,[58] scattering all beneath it with its hooked claws. Thus did *all-powerful Fortune and the inescapable Fates* ordain for you mortals."[59]

23

24 Tum ego ad certissima dei dicta suspirans, pauca haec Sophocleo de more retuleram:

ὁρῶ φάρ ἡμᾶς οὐδὲν ὄντας ἄλλο πλὴν
εἴδωλα⁹ ὅσοιπερ ζῶμεν ἢ κούφην σκιάν.

Sed iam aliqua nostro de Caesare cupio te canente audire.' Et talia quom dixissem, coepit inde talia δαίμων: 'Magnam quidem, ὦ παλαιόφιλε, rem et inenarrabilem novimus te flagitare, sed enim a me vobis perpollicitam quidem. Nam quis adeo iam sub umbra palluit Parnasi aut suavissimum laticem e *caballino fonte* potavit, volens huic loco satis officio facere, ⟨ut⟩¹⁰ non multis vatisonis laboraret Camenis? Nam et plerique vestri clarissimi auctores, historiae conscriptores atque excellentissimi vates, quom saepe et multum suis¹¹ in laudibus laborassent, exiguam tamen virtutum suarum partem commendare litteris potuere. Nam quis attingeret verbis ab ineunte aetate mirabile suum et prope divinae mentis ingenium? Quis ineffabilem eloquentiam suam latinae ve linguae facundiam narret? Quid virtutem, constantiam, mirabilem ve providentiam memorem? aut sublimitatem omnium capacem quae caelo continentur? Dicam ne proprium animi vigorem celeritatemque quodam igne volucrem? Scribere simul et legere, dictare et audire solitum accepistis; epistolas tantarum rerum quaternas septenasve quandoque per ocium pariter dictare librariis memoriae commendatum est.

25 'Nam et sua de fortitudine dicere si forte velimus, quantus inter milites Siccinus aut Sergius, tantum vel longe praestantior inter duces omnes aut inter viros, dictator iste Caesar perstrenuae militiae claritate emicuit. Signis collatis supra quinquageties cognovimus dimicasse, M. Marcellum supergressus, qui unum de

Sighing at the god's infallible words, I replied in a Sophoclean   24
mode,

"I see that we, the living, are nothing
but images and empty shadow.[60]

But now I would like to hear you sing something about our Caesar." When I had said this, the daimon[61] began as follows: "It is a
great and inexpressible request you make of me, lover of antiquity,
but one I have repeatedly promised to fulfill. For who has ever
grown so pale in the shadow of Parnassus or drunk sweet water
from *the horse's spring*,[62] wanting to do his duty to this subject, that
he did not toil under the inspiration of many prophetic Muses?
For your most illustrious authors, both writers of history and excellent poets, though they labored often and hard on their enco-
mia of Caesar, were able to put down in writing only a tiny portion of his virtues. For who could approximate in words his
amazing and nearly divine intelligence from his earliest age? Who
could tell of his inexpressible eloquence and mastery of the Latin
language? Why need I mention his courage, his steadfastness, his
admirable foresight, or his eminence, capable of anything under
the sun? Shall I speak of his characteristic power and his quickness of mind, swift as fire? You have understood that he was wont
to write and read, dictate and listen simultaneously. Tradition has
it that in his free time he would dictate to his secretaries four to
seven letters at a time on matters of great importance.[63]

"If perchance one should choose to speak of his courage, Cae-   25
sar, as dictator, outshone his officers and men in vigorous combat
as much or far more than Siccius and Sergius[64] excelled among
their fellow soldiers. We know he fought more than fifty pitched
battles, surpassing Marcus Marcellus, who had engaged in thirty-

quadragies pari modo fuerat proeliatus. Sed heus! Quid hominum
strages commemorem? Quom et ab eo ipso Caesare in proeliis XI
centena et XCII caesa sunt hostium milia, praeter quos non ipse
memorare censuerat, quantos invitus fuderit civile bello?

26   'Ast enim eius si magnis de trophaeis audire velitis et quantum
suis cum et Pompeianis legionibus in Gallos trans et citra Rhe-
num quantum ve in Germanos, Brittanos, Afros et Numidas terra
marique gesserit, reticeam quidem ego et sua ipsa suis de rebus
commentaria loquantur. Quae ita ab eo ornate et elegantissime
condita sunt, ut ea, si forte aliorum de gestis conscripsisset, ex iis
et insignibus aliis eius litterarum studiis, nullo a se armis peracto
facinore egregia inter auctorum nomina Latinorum celebratissi-
mum suum haberetur nomen. Animi vero magnitudine, pietate,
benignitateque adeo praeditus, ut quos armis subegerat clementia
magis vicerit, iniuriarum omnium semper immemor.

27   'Et enim postquam exactis rebus ad urbem quinos insignes et
amplissimos triumphos egerat, a patribus patriae patrem saluta-
tum et ante sacram almae Veneris aedem sacrosanctum et perpetuum dictatorem dictum audivimus. Spectacula quidem ab eo
edita effusasque opes aut opera magnifica hac in parte recensere
luxuriae faventis est. At et si non dira ambitio illa civium atque
edacissimus livor impias in eum et sacrilegas manus iniecissent, ad
ipsam exornandam urbem atque imperium propagandum multa
atque maiora destinasse praescivimus. Quae inter et nostro Marti
belligero quantum nusquam esset dicare delubrum, et Parthis per
Harmeniam inferre ingens et lacrimabile bellum, leges emendare,
bibliothecas per urbem omnigenum litterarum instruere, et alia
quae vobis non pauca auctorem haud ignotum novimus detexisse.

nine battles in the same way. But alas! why should I recall the slaughter of human beings when 1,192,000 of the enemy were slain by Caesar in battle, not counting those he saw fit not to record— all those whom he slew reluctantly in the Civil War?[65]

"But should you wish to hear about his great victories, his ex- 26 ploits by land and sea, with both his and Pompey's legions against the Gauls on both sides of the Rhine, against Germans and Britons, Africans and Numidians, I for my part would prefer to keep quiet and let his *Commentaries* speak for themselves. They are composed with such rhetorical excellence that if it were someone else's exploits he had recounted, just on the basis of these and others of his literary efforts, with no military achievement of his own, he would be ranked among the most celebrated of Latin writers. So high-minded was he, so dutiful, so generous, that those whom he had subdued by force of arms he conquered more by his clemency, ever ready to forget the wrongs done to him.

"For we are told that after he had achieved his goal and cele- 27 brated five grand triumphs in the City, the Senators saluted him as Father of His Country and before the sacred temple of fostering Venus proclaimed him inviolable and dictator in perpetuity. As to the public entertainments he put on, the wealth he lavishly expended, or the grand public works, to rehearse them would be the work of someone who loves extravagance.[66] But if the dreadful ambition and consuming envy of his fellow citizens had not laid impious and sacrilegious hands on him, we know he had planned many works of greater scope to adorn the city and extend the empire. Among them were plans to dedicate a temple, larger than any other anywhere, to our warrior Mars; to wage through Armenia a major, tearful war against the Parthians, to revise the laws, to build libraries throughout Rome in every branch of literature, and many other projects, as an author well known to you has disclosed.[67]

28   'Nam et ingentes quae de nobilissimo Affricano a vobis recensi-
tae sunt laudes, vere et longe maiores aeternis suis coram Iove
meritis in auro a caelicolis commendatae litteris videntur adaman-
tinis; sed inter nobilissimas suos ipse annos virtute praeteriens
Hanibalem Poenum, insignem et praecellentissimum bello ducem
ac perniciosissimum populi Romani hostem, egregia virtute su-
perasse ad pacemque sibi petendam coegisse ac eo duce potentis-
simum populum Cartaginensem Romanae dicioni magna cum
S.P.Q.R. dignitate subegisse: Non et Dardanius ille vestrae caput
gentis filio ostentarat Anchises amplum per Aelisium venturam
sub caelo Scipiadum gloriam? Quam etsi maiorem in modum eum
ipsum intellexisti, inclytae Iuleae Caesareae gentis nomina sancta
ferentem, ut insignis ille Latinorum vates vos inter gloriose cecinerat.

29   'Nam et audiendi venerandique sunt poetae, quorum divino atque perpetuo carmine non modo viri antiquissimi heroes ut inter
posteros viverent, indigerunt, sed nostrorum quoque caelicolum
tanta maiestas eorum quandoque laboribus indigere videbatur.
Nam et ab iis ea dignissima quae per longinquam aevi vetustatem
homines inter et divos dicta factaque fuerint veluti praesentia nobis et venturis utique nepotibus extant. Tantum enim praevaluerat
eis praecellentissimum illud et venerandum litterarum munus, humano generi ab ipso Iove optimo magna liberalitate largitum. Quo
quidem egregio beneficio qui penitus a disciplina remoti sunt,
carentes, debiles caecique, maestam et lugubrem vitam agere mani-
festissimum est, quamvis fere plerisque accidit ut praesidio litterarum diligentiam in perdiscendo ac memoriam remittant.

30   'Sed quom *labentia* iam me *sydera* repetant ut nostro Iulio de
Caesare quodammodo finem faciam, ne quidem laeta serenitas
caeli tantae esset hominis extimationis, si numquam Olympus ipse

"Indeed, the marks of praise you have listed in regard to the 28 renowned Africanus are also vast; and truly, because of their eternal merit, they seem far greater praises in the eyes of Jove, recorded in gold by the angels in letters that will never fade. But among the noblest was that he himself, more resolute than his years would warrant, overcame by his extraordinary valor that distinguished and eminently capable war leader, most deadly enemy of the Roman people, Punic Hannibal, forced him to sue for peace, and, under his own leadership, subjected the mighty nation of Carthage to Roman domination, to the great glory of the Senate and People of Rome. Did not Dardanian Anchises, the fountainhead of your race, show to his son the future glory of the Scipios striding beneath the sky through broad Elysium? And yet you have heard him pronouncing himself the sacred names of the celebrated family of the Julian Caesars, as your peerless Latin seer gloriously sang.[68]

"As you know, the poets should be listened to and revered, for 29 not only do the ancient heroes need their inspired and everlasting song in order to live among those who come after them, but even the great majesty of our gods themselves seems to require their services from time to time. For it is by them that worthy deeds and words among men and gods in ages long past are in a sense present to us and to our posterity, so much advantage have they had from that preeminent and revered gift of letters that mighty Jove bestowed most lavishly on humankind. Indeed, it is perfectly clear that those who are utterly barred from instruction, lacking this remarkable gift, are doomed to live sad and melancholy lives, weak and blind, while it happens that many, under the protection of letters, slacken their diligence in learning and their memory.

"But the *setting stars*[69] are now calling me back home. Therefore, 30 to conclude about Julius Caesar, not even the joyful brightness of the sky would be so esteemed by mankind were Olympus itself

caerula aliqua obtexeretur nube, nec tam spectatae conspicuae ve pulchritudinis videretur regium quodcumque nobilissimum diadema si totum gemmis contextum praeciosissimis non aliqua ex parte raresceretur inferioris praecii variarum aspergine rerum. Ita et si Caesareis divinis operibus non aliqua humana immisceretur voluptas, minus insignia atque admirabilia eius albescerentur facinora. Ea quidem voluptuosa aliqua iocanda veluti solatii loco saepe inter iocundissima sibi milites iactabantur. Quod et si deteriorem in partem ab aliquo eo de divino homine ad dedecus damnosae lubidinis humanae ve quoiuscunque tabediae,[12] aut turpia aut minus digna viro verba admissa perlatave essent, Latini atque humani nominis de re censeo eam quoiuscunque infandi hominis temerariam vocem summo omnium silentio praetereundam, opprimendam, non pro dicta aut excogitata quidem habendam, ac ab omni hominum memoria delendam esse.'

31   Et haec ubi caducifer dicta dedit, postquam aperta nube Caliopen solverat, propriam resummens formam Argiphonteam, ubi mille dei volantum vitae gloriam almae Trini Numinis maiestati cecinerant, *in tenuem auram nostris ex oculis* evolavit. Exin ego *sopno solutus* calamum cepi et tibi, ut ad quem semper Latini nominis gloriae exornatorem cognovi, portentum hoc inscribere, praedignum amiciciae nostrae munus existimavi.

32   Vale ex Argo Amphilochia antiquissima Epiri et vetustate diruta apud Acheloum amnem civitate. III Kalendas Februarias 1436. Ex Liburnea Iadera XII Kalendas Decembris MCCCCXXXV.

never veiled by a dark cloud; nor would the noblest royal diadem seem so remarkably, strikingly beautiful if precious gems covered it entirely instead of being spaced to some extent by a sprinkling of a various less costly ornaments. In just the same way, if the human pleasures of the flesh had not mingled with Caesar's godlike achievements, his outstanding and admirable deeds would shine less brightly. Indeed, there were those bawdy jestings, uttered often as a source of relaxation among his soldiers. But if his toleration of obscene or inappropriate language had detracted to any extent from this godlike man to the point of ruinous disgrace or any sort of moral decay, I think that in respect for the good name of the Latins and of humanity itself, that kind of reckless speech on the part of any unspeakable individual would have to have been passed over and suppressed in unanimous silence, would have to have been considered unworthy of verbal expression or thought, and would have to have been erased from the memory of mankind."

When the staff-bearer had finished speaking and had opened   31
the cloud and released Calliope, he resumed his Argos-slaying shape and, as a multitude of God's flying creatures sang the glory of life to the majesty of the fostering Trinity, *flew from our sight into thin air*.[70] Then, released from sleep, I took up my pen and, to you, knowing you to be ever an ornament of the glory of Latinity, I reckoned I would dedicate this poetic fiction, a gift eminently worthy of our friendship.

Farewell from Amphilochian Argos, an ancient city of Epirus   32
on the river Achelous, ruined with age. January 30, 1436.[71] From Liburnian Zadar on November 20, 1435.[72]

: V :

Leonardo Aretino viro clarissimo optimoque
Florentinae Rei secretario salutem.[1]

1 Ἐπίγραμμα, εἰς Ἀθήνας ἐπὶ σημείου[2] τῆς Ἀττικῆς πόλιν.
Ad fauces aqueductus extra civitatem, ad unum miliare.

> IMP. CAESAR. T. AELIVS. HADRIANVS
> ANTONINVS. AVG. PIVS. [COS.] III. TRIB. POT.
> II. P.P.
> AQVEDVCTVM IN NOVIS. ATHENIS. CEPTum
> A DIVO HADRIANO. PATRE. SVO CONSumauit
> DEDICAVITque.

Latinam hanc inscriptionem ex me nuper Athenis compertam dignissimae spectationi tuae hoc loco rescribendum delegi, Leonarde latinorum elegantissime vir, ut et per eam facilius videas quanta diligentia curaque maiores nostri latini ue nominis cesarei principes providentissime, pie atque magnanimiter, non per Italiam modo, sed et per Graeciam ac magnum undique fere per orbem cadentes nobilissimas urbes cum omni cultu restituere.

2 Optabam praeterea te felicem reuisere tecumque non pauca conferre de rebus memoratu dignissimis meo ex hoc itinere per Illyriam, Macedoniam, Epyrum, Achayam, Euboiam, Peloponesumque visis, sed ab eo me desiderio res haud importune cohercent. Vale, et subsequens atthicis litteris epigramma, quod apud

: V :

Cyriac to Leonardo Bruni
?Greece, shortly after April 7, 1436[1]

To Leonardo Aretino, an excellent and distinguished man,
chancellor of Florence.

Epigram [found] in Athens, the Attic city, at the marker, nearby   1
the outlet of the aqueduct, one mile outside the city.

Emperor Caesar Titus Aelius Hadrianus
Antoninus Pius Augustus, [*consul*] for the third time, with
tribunician power
for the second time, father of his country,
completed and dedicated the aqueduct in New Athens
which was begun by his father,
the divine Hadrian.[2]

I chose to transcribe this Latin inscription I recently found in
Athens for your most worthy consideration, Leonardo, most judi-
cious of Latin writers, so that through it you might more readily
see the great care and effort our ancestral princes of the Latin
name took to restore in all their adornments, with immense foresight, reverence, and greatness of soul, the noblest cities fallen into
decay, not only throughout Italy, but throughout Greece and almost everywhere throughout the world.

It has been my wish, moreover, to see again your fortunate self   2
and to discuss with you in some detail the memorable sights I
encountered on this visit to Illyria, Macedonia, Epirus, Achaea,
Euboia and the Peloponnese. But distressing events prevented me
from achieving my wish. Farewell, and may the following epigram

nobilem et vetustate collapsam Delphorum civitatem alia inter
comperi, utique lectitare placeat. τὸ μὲν γὰρ εἰς τὴν τοῦ Πυθίου
Ἀπόλλωνος ἱεροῦ πλευρὰν γεγραμμένον ἐστίν.

ΕΠΙ ΑΡΙΣΤΑΓΟΡΑ ΑΡΧΟΝΤΟΣ ΕΝ ΔΕΛΦΟΙΣ
ΠΤΛΑΙΑΣ . ΗΡΙΝΗΣ . ΙΕΡΟΜΝΗΜΟΝΟΤΝΤΩΝ
ΑΙΤΩΛΩΝ³ ΠΟΛΕΜΑΡΧΟΤ ΑΛΕΧΑΜΕΝΟΤ
ΔΑΜΩΝΟΣ.

3   Desiderabam insuper abs te certiorem fieri an libellum exceperis
quem adversus indignam Poggii nostri divo de Caesare opinionem
integerrimo tuo amplissimoque iudicio ex Epyro hisce nuper diebus transmisi. Vale iterum.

: VI :

1   Poggius plurimam salutem dicit Leonardo Aretino viro clarissimo.
2   Oblata est mihi nuper, mi Leonarde, insulsi ac ridiculi hominis,
tibi vero notissimi, Ciriaci Anconitani epistola quaedam, scripta
ad te aureolo minio, quam stultus ille ac mentis inops Caesaream
appellat. Eam cum legissem, nescio risune an stomacho maiore
commotus sim videns et vesani hominis verbosam loquacitatem
et impudentiam scribendi. Risi quidem primo non mediocriter
hominem levem, insulsum atque inconstantem tam verbosam
congeriem adeo inepte conglutinasse, ut quid dicatur neque qui
scripsit sciat neque qui legant, nisi divinare velint, queant intelligere: Graeca plurima Latinis mixta, verba inepta, Latinitas mala,

in Greek, which I found among others in the ruined city of Delphi, give you pleasure to read. It was inscribed on the wall of the temple of Pythian Apollo:

> When Aristagoras was archon in Delphi,
> spring session, Polemarchos, Alexamenos
> and Damon were delegates of the
> Aetolians.[3]

I would also like to know whether you have received the little 3 book I submitted to your incorruptible and generous judgment from Epirus in these recent days, a work directed against Poggio's unbecoming views about the godlike Caesar. Farewell.

: VI :

Poggio Bracciolini to Leonardo Bruni
Ferrara, March 31, 1438

Poggio sends best wishes to the distinguished Leonardo of Arezzo. 1

My dear Leonardo, I was recently shown a certain letter, writ- 2 ten to you in reddish gold letters by a tasteless and laughable man, well known to you, Cyriac of Ancona, which that stupid and empty-headed man calls Caesarean. When I had read it I did now know whether I should be more moved to laughter or anger, recognizing in it both the loquacity of a madman and the impudence of his writing. In fact I laughed at first quite a bit that such a frivolous, tasteless and capricious man had stuck together so absurdly such a pile of verbosity that neither the writer nor his readers could understand what he wrote, unless they wanted to guess: a lot of Greek mixed with Latin, words improperly used, bad

constructio inconcinna, sensus nullus, ut vere responsa Phoebi
subobscura aut dicta Spingae esse videantur, quae praeter Sybillam
intelligat nemo.

3   Indignatus sum vero paululum quod stultus ille, quem numquam ne verbo quidem offendi, petulanter ac proterve in me impetum faciat, scripsisse me insane et temerarie dicens quod Scipionem in quadam disputatione inter me et Guarinum nuper habita
praetulerim Caesari. Rationem vero nullam affert suae sententiae
neque Caesarem ipsum laudat, sed solummodo putat summum
esse sacrilegium contra Caesarem loqui, idque pro ratione ducit,
quod secum sentire ait quosdam homines inauditos, obscuros, qui
vivantne an mortui sint Apollo esset Delphicus consulendus. Sed
tamen cum totam fabellam odiosam atque ineptam uno spiritu
decurrissem, deposito stomacho, animum meum ad risum con-
verti, considerans quot monstra hominum sint et quanta stultitia
versetur in terris, ut iam alter Hercules esset ab inferis excitandus,
ad perdomanda haec prodigia, quae non verbis reprimenda sunt,
sed clava et fustibus castiganda.

4   Sciebam Ciriacum hominem esse loquacem, stolidum, verbo-
sum, et tamquam molestam cicadam auribus hominum perstre-
pentem; sciebam eum indoctum, dicacem, et veluti scurram quendam infestum, vagum atque instabilem, tamquam Scytham,
nullam habentem neque animi neque corporis quietem, qui in
Latino sermone saepissime ut puerulus labitur, nulla in re doctus
praeterquam inani verborum iactantia et sono, sed tamen non cre-
debam adeo progressuram dementiam suam, ut etiam in me vellet
incursare.

5   Est profecto maximus omnium morbus stultitia, qua qui labo-
rat, parum distat a beluis. Quis unquam opinatus esset hunc bar-
batum satyrum bellum mihi sine causa indicturum pro Caesaris
mortui causa, qui ne se vivum quidem tueri potest, famelicus,

Latin, awkward constructions, no sense, so that really they seem to be the unintelligible responses of Apollo or the words of the Sphinx, which no one but the Sibyl could understand.

I was a little angry that this fool, whom I had never offended even by a word, impudently and wantonly attacked me, saying that I had written madly and rashly because I had preferred Scipio to Caesar in a recent discussion between me and Guarino. He does not adduce any reason for his opinion, nor does he praise Caesar himself, but only thinks it is the highest sacrilege to speak against Caesar, and he thinks it counts as an argument that some obscure, unheard-of men (you would have to consult Delphic Apollo to know whether they were dead or alive) share his opinion. But when I had finally gone through in one breath his wholly odious and silly little tale, I put aside my anger and changed my mood to laughter, bethought myself of how many monstrosities there were among mankind, and how much stupidity there is in the world, so that another Hercules would have to be called up from the underworld to overcome these monsters, which are not to be subdued by words but punished with a club and cudgels.

I knew that Cyriac was a talkative, dull, verbose man, like an irritating cricket noisily disturbing men's ears; I knew he was uneducated and sharp-tongued, like some troublesome buffoon, aimless and inconstant, like a Scythian,[1] restless in mind or body, who very often stumbles in the Latin language like a small child, skilled in nothing beside an empty boasting and sound of words. Even so, I did not believe his madness would go so far that he would want to attack even me.

Truly the greatest disease of all is stupidity: whoever suffers from it is not very different from the animals. Who would have thought that this bearded satyr for no reason would declare war against me on behalf of a dead Caesar — a starving beggar who lives off other people's money and cannot even keep himself alive?

227

mendicus, et aere alieno vivens. Atque hunc, si Caesar viveret, pro eius stultitia veluti abiectum servum ad bestias deputaret.

6   Vir doctissumus Guarinus noster, cum contra me causam Caesaris suscepit, aliqua verborum moderatione usus est. At vero hic musca importunior, molestior culice, indoctus, insulsus, loquax insanum me, dementem, temerarium existimat, quod videar sentire contra institutorem, ut ait, monarchiae, quam necessariam putat ad regimen gentium, laudans imperatores et rem publicam Romanorum vituperans. Quid huic asino respondeas bipedali, tardo atque imcomposito, nato ad servitutem, qui esset non verbis, sed baculis cohercendus?

7   At hic me quondam amicum sibi fuisse dicit, ac si maxima a me sit iniuria affectus quod contra Caesarem scripserim pro laude Scipionis. Sed, dii boni, quam ridicule suam hanc contexuit loquacitatem. Fingit somniasse se redeuntem e Graecia, ex qua levitatem et insaniam asportavit, atque in somniis astitisse sibi musas nescio quas, ac contra me pro Caesare locutas, deinde missum ad se ab Iove Mercurium, qui Caesarem tueretur, et fuisse illum eloquentem, prudentem, humanum, et multa praeterea doceret. De iis, quae a me scripta erant, verbum nullum.

8   Tota confictio ridicula et somniis Cyriaci digna, qui, si ea nocta paulum quid plus bibisset, ipse in caelum ad Iovem ipsum advolasset, non Mercurium stultitiae suae finxisset nuncium. Sed erravit aspectu paulum homo vesanus gravi oppressus somno. Quas enim musas putavit corniculae et ranae extiterunt, quarum alterae cohaxantem illius loquacitatem, alterae mentis vertiginem repraesentabant. Nam quid stulto illi commune cum musis, qui nihil nisi garrire novit, imperitissimus omnium qui vivant? Orpheum se aut Museum existimavit, ad quem musarum chorus tanquam ad vatem suum proficisceretur, Iovem praeterea nimis otiosum, cui

If Caesar were living, he would condemn this fellow, like the mean slave he is, to the wild beasts because of his stupidity.

When our very learned Guarino took up the cause of Caesar 6 against me, he used a certain moderation in his language. But this troublesome fly, more irritating than a mosquito — uneducated, tasteless, verbose — thinks that I am mad, out of my mind, and rash, because I seem to have an opinion against the founder, as he says, of monarchy — which he thinks is necessary for ruling nations — praising the emperors and defaming the republic of the Romans. What can you say to this two-legged donkey, slow-witted and disorganized, born to servitude, who should be restrained not by words but by sticks?

But this one says that I was once friends with him, as if he were 7 suffering the greatest injury from me because I had written against Caesar in praise of Scipio. But, gods above! how laughably he has woven together his garrulous twaddle. He pretends that he had fallen asleep as he was returning from Greece (from which he brought his lunatic frivolity) and that some Muses stood near him and spoke against me in favor of Caesar, then that Mercury was sent to him by Jupiter to defend Caesar, and *declared* that he was eloquent, wise, human, and much else; but not a word about what I had actually written.

This whole fabrication is ridiculous and worthy of the dreams 8 of Cyriac, who, if he had drunk a bit more that night, would himself have flown to Jupiter, and not made Mercury the messenger of his stupidity. But this lunatic, sunk in deep sleep, made a mistake in what he saw. For what he thought were the Muses were actually crows and frogs, some of them portraying his croaking verbosity, others his giddiness of mind. For what could that fool, who knows only how to chatter, have in common with the Muses? The greatest ignoramus alive thought that he was some Orpheus or Musaeus to whom the chorus of the Muses would come as though to their bard, and that Jupiter furthermore had so little to do that he

magnae curae essent fanatici hominis somnia. Recte tamen per somnium musas servum locutas simulat. Si enim ad hominem vigilantem verba fecissent, aliquid forsan ab eis discere potuisset.

9   Nunc cum nihil litterarum sciat, cum sit omnium quos norim stultissimus, quicquid novit, cum parum id existat, rectissime somnium esse testatur; et ne homines fraudet, homo liberalis ipse etiam hoc litteris mandavit. Numquam quicquam verius aut scribere aut loqui potuit Ciriacus, quam se somniare cum scribit aut loquitur. Quae cum vere somnia sint levia et Ciriaci digna, indignissima sunt quibus respondeatur.

10   Haec vero post risum ad retundendam illius petulantiam ad te scripsi, ut tu quoque rideas, si epistolam, quam circumferre ad ostentationem coepit, ad te destinavit.

Vale. Ferrariae, pridie Kalendas Aprilis.

concerned himself with the dreams of a madman. Rightly, though, he pretends that the Muses spoke to him in his sleep. For if they had directed their words to a man who was awake, he might perhaps have learned something from them.

Now, since he knows nothing of literature, since he is the stu- 9 pidest of all the people I know, whatever he knows, since that is very little, he rightly calls a dream and, so as not to deprive mankind of it, the generous man has entrusted even this to writing. Cyriac could never write or say anything truer than that he was dreaming when he writes or speaks. Since these dreams are really trivial and worthy of Cyriac, they are completely undeserving of a response.

I have written you this, after laughing, in order to blunt his 10 impudence, so that you too can laugh if he has sent you the letter, which he has ostentatiously begun to circulate.

Farewell. Ferrara, March 31.

CYRIAC OF ANCONA
THE KING'S NAVAL BATTLE

Praefacio

1 Vellem, o quam lubentissime, praestantissime Francisce eques, ut quemadmodum de Christianissimi atque optumi Regis conflictu hodierno die me tibi scripturum scio, ita victores simul et victos aliosque generosissimae gentis Italae potentatus (ut iam plus quam exacto biennio, ipsi primum Lyguro Philippo duci, exin ad urbem inclyto Sigismundo Caesari atque max[imo] E[ugenio] pontifici meis plerisque orationibus persuaserim), uno et sanctissimo foedere iunctos, adversus truces Afros, Getulos, Numidas, Bistones, Thracas, Adiabenos, Arabes et Parthos atque inphandos alios plerosque almae religionis nostrae barbareos hostes rem gesisse, et, ut pluries maiores nostri praeclarissime fecerant, insignes ex iis triumphos retulisse, laeto magis calamo dicerem.

2 Ne quidem aetatis nostrae inertiae sortes nostrae dedissent infelices, ut, quemadmodum adversus barbaricas Cartaginensium incursiones primores nostri insignem maritimae rei gloriam magnis et constantissimis animis vendicarunt, ita et potentes quoque nostri de profanis nunc hostibus triumpharent!

3 Nam, ut auctore Pollibio memoriae conmendatum est, primo punico bello, quanquam naumachiae inexperti, C. Duellius Hanibalem, Attilius Hamilcarem, Catulus denique Barcham Hamilcarem alterum plerisque apud Siceliam et Lilybeum navalibus

*Cyriac of Ancona's Account
of the King of Aragon's Naval Battle of Ponza,
Dedicated to the Most Excellent Knight,
Francesco Scalamonti*

Preface

How happy I would be, most excellent knight Francesco, knowing   1
that today I am going to write you about the battle of the most
Christian, excellent king [Alfonso], if I could rather write you
with joyful pen that all the participants, both victors and vanquished, along with the other rulers of the most noble people of
Italy, had joined in a single, most holy alliance and had waged
war against the cruel Africans, Gaetulians, Numidians, Thracians,
Adiabeni, Arabs, and Parthians and other numerous unspeakable
enemies of our fostering religion and had brought back news of
signal triumphs, as on so many occasions our ancestors most gloriously had done. (I had argued for this in several speeches more
than two years ago, first to Duke Philip of Milan, then, in Rome,
to the glorious Emperor Sigismund and the Supreme Pontiff Eugene.)

Not even the sluggish, unlucky fates of our own age would have   2
brought it about that, just as our ancestors earned signal glory in
naval warfare against the barbarous invasions of the Carthaginians
by their resolute great courage, so our own rulers would also triumph now over the infidel foe!

For, as the writer Polybius transmitted to history, in the first   3
Punic War, although Gaius Duilius, Attilius, and finally, Catulus
were unpracticed in naval warfare, by overcoming with their great
courage Hannibal, Hamilcar, and the second Hamilcar Barca in
numerous naval battles off Sicily and Lilybaeum[1] and remarkably

praeliis magna virtute superantes, innumeris hostium classibus insigniter expugnatis ad sublime rei navalis gloriae fastigium evasere.

4   Decet set enim ea spectationi tuae scribere, quae hac in tempestate infesta nobis et ineluctabilia fata molierant.

1.1   Itaque, dum superioribus diebus dumque proxima ferveret aestas, Alfonsus, inclytus Taraconensium Rex, Neapolianum regnum sibi re viae adoptionis iure debitum affectans, suo cum nobilissimo exercitu atque ingenti omnigenum navium classe Caetam, civitatem Campaniae vetustissimam, plurigenis undique missilibus armis atque muralibus machinis magna obsidione terra marique premeret, Philippus, magnanimus Lyguriae dux, ubi Neapolitanis nunciis ac frequentibus literis et oratoribus legatis regnum Ranerio Gallico duci, affini suo, regio testamento relictum lacessiri vastarive percepisset, eique magnanimiter opitulari decrevisset, missa primum Caetam in auxilium delecta sub Placentino tribuno balistariorum militum cohorte, extinguere maritimam Regis potentiam providentissme cogitarat.

1.2   Proinde hortati ab eo Genuenses, viri rei maritimae peritissimi ac magnarum gerendarum rerum expertissimi, quom esset primum Caietam navali oppressione solvendum ac alias Regni maritimas urbes orasve tutandum, suam quam celeriter classem instruere pararive solertissime curavere.

1.3   Itaque tres et decem ceteas onerarias ac tres rostratas, una cum bireme, triremes omnifariam machinis instructas munitasque armato milite compleverant, hisque praefecerant militibus Guidonem Taurellium, virum quidem perstrenuum ac militae longa exercitatione doctissimum.

capturing countless enemy fleets, they rose to the highest pinnacle of glory in naval warfare.

But it is proper to write to your Excellency of the events that 4 the Fates, hostile to us and irresistible, set in motion in our own time.

And so, while in the preceding days, while the recent summer was 1.1 still seething, Alfonso, renowned King of Aragon, aspiring to the throne of Naples as due to him by right of royal adoption, was conducting a great siege by land and by sea of Gaeta, an ancient city of Campania,[2] with his most noble army and a huge fleet of every kind of ship, with many kinds of missile weapons and siege machines, Philip, the greathearted Duke of Milan, having learned from Neapolitan emissaries and from frequent written and oral dispatches, that the kingdom, which had been left by royal testament to his relative, the French prince René, was being attacked and laid waste, decided generously to help him by first sending to the aid of Gaeta an elite cohort of artillerymen under the command of a tribune from Piacenza. His most providential plan was to destroy the naval power of the king.

Therefore, the Genoese, a people highly skilled in naval warfare 1.2 and highly experienced in great undertakings, urged to it by Philip, mustered a fleet as quickly as they could and very skillfully attended to its readying, since the first priority was to free Gaeta from naval attack and to safeguard the other coastal cities and shores of the Kingdom.

So they outfitted thirteen cargo ships, three beaked triremes 1.3 and one bireme, outfitted with all kinds of machines and defended with armed soldiers, and they put the soldiers under the command of Guido Torelli,[3] a very vigorous man and most knowledgeable in warfare because of his long experience in the field.

1.4   Classi quidem omni praefectus ab iis fuerat Blasius Agereus, scriba quidem homo et in primis audax, quem iusserant Caietam quam primum recto navigare itinere ibique cum applicuisset, classem omnem Francisco Spinolae, nobilissimo nempe homini, quem eo antea ad confovendos civium animos, ut permanerent in fide, praemiserant, exinde maritimae expeditionis imp[eratorem] designaverant, omnibus cum rebus exercitibusque committere.

1.5   Sic igitur instructis paratisque copiis, postquam ad naves magno strepitu frequentive civium plausu conscendere, ad X K[alendas] Aug[usti] solutis ancoralibus et datis afflanti zephyro velis Genuensem portum praeterlinquentes et Caietam versus lato aequore navigantes in altum deferebantur.

2.1   Per idem fere tempus apud Caietanum agrum serenissimus Rex his percumptatis rebus, accitis ad castra primatibus suis regnicolis plerique maiestatis suae fautores, principes, heroes ac nobiles, innumeri equites et armagerentes ad eum incredibili splendore, ingenti pompa ornatuve convenere; quos enim vero dum laetis oculis conspexisset, ingentemque sibi animum spemque simul et vires attollere tantorum praesentia heroum cognovisset, concione habita, quom multa ad excitandos eorum rei gerendae animos fortiter egregieque disseruisset et exploratam tandem adversus adventantem Genuensium classem mari obviam congrediendum placuisset, magnam exercituum eius partem ad navalem expeditionem pararat.

2.2   Divisis itaque copiis, Christoforo Caietaneo, Francisco Ursino atque Barceloneo quodam sibi fido exercituum praesidente cum quinque equitum atque peditum milibus in castris ad obsidionem relictis, ipse aliis cum omnibus herois et principibus suis, cum et cohortibus reliquis regniculis Siculis et Hispanis, in quibus fuerat ex equitibus peditibusque clipeatis ad undecim hominum milia,

Biagio Assereto,[4] the chancellor (of Genoa) and especially dar-   1.4
ing, had been placed in command of the entire fleet. They had
ordered him to sail directly to Gaeta as quickly as possible, and
when he had landed there, to entrust the whole fleet with all its
equipment and soldiers to Francesco Spinola,[5] a man of highest
nobility, whom they had previously sent ahead to fire up the hearts
of the citizens to remain loyal, then had designated him commander of the naval expedition.

With their forces drawn up and readied, after they boarded the   1.5
ships to great clamor and frequent applause of the citizens, they
weighed anchor, and on 23 July gave sail before a stiff west wind.
And leaving behind the port of Genoa, they put out into the deep,
sailing for Gaeta over the open sea.

At about the same time, in the territory of Gaeta, the most se-   2.1
rene king, having investigated these matters, summoned his foremost subjects. Numerous supporters of his majesty, princes, heroes and noblemen, countless knights and armor bearers, gathered
in his presence with unbelievable splendor, great pomp and cir-
cumstance. The sight of them brought joy to his eyes and he recognized that the presence of such great heroes uplifted his own
great courage and hope and strength. He spoke to them at length
and with admirable power to arouse their enthusiasm for the campaign. Finally, having decided on the basis of intelligence that he
should meet and engage the approaching Genoese fleet, he readied
the great part of his forces for a naval campaign.

So he divided his forces: to carry on the siege, he left behind in   2.2
camp 5,000 cavalry and infantry under the command of Cristoforo Gaetani,[6] Francesco Orsini,[7] and a man from Barcelona[8] who
was loyal to him. And on the third of August, he himself, with
all his all his other heroes and princes and the remaining cohorts
of his Sicilian and Spanish subjects, among whom there were
about eleven thousand cavalry and infantry armed with shields, in

supra quos habuisse fertur balistarios et funditores circiter quatuor
milia, ad III Nonarum Augustarum diem, magno imposito com-
meatu regali luxu splendidissimisve cum apparatibus confertas copiarum naves conscendunt.

2.3 Ilico laeto atque frequentissimo omnium plausu sua cum omni
classe, instructis paratisque omnibus, quibus ad praelium opus
fuerat, magna nautarum, ut mos, vociferatione sublata, Caietano
portu solventes plano in aequore solutis velis in altum ingentibus
animis properabant in hostem.

3.1 Et enim postquam per biduum aequor placidum percurrere,
quom a Caietanis moenibus ad miliaria quadraginta distarent secus Pontianam insulam, primum iam venereo albescente olympo
hostilium advenientem classem ex altissimis navium arcibus conspexere.

3.2 Rex itaque primo impetu decertare quom decrevisset, quatuor
primum in partes discreverat copias: primam igitur classem praetoria vectus navi Alfonsus Rex ipse regebat, deinde vero Iohanni
germano suo, nobilissimo Navariae Regi, secundam, et Tarantino
Principi tertiam commiserat, quartam vero triarii nominis ad
instar domnus Henricus Infans, regius et ipse frater, magnus et
ecclesiae apostoli Jacobi magister, ingenti splendore ornatuve ducti-
tarat.

3.3 His omnibus quidem quatuor supra decem onerariis navibus
tres et decem rostratae triremes, biremesque una de decem, Petro,
regio et ipso fratre atque Hispanae Castiliae magnanimo Infante,
praefecto, veloces ad insectandum ac circumveniendum hostem, ad
omnia expeditissimae, subsequebantur.

3.4 Atqui iussu regio primae Taraconensium navium in altum dela-
tae, protenso longius sinistro cornu ac velut hostem circumventu-
rae, pertendebant.

3.5 Reliquae enim puppes fere omnes ad dextrum cornu proris
omnibus in hostem conversae navigabant.

addition to whom he is said to have had about four thousand artillerymen and slingers, after a great quantity of supplies had been
loaded, boarded the ships that were filled with troops, with royal
magnificence and splendid equipment.

At that moment, when everything had been organized and 2.3
made ready that was needed for battle and the sailors had raised
the customary cheer, to the joyful and frequent applause of all,
[Alfonso], with his whole fleet, left the port of Gaeta under full
sail on a smooth sea and hurried out into the deep in high spirits
to encounter the enemy.

To go on, after a two-days' quick run over a calm sea, they were 3.1
alongside the island of Ponza, some forty miles distant from the
walls of Gaeta, when, as Venus' sky was growing bright, they first
caught sight from the highest of the ships' poops of the advancing
enemy fleet.

Therefore, since the king had decided to fight to the finish by 3.2
attacking first, he divided his forces into four units: the first fleet
King Alfonso himself commanded aboard the flagship; the second,
he entrusted to his brother John, the noble king of Navarre,[9] and
the third, to the prince of Taranto;[10] the fourth, as a kind of re-
serve unit, the Infante led, Lord Henry,[11] the royal brother, Grand
Master, Church of the Apostle James, with grand splendor and
display.

Following all these fourteen transport ships were thirteen 3.3
beaked triremes and nine biremes, under the command of Peter,[12]
himself a brother of the king and the greathearted Infante of
Spanish Castile. These were swift for pursuing and surrounding
the enemy, ready for every kind of action.

And so, at the king's order the foremost of the Aragonese ships, 3.4
brought into open water, continued on, with the left wing extended longer, as though they were going to surround the enemy.

Meanwhile almost all the remaining ships turned and sailed to 3.5
the right wing with all prows facing the enemy.

4.1   Haec enim dum ita geruntur, Genuenses, aequatis velis propin-
quantes, conspicati regiam classem, bipartita tantum acie bifariis
suis omnibus vehebantur navibus.

4.2   Nam trium omnium et decem onerarium navium unicum age-
bant agmen; in altera quidem parte, una cum sola bireme tres
tantum rostratae naves longae triremum inter ordines velocissimae
erant.

4.3   Omnem quidem Genuensium classem, ut supra diximus, curabat Agereus ille Blasius, quem audacissimum hominem Genuenses, viri providentissimi, pro Francisco Spinola, classis huiusce
designato imp[eratore] absente universae huic expeditioni praefecerant, Guidone Taurellio legionariis militibus et decurionibus
imperante: exiguae quidem numero classis huius copiae videbantur, sed iuventutis robore et egregia animi virtute tam et terrestri
quam maritimo bello idonei viri et quam expertissimi ac omni in
re validissimi praestiterant.

4.4   Itaque Genuensium primarios inter quam primi, Blasius ipse
praeses Agereus, Philippus Iustinianus atque De Mare Cyprianus,
viri quidem et longa maritimarum rerum naumachiarumve experientia doctissimi et summa cum Neapolitanis civibus benivolentia
coniuncti, ante alios omnes ardentissimis in hostem animis de-
vehuntur, nauticis primum suis gubernatoribus imperantes, ut
dato signo in exploratam e cymba regiam occurrentem navim
quam maximo possent impetu ruant.

4.5   Et Taurellius, una conversus, dignissimis verbis et opera arei-
philos mil[itum] animos ad pugnam accendit.

4.6   Igitur tribus praetoriis quibus vehebantur turritis navibus dum
in propinquo essent, horrisono et ingenti clamore sublato, plenis et
omnibus tumescentibus velis, infestissimo stridentibus rostris impetu primam Taraconensium classem invadunt.

While this was going on, the Genoese, approaching with lev-   4.1
eled sails, spotted the royal fleet, and sailed along with all their
ships divided into a double line only.

For all thirteen of the transport ships were forming one single   4.2
line; on the other side, with one bireme only, were only three
beaked war ships, the fastest among the classes of triremes.

As we said above, Biagio Assereto, an exceptionally daring man,   4.3
was in charge of the whole Genoese fleet, whom the Genoese,
men of considerable foresight, had appointed commander of this
entire operation, as replacement for the absent Francesco Spinola,
the admiral-elect of this fleet, with Guido Torelli commanding the
legionary soldiers and squad officers; the forces of this fleet seemed
small in number indeed, but the men were suited to both land and
naval warfare by the vigor of their youth and their outstanding
mental toughness, and were highly experienced and formidable in
every undertaking.

And so, the foremost among the leading men of the Genoese,   4.4
the commander Biagio Assereto, Filippo Giustiniani,[13] and Cipri-
ano De Mari,[14] men highly skilled by their long experience of
maritime matters and naval warfare, and united to the citizens of
Naples by the greatest goodwill, sailed before all the others against
the enemy with fiery courage, first ordering their helmsmen that,
on a given signal, they charge with the greatest force possible the
approaching king's ship, which had been identified from a small
boat.

And Torelli, turning together with them, fired the war-loving   4.5
spirits of his forces to battle with appropriate words and deeds.

Therefore, when they were near the turreted ships that carried   4.6
the three admirals, they raised a loud, frightening shout, withal
the sails were full and swelling, they attacked the first fleet of the
Aragonese in the most hostile manner, the beaks of the ships
shrieking.

4.7   Reclamatur a Taraconensibus horrendissime, nec minore impetu illis occurritur.

4.8   Committitur ingens et atrox praelium ac ancipiti Marte aliquamdiu pugnatur.

4.9   Eo quidem certamine quos clamores, quos strepitus tubarumve clangores, quos horrores, quae tela, quos gladios, quas denique navium immissiones!

4.10   Et Genuensi calliditate regias inter puppes ad coercendum inexpertos navalis rei milites fumiferas caliginosasve sparsarum calcium nubes ac flammarum attollere globos aspiceres.

4.11   Hinc utique machinarum aere impetu quassatas, illisas, confractas saloque semimersas naves, naufragos denique victores per undas tabularia interve remigia scutaque labantes atque cadavera inter rubescentes cruore fluctus miserandum in modum videres.

4.12   Tollitur ingens ad caelum clamor, fit eo denique loco magna nautarum atque mil(itum) caedes et ardentissimis utrorumque animis pertinacissima pugna ab orto die ad occiduum usque solem ingens et terribile bellum traxere.

5.1   Tandem rei peritia Genuenses superiores, ubi magna vi primam Taraconensium classem expugnarunt, Regia primum navi ipso cum inclyto Rege capta, perculsas metu reliquas onerarias omnes, praeter binas, Encantoneam scilicet et Enconilianam, quae primo congressionis impetu, ingenti formidine territae, Sicaniam versus fugam plenis velis arripuere, brevissimum inter tempus et parvis inter se disiunctas spaciis modico discrimine expugnatas excepere.

5.2   Petrus vero Infans, regius frater magnus, ubi superiores bello Genuenses conspexerat regiamque primam classem parvo medio expugnandam cognoverat, dum ab utroque etiam latere magna vi

The Aragonese shouted most fearfully in response and they met 4.7
the attack with no less an onset.

A great and fearful battle was fought with its outcome in doubt 4.8
for some time.

What outcries in that struggle, what a noise and blaring of 4.9
trumpets, what horrors, what weapons, what swords, what crashing together of ships!

And you would see flame-bearing and mist-creating clouds of 4.10
sprayed lime and balls of fire rise up among the king's ships, a cun-
ning Genoese device to keep under control soldiers inexperienced
in naval warfare.

As a result, you would see ships shaken, crushed, broken, and 4.11
half-sunk in the sea by the violence of the bronze engines of war,
and finally you would see shipwrecked [sailors] carried piteously
through the waves, sinking amid benches, oars and shields, and
corpses among the billows that were turning red with blood.

A loud cry was raised to the sky; there was, in short, a great 4.12
slaughter of sailors and soldiers in that place, a stubborn fight between fiery souls on both sides; they carried on a huge and fright-
ful war from the dawning of day to the setting of the sun.

Finally, when the Genoese, because of their superior expertise, 5.1
had overcome the first fleet of the Aragonese with great force, first
capturing the flagship along with the renowned king himself, they
caught all the remaining transport ships in a very short time, except for two, the *Encantonea* and the *Enconiliana*, which, terrified
with fear at the first onset of the encounter, fled under full sail
toward Sicily. They achieved this because [the ships] were separated from each other by small distances, [and] captured with little
danger.

When the Infante Peter, the king's great brother, saw the Geno- 5.2
ese had the upper hand in the battle and realized that in a short
interval of time the royal fleet was doomed to be defeated, while
the remaining ships on both sides were being attacked with great

reliquae oppugnabantur naves, saluti suae fuga consuluit ac, celeritate fretus, tres omnes et decem rostratas triremes atque velocissimas novem biremes ducens, in altum defertur.

5.3   At enim vero antea ditissimus ille Salerni princeps Antonius, qui felix olim max[imi] Martini pont[ificis] nepos fuerat, eo praelio et prima hostium incursione ingenti metu perculsus, exigua indutus pharea, e navi qua vectus erat mediis hostibus delapsus, in scapham prosiliens ac inde protinus in fugientem quandam et velocissimam biremem conscendens, fugam et ipse quam primum arripuit simulque cum triremibus ab Infante ductis primum Hyscheam ad insulam una cum magno Regni cammerario in tutum se receperat.

5.4   Exinde refectis navibus Infans, Neapolitanis primum, quae fratris in dicione manebant, arcibus revisis, nobilissimam Sicanum insulam, ut in re dubia Siculos conservaret in fide, acceleratissimo cursu petierat.

5.5   His itaque rebus auditis, qui apud Caietanum agrum castrametati civitatem obsidebant, quos inter fuere primarii Christoforus Caietaneus, Franciscus Ursinus atque Colunneus Lodovicus, viri quidem bello perstrenui, extemplo plenis copiarum castris relictis, nullo praecone obsidione soluta suos hinc inde quisque lares petentes fugam arripuere.

6.1   Atqui Genuenses interea compoti voti sui eaque insigni victoria potiti, duabus supra decem munitis atque refertis navibus captis, quibuscum, innumeros inter captivos, duobus ipsis cum potentissimis gemellis Regibus, cum et altero utique fratre regio, magnoque et verendissimo sancti Jacobi ecclesiae magistro, hos primarios ex regnicolis habuere: binos imprimis Iohannes Antonios, principem scilicet Tarentinum atque Suessanum ducem ingenuas Ursinae Martianaeque domus proles, post hos Josiam Aquaevivianum atque Menecucium Aquilaneum, haud inexpertos bello iuvenes et praeclaros; quos praeter ex Hispanis, Barceloneis, Siculis atque

force, he looked to his own safety in flight and, relying on speed, led all thirteen triremes and the swiftest nine biremes, and put out into the open sea.

What is more, prior to this, Antonio,[15] the famous, very wealthy 5.3 prince of Salerno, the fortunate nephew of the late Pope Martin [V], struck with a great fear at the first assault of the enemy in that battle, put on a small cloak, slipped from the ship on which he was sailing, in the midst of the enemy, leaped into a small boat, climbed immediately from there onto a fleeing, very fast bireme and, along with the triremes led by the Infante and the great chamberlain of the kingdom,[16] withdrew first to the safety of the island of Ischia.

After that, once his ships had been repaired, the Infante first 5.4 visited the fortresses of Naples which remained under his brother's control, then made for the noble island of Sicily with the utmost speed to preserve the Sicilians' loyalty in an uncertain situation.

When this news reached those who were encamped in the ter- 5.5 ritory of Gaeta besieging the city, the foremost of whom were Cristoforo Gaetani, Francesco Orsini, and Ludovico Colonna,[17] men surely very keen on war, immediately they left a camp full of soldiers, dissolved the siege without any announcement, and took flight, each one heading for home, in this direction or that.

Meanwhile, the Genoese, having achieved their purpose and 6.1 obtained that signal victory, having captured twelve ships that were equipped and full, with which, among the innumerable prisoners, along with the two most powerful twin kings, with also the other brother of the king and the great and revered Master of the Church of St. James, they held the leading men of the realm: first, the two Giovanni Antonii, i.e., the prince of Taranto and the duke of Sessa,[18] the noble scions of the Orsini and Marzano houses; after them, Giosia Acquaviva[19] and Menicuccio Aquilano,[20] youths not inexperienced in war and illustrious; besides them, of the Spaniards, Barcelonans, Sicilians, and

nuper exostratis Neapolitanis, nobiles supra centum equestris ordinis viros et belligeros eo praelio victos tenuere.

6.2   Confectis itaque rebus, tribus cum regiis splendidissimis supel-
lectilibus magna auri et omnigenum praedarum copia ditati, velis
denique in altum sublatis, postquam tranquillo cursu placidi Nep-
tunni liquidum sulcavere campum tandem ad Caietanum portum
tota cum felicissima classe tanta exultantes victoria, laeti in tutum
se receperunt.

6.3   Ubi a Francisco inprimis designato imp[eratore] cum et Caietanis Neapolitanisque obviantibus civibus magna undique fremente
laetitia complexi, aliquos per dies ad reparandam classem atque
curanda corpora morabantur.

7.1   Erat itaque captas inter regias puppes Anconitana quaedam
navis, quae, cum onerata frumento Benuto Scacchio ductore, ut,
ad quas eo indigentes urbes applicuisset mercemonii gratia, venun-
daret, ad orientales Siciliae oras transmeasset, a navi quadam
Encantonea duabusque Taraconensium triremibus, ob singularem
cum Rege amicitiam nullo obsistente capta, ab eo ipso Rege huius
utique fiduciae gratia suae adiuncta classi, tanta in expeditione
navigarat; quam, simul aliis cum navibus eodem expugnationis die
captam, optumi Genuenses viri, inveteratae cum Anconitanis civibus benivolentiae memores, regio intermiscente rogatu, reposcenti
patrono suo quam placide liberam reddiderunt.

8.1   Per idem tempus nunciatum est septem onerarias naves Messanam applicuisse, quas, munitas copiis, Bernardo Encaprario duce,
Maria, splendidissima uxor, ab urbe Barcelona Regi optimo con-
iugi in supplementum suae classis magna cum affectione trans-
miserat; quae, quom adverso fato adversisque flatibus aegra navigatione tardantes, post rem confectam advenissent, Siceliam ad se
tutandum Bernardus dux ipse petierat.

recently ennobled Neapolitans, they held over a hundred warlike men of the equestrian order, defeated in that battle.

And so, with these matters concluded they finally raised sail for 6.2 the open sea, enriched by a great abundance of gold and all kinds of booty, including three superb pieces of the king's furniture. At last, after plowing the watery field of tranquil Neptune in a peaceful voyage they arrived joyful in safety at the port of Gaeta, exulting with the entire happy fleet because of such a great victory,

When they had been embraced, especially by Francesco [Spi- 6.3 nola], the commander designate and by the citizens of Gaeta and Naples, who came to meet them with a great roar of joy on all sides, they lingered there for several days to get the fleet repaired and to recover their strength.

Among the captured royal ships was an Anconitan vessel. Skip- 7.1 pered by Benuto Scacchio, she had crossed to the eastern shores of Sicily loaded with grain, intending to sell her cargo commercially to any of her port cities that might need it. Captured by the *Encantonea* and two Aragonese triremes without resistance because of a particular friendship with the king, she was joined by that king to his own fleet, surely because of that trust, and sailed in this great expedition. When she was captured along with the other ships on the same day of defeat, the noblest Genoese, mindful of their long-standing goodwill toward the citizens of Ancona, at the request of the king, acting as intermediary, returned her, peacefully free, to her owner, who was demanding her return.

At the same time news came that seven cargo ships had put in 8.1 at Messina, supplied with troops under the command of Bernardo Emcaprareo. Maria,[21] the illustrious queen, had sent them over with great affection from the city of Barcelona to her excellent husband, the king, to supplement his fleet. When, they, slowed down by an adverse fate, adverse winds, and unsound navigation, had arrived after the battle had been settled, Bernardo, their leader himself, made for Sicily for his own protection.

9.1   Ast enim interea Genuenses, curatis refectisque rebus, magna animi cupiditate Genuam, patriam civitatem, revisere tanta cum insigni victoria properantes, extemplo deductis e Caieta navibus in salum, postquam sublatis velis atque remigiis agitatis aequor omne medium acceleratissimo cursu transiecerant, tandem ad V K[alendas] Septembr[is] Genuensem ad portum ovantes applicuere.

9.2   Ubi, postquam Lamponeanus ipse nobilissimus praeses Oldradus omnesque alii pro Anguigero Philippo duce magistratus ac Genuenses plerique praestantissimi cives, summa iocunditate conspicuo atque amplisssimo ordine obviam, Blasium praefectum aliosque, victores simul et victos, reges atque heroes complexere, una omnes e navibus desilientes, in urbem ad sacras se primum aedes religose contulerant.

9.3   Ubi nam pientissimo cultu peractis immortali deo Genuensiumque numinibus votis, sacratissimis de more hostiis oblatis, ultimum Nonarum Augustarum diem, qua nobiliorem longe quam antea nusquam per aevum maritimarum rerum gloriam consecuti fuere, faustos inter felicissimum dedicarunt.

10.1   Quam laeto deinceps animo amplissimove ore, optume Francisce, inclita Philippi magnanimi ducis facta sint personanda?

10.2   Qui, quom hac in re, ut vel certissimam magis et inextinguibilem tanti facinoris gloriam posteros inter conspiceret, solita sui animi magnitudine haberi se decrevisset, postquam ad se quam primum captivos omnes primarios mittere literis Oldrado ac Genuensibus civibus imperarat, ad hos praedigne excipiendos nusquam regio tali luxu tantove splendidissimo rerum apparatu atque ineffabili iuvenum pompa suam Mediolanum, nobilissimam Insubrium urbem, creditur perornasse.

Meanwhile, the Genoese, [their strength] recovered and [their 9.1
ships] repaired, their hearts set greatly on hurrying back to their
home city Genoa after such an outstanding victory, immediately
brought their ships from Gaeta to the salt sea, raised sails and set
the oars in motion, crossed the intervening sea in an extremely fast
voyage, and finally, on the twenty-eighth of August, put in rejoic-
ing at the port of Genoa.

There, Oldrado Lampugnani,[22] the most noble governor, and 9.2
all those who held public office in the name of Duke Filippo the
Serpent Bearer,[23] and very many of the most distinguished Genoese citizens, came to meet them with great joy and in a striking
and most splendid procession. They embraced Admiral Biagio and
the others, both conquerors and conquered, kings and heroes, as
all together they disembarked from the ships. After that, the first
thing they did was to go devoutly to a church in the city.

There, in a devout ritual, having fulfilled their vows to Immor- 9.3
tal God and to the patron saints of Genoa, they offered the Holy
Sacrifice [of the Mass] as is customary, and dedicated the fifth of
August, the day on which they won glory in naval warfare far
more noble than ever before, as the most happy among auspicious
days.

Excellent Francesco, with how joyful a spirit and fullness of 10.1
expression should the famous achievements of greathearted Duke
Philip be sounded?

In this matter, in order to contemplate a sure and indestructible 10.2
glory for such a great deed as this among his descendants, he had
decided to behave with his customary magnanimity: he ordered
Oldrado and the Genoese citizens in writing to send all the highest ranking prisoners to him as soon as possible. Then, it is believed, he had his Milan, the most distinguished city of the Insub-
rians, adorned for receiving these men in such royal luxury and
with such brilliant surroundings and inexpressible display of young
people as nowhere else.

10.3   Sic igitur, vir generose, perquam consentaneum habeto captivos hos serenissimos reges, suis cum praeclarissimis omnibus principibus herois, post insignes habitos apud Medioalnum honores, a magnanimo ipso duce liberos atque magnificentissime donatos, ad sua quaeque regna omni cum decore conversuros.

10.4   Tu denique, praeclarissime eques, qui mecumque diu regiae Alfonsi inclytae maiestati dicatissimus fuisti, ex adversis confractisve tantae expeditionis suae rebus de immensa victoris magnitudine animi et amplissima magnis in rebus liberalitate, ut quem ad modum mihi persuaserim, spem haud exiguam haurire velis.

Exactum Anconi Idibus Septembribus.

As a consequence, noble sir, consider it entirely appropriate that 10.3
these most serene captive kings along with all their most illustrious princes and heroes, after the extraordinary honors shown
them in Milan, will be freed by the greathearted duke and, provided with most magnificent gifts, will return, each to his own
kingdom in all honor.

Finally, you, most illustrious knight, who, with me, have long 10.4
been devoted to the renowned majesty of King Alfonso, might
wish to draw no little hope from the adverse and disastrous outcome of such an important expedition, and the enormous great-
heartedness of the victor and his supreme generosity in delicate
circumstances, which is exactly my conviction.

Finished in Ancona, September 13, [1435].

APPENDICES

APPENDIX I

Chronology of Events in Scalamonti's Life of Cyriac

The reader may find useful the following chronology of events recorded in the *Life*, constructed on the basis of internal evidence in the narrative itself and verified, wherever possible, by reference to fixed dates known from other sources. The text of the *Life* is cited by paragraph numbers, given here within parentheses. External evidence is presented in the notes to the corresponding paragraphs of the translation.

1391	Cyriac is born on July 31 (§5).
1401	April 13: visits Venice with his grandfather (§§5–6) and Padua (§7).
1401–3	In Ancona, receives some schooling (§8).
1403–4	Early in 1403, his grandfather takes him to the Kingdom of Naples. Passing through Apulia, Samnium, Lucania, and Campania and stopping at Teano and Sessa Arunca, they reach Naples, then travel on to Salerno, Amalfi, Paestum, Tropea, Laconia, and Maida (§§8–11). For a year he studies the rudiments of grammar at Maida (§§11–12), after which they return to Naples (§12). They return to Ancona by way of Sessa (§13).
1404	Begins an apprenticeship in Ancona (§14).
1406	Put in charge of Pietro di Jacopo's business (§14).
1411	Elected to the board of six *anziani*, the governing body in Ancona, and becomes a senator (§15).

1412   Finishes his apprenticeship (§15). Before April, he takes a voyage to Egypt and sees antiquities in Alexandria (§17). On the return voyage, he visits Rhodes and Chios (where he is promoted to senior clerk); he visits Miletus—passing Samos and Icaria along the way—(§18) and visits the Cypriot cities of Kirini, Paphos, Famagusta, and Nicosia as well as nearby Beirut, then Reggio in Calabria (§19), Messina, Gaeta, and Castellamare (§20).

1413   Returns with a new cargo to Alexandria after being blown off course by a storm that drove them past Ustica to take refuge in the Sicilian port of Trapani on February 26 (§21). He is back in Ancona before September (§22), rich enough to augment his sister's dowry. On October 7 he takes part in repelling an assault on Ancona by Galeazzo Malatesta, afterward writing his first literary composition, an account in Italian of the event (§23).

1413–15   Spends nearly two years in Ancona (§31), partly in private life, partly as an *anziano*. He reads Dante, Petrarch, and Boccaccio and engages in poetic correspondence with humanist friends (§§23–30).

1415   Embarks on a journey to Sicily, stopping at Scilla in Calabria. He sees the antiquities of Taormina, then travels via Messina to Palermo, inspecting the antiquities of Palermo and the surrounding country, including Monreale (§§31–34).

1417   On his return voyage to Venice, he visits Zara in Croatia (§35), where he hears of the election of Martin V (after November 11, 1417) (§35). Disposing of his merchandise in Venice, he is back in Ancona by the end of the year (§§36–37).

1418   Embarks early in September on a merchant ship headed for Constantinople, stopping along the way at Suasna in Epirus (September 11), Delos, and Sestos near Gallipoli, arriving at Constantinople on October 7 (§37). The antiquities of the city are described (§§38–42). He visits the Genoese colony of Galata/Pera (§43).

1419   Returns to Ancona, where he stays for some time, after which he visits Pola, inspecting its antiquities (§44). After a few days in Ancona, he returns to Chios, Gallipoli, Constantinople, stopping at Albuneo in Dalmatia on the way (§45). Back in Ancona, he engages in various business, including a commission to balance the books of a local merchant, which he does successfully (§46).

1420   Cardinal Gabriele Condulmer is appointed legate of the Marches on February 7, 1420 (§47). During June and July, Cyriac serves as *podestà* in Varano, while the plague is raging in Ancona (§46, note).

1421–23   Financial officer in the project to repair the harbor of Ancona (§47). During this time he begins to study Latin (§53), and his interest in antiquities is sparked by close inspection of the Arch of Trajan at the harbor of Ancona (§54). On August 6, 1423, he resigns his financial post when Condulmer leaves for assignment in Bologna (§48). He exchanges poems with Serafino of Urbino (§§49–52).

1424   December 3: goes to Rome, where he stays for forty days as a guest of Cardinal Condulmer, inspecting and recording the antiquities (§55); he realizes their importance as historical evidence (§56) and laments their ruinous state (§§56–57). He composes a poem in praise of Pope Martin's nephew, Antonio (§58). He remains in Rome through Christmas and New Year's Day (§59). It was during this period in Rome that he may have met Leonardo Bruni (§78 and note).

1425   January 1: leaves Rome for Ancona, stopping at Sutri, Viterbo, and Orvieto (§60).

1426 or 1427   Elected *anziano* of Ancona (§61).

1427   May 13: at Ancona (?), where he finishes copying Ovid's *Fasti* (§76, note). 21 December: letter from Filelfo in Venice to Cyriac in Ancona (?) (§68, note).

1428   Sets out from Ancona as commercial representative of Zaccaria Contarini in Cyprus (§61); after stops at Monopoli, Bari, and ancient Anterium in Apulia, he arrives in Constantinople, where he picks up the rudiments of Greek (§62). Sailing on to Chios, he meets Andreolo Giustiniani-Bancha for the first time and buys a Greek New Testament (§63). He then travels by way of Rhodes to Beirut and Damascus (§§64–66); then from Beirut to Famagusta in Cyprus, where he serves as vicar for the *podestà*, making decisions based on Roman law (§67).

1428–29   Reaches Nicosia later in 1428 (§68, note), where he is received by the majestic King Janus Lusignan, who takes him on a hunt. He completes Zaccaria's business within a year and purchases manuscripts of the *Iliad*, *Odyssey*, Euripides, and Theodosius (§§68–71).

1429   Leaves Nicosia after composing an inscription honoring King Janus (§72) and sails from Famagusta to Rhodes, where he inspects the antiquities, purchasing three recently excavated fragments of sculpture (§73). Making for Thrace by way of Chios, he translates a life of Euripides while awaiting favorable winds at Kardamyla (§74). He then travels by way of Tenedos to Gallipoli, where he unloads Zaccaria's goods and brings them by camel to Adrianople, the Turks' European capital (§75).

1429–30   Winters in Adrianople, selling his merchandise and listening to Greek lectures on Homer and Hesiod (§75). After March 29, 1430 (the date of the fall of Salonica), he buys Greek manuscripts (Ptolemy's *Geography*) and an Epirote slave girl from the Turkish plunder of that city and plans a journey to Persia (§75). At Gallipoli he ships goods on to Ancona, then travels overland to Philippi to see its antiquities (§76); he then travels on to Salonica, where he views its pagan and Christian monuments and buys more manuscripts (§77).

1431   Returning to Gallipoli some time after March 3, he hears news of Gabriel Condulmer's election on that date to the papacy as Eugenius IV (§78). Canceling plans for travel to Persia, he sends off letters to influential friends in Italy and Dalmatia expressing his pleasure and sets out to collect intelligence to support his projects for union with

the Greek church and a crusade against the Turks
(§§78–79), with the aid of Memnon, a seasoned
military advisor. Their first stop is Bursa, the Ottoman capital in Asia, where he pleads with the
governor, Canuza Bey, to put a stop to the gradual
spoliation of the temple at Cyzicus (80–81). After
revisiting Cyzicus (§§82–83), he makes for Constantinople by land, stopping to inspect the antiquities of Nicaea (§84), before crossing the Bosporus at Scutari. (§85). In Constantinople, learning
that the next ship for Ancona would not be leaving for a month (§85), he uses the intervening
time to continue reconnoitering locations in
Turkish-held Anatolia that might be of strategic
as well as antiquarian interest, sailing first to Lesbos, where he inspects the cities of Mytilene,
Pyrra, and Methymna (§86), then crossing to the
mainland to see Pergamum (§87), then the ruins
of ancient Cyme and Smyrna (§88), before pro-
ceeding on to Vecchia and Nuova Foglia (ancient
Phocaea) on the mainland, and thence over to
Chios to await his ship (§§89–90) for Ancona
(§91). Between October 31 and November 6 (§91,
note), he leaves Chios for Ancona. After a few
days at home, he hastens to Rome to see the new
pope, whom he urges to call a council of union
with the Greek Church and to proclaim a crusade
against the Turks (§92).

1432[1]   During this visit to Rome, he inspects the antiquities of Tivoli and Ostia (§§93–96). He returns
to Rome to see the pope (§204); then, when he
hears of rebel Anconitans practicing piracy, he hur-
ries to Gaeta to advise a friend, the captain of an
Anconitan ship sent to join the fleet, charged with
the mission to bring them to justice (§§204–5);
when this ship leaves Gaeta for Naples, he travels
by land, keeping an eye out for antiquities, from
Gaeta by way of Terracina, Minturno, Sessa, Capua, and Aversa (§§206–9). He returns to Naples,
where he visits the Vergilian landmarks in Pozzuoli, Lake Avernus, Cumae, Baiae, and Cape
Miseno (§§209–10); after an excursion through
Naples to Benevento (§§211–214), he returns to the
port city, where he boards his friend's ship, which
first conveys to Messina emissaries sent by the
pope to King Alfonso (§§215–16), then sails to the
Gulf of Taranto to join the Anconitan fleet; there,
unable to attack the pirate ship because it was
protected by Queen Maria d'Enghien, the fleet returns to Ancona with him aboard (§§216–17).

1432–33   Some time between July 8, 1432 (§97, note), and
April 1433, he goes to Siena with two papal ambassadors to meet emperor-elect Sigismund,
whom he presents with a gold coin of Trajan as a
model of a good emperor, and is received into his
court (§97).

1433   Before April 25 (§97) he returns to Rome, presumably in the entourage of the emperor-elect.
After Sigismund's coronation in Rome (May 31),
he again lobbies the emperor to press the pope for
a council of union and a crusade against the Turks
(§98). While touring the city's ruins with Sigismund, he deplores the practice of burning up into
lime the ancient sculptures, architectural pieces,
and inscriptions (§99). Leaving Rome for points
north, he first visits Pisa (§100), then Florence,
before September (§101, note). Brunelleschi con-
ducts him around his dome, then under construction; he sees the baptistery and the public buildings, not omitting the ancient walls and theater of
Fiesole (§104) and meets the political and intellectual leaders of Florence as well as its leading art-
ists (§101–3). A northern journey brings him to
Bologna and Modena (§§105–10), Parma (§111),
Piacenza and Pavia (§112, note).

1433–34   Arriving in Milan, he inspects its monuments and
copies inscriptions in the city and its surrounding
area, including the castle and monastery of Pavia
(§§113–51), then travels on to Brescia (§§152–64)
and Verona (§§165–89). After returning to Milan,
where he spends several days with the duke
(§190), he goes on to Mantua (§§191–97) and Genoa (§§198–204).

NOTES

1. For the chronological anomalies occurring in this section of the *Vita*
see the notes to §§215–17 of the translation.

APPENDIX II

Cyriac's Drawings of Hagia Sophia in Constantinople

It is impossible to determine the actual date on which Cyriac made the original drawings of the former Patriarchal Basilica of Hagia Sophia. He visited Constantinople often in his travels — in 1418–19, 1428, 1431, and several times in the year 1444.[1] Although the only lengthy verbal description of Constantinople's antiquities attributable to Cyriac occurs in the *Life* in connection with his earliest visit in 1418, it is unlikely that Cyriac knew enough Latin at that time to be able to write either the detailed description reported in the *Life* (§§38–43) or the headings to the drawings of Hagia Sophia recorded here. Nevertheless, we include the headings here on the chance that they are contemporaneous with the description in Cyriac's lost diary on which §§38–43 are based, whenever that may have been written.

The texts are preserved in a fifteenth century manuscript in Parma (Bibliotheca Palatina, MS. Parm. 1191), where the headings for the eight drawings occur on a separate gathering, ff. 61r–66v. Space is left on each page for the drawings, which were never inserted. A Vatican manuscript (Barb. lat. 4424), however, includes two drawings by Giuliano da Sangallo (1443–1516), with the same headings as two of Cyriac's. These correspond to numbers 1 and 5 here, but they do not reproduce Cyriac's drawings, for Sangallo, a professional architect, revised the sketches to represent how he thought the building should appear.[2]

CYRIAC'S HEADINGS IN MS. PARM. 1191[3]

FOL. 61V

Introductory paragraph

Almae Sophiae sapientiaeve sacrum in Bizantio a Iustiniano Caesare Templum maximum et CIIII porfireis serpentinis ac marmoreis columnis diversorumque nobilium et conspicuum lapidum insigne, Anthemio Tralleo et Isidoro Milesio nobilibus architectorum principibus.

The great temple dedicated in Byzantium to fostering Sophia, i.e., wisdom, by Caesar Justinian. Notable for 104 porphyry, serpentine, and marble columns of various noble and remarkable stones. By Anthemius of Tralles and Isidore of Miletus, noble princes among architects.

Heading for drawing no. 1

Ab externa templi et occidua parte figura a qua primum vestibulum atque ingressum habuisse videtur: cuius amplitudo per lat[itudinem] cubito[rum] C et L, altitudo vero cubi[torum] CXX metita est.

A figure from the exterior and western part of the temple, from which it is seen to have first had a vestibule and entrance: the dimension is 150 cubits wide and 120 cubits high.

The rest of the page was left blank, presumably in order to accommodate the drawing of the church's exterior from the west, showing also the front of the atrium. This is one of the two drawings reproduced by Giuliano da Sangallo.

Heading for drawing no. 2

Pronaon Pentapilon Bizantiani maximi Sophiae sapientiaeve delubri nobile. Longitudo cubi[torum] XC, la[titudo] X, alt[itudo] p[edum] XX.

The noble five-doored vestibule of the greatest Byzantine temple of Sophia, or wisdom. Length 90 cubits, breadth 10, height 20 feet.

The rest of the page is blank, to leave room for a drawing, presumably of the first narthex, or vestibule.

Heading for drawing no. 3

Propylea templi IX portarum diversorumque conspicuum lapidum et aurea testudine insigne. Lon[gitudo] cu[bitorum] XC, lat[itudo] XV, altitudo cub[itorum] XXV.

The entrance of the temple, of nine doorways and diverse, noteworthy stones and remarkable for its golden vault. Length 90 cubits, breadth 15, height 25 cubits.

The rest of the page is left blank for a drawing, presumably of the second narthex, whose measurements are about the same as those of the first.

Drawing no. 4

Opus inimitabile tempus minatur destruere. Prohibetur autem nostram per curam. Sed, o rex excelse, aperi nobis domum quam tempus non tangit.

Time threatens to destroy the inimitable work. This we pre-
vent through our efforts. But, most-high king, open to us a
mansion which time does not touch.

Not a caption, but "Cyriac's Latin version of an inscription once in
the north tympanum of Hagia Sophia."[4] The rest of the page is
left blank for a drawing, probably not of the north wall, as the inscription might lead us to expect, but "a general, perspective view
of the interior looking toward the apse."[5]

FOL. 63V

Heading for drawing no. 5

*Ad alta templi ab interiori parte deambulatoria quae catacumina
vocitant in medio primariae partis pavimento.*

Toward the high ambulatories, called catacumina, from the
interior of the temple in the middle of the pavement of the
most important part.

The rest of this page is left blank for a drawing of the interior of
the west facade, i.e., the whole front third of the church viewed
from under the dome looking west, including the two western
piers that support the dome, which in the drawing — also copied
by Sangallo — are made to appear as if they are on the same plane
with the two piers on either side of the entrance. The drawing also
shows the "high ambulatories, called galleries" ($\kappa\alpha\tau\eta\chi o\acute{u}\mu\epsilon\nu\alpha$)
mentioned in this heading and, in the galleries, the "porphyry and
serpentine marble columns" of the introductory paragraph (and
the *Vita*, §40), which either Cyriac or Sangallo misinterpreted as
"twisted porphyry and marble columns."[6]

Heading for drawing no. 6

Pavimentum media testudine templi DC marmoreis expolitis tabulis insigne et suacte natura.

The pavement [beneath] the temple's central dome: noteworthy for its 600 dressed marble slabs and its singular character.

The rest of the page is left blank for a drawing, perhaps of a detail of the pavement under the dome, perhaps as seen from the gallery, though more likely it accompanied "the ground plan reproduced on fol. 44r of the Barberini Codex."[7]

Heading for drawing no. 7

A summo testudinis culmine ad pavimentum cubitorum C, lat[itudo] p[edum] LX, diametrum p[edum] IIII.

From the very top of the dome to the pavement 100 cubits, breadth 60 feet, diameter 4 feet.

The whole page is left blank, probably for a drawing showing the elevation from the top of the dome to the floor, i.e., a longitudinal section through the building, including the nave arcade and the dome, with the following subscript at the bottom:

Headings for two inscriptions, side by side

Ad magnam de marmore   *Latinis litteris inscriptio:*
basim ad marmoream columnam.   *in Neronem Caesarem epigramma*

On a large marble base by a   A Latin inscription: epigram
marble column.   against the emperor Nero.

The rest of page is left blank, presumably for two Greek inscriptions.

Heading for drawing no. 8

Latitudo cubitorum C et similiter ad summum testudinis culmen altitudo cubi[torum] C. Ab interiore parte.

Width, 100 cubits. Similarly, the height to the top of the dome is 100 cubits. Interior view.

This looks like the heading for an eighth drawing of Hagia Sophia showing, perhaps, a view up into the dome from floor level, or possibly, the half-dome over the apse. This latter interpretation would supply the one element missing from the description: the eastern interior wall with its apse and altar table. Otherwise, we may have to say that he considered the east interior wall too much like the western one, which he did represent, to repeat.

NOTES

1. See Appendix I in this volume, and *Later Travels*, 53–59, 85–94.

2. Brown and Kleiner, "Giuliano da Sangallo's Drawings." For further reference, see Smith, "Cyriacus of Ancona's Seven Drawings" (whose translations, slightly modified, are reproduced here), and Scalamonti, *Vita viri clarissimi*, 208–12. One of these drawings is reproduced in *Later Travels*, xxviii, pl. III.

3. Ff. 61r and 65r are blank.

4. Smith, "Cyriacus of Ancona's Seven Drawings," 22.

5. Ibid.

6. Ibid., 23.

7. Ibid.

APPENDIX III

Letters of Francesco Filelfo to and about Cyriac, 1427–34

The texts below, illustrating the early career of Cyriac, come chiefly from Francesco Filelfo's epistolary in forty-eight books, collected and arranged by Filelfo himself with the help of various amanuenses, in Milan, Biblioteca Trivulziana MS. 873. The first thirty-seven books were printed in the Venetian edition of 1502 used by Bodnar in Scalamonti (pp. 191–93; his Appendix 3), checked against editions of dubious value excavated from various secondary sources. The first four texts below, however, do not reproduce the Bodnar texts, but have been kindly supplied to serve as provisional texts by Dr. Jeroen De Keyser, who is preparing the critical edition of all Filelfo's letters in the forty-eight-book collection. They are based directly on the Trivulziana MS., collated with the 1502 edition. We reproduce his text without apparatus and refer the reader to the eventual critical edition for more philological detail.

The fifth letter in the appendix follows the text published by De Keyser in his article *"Nec tibi turpe tuum ducas audisse poetam"* (p. 57), rather than Bodnar's text in Scalamonti (p. 194).

The English translation of the Latin letters is by James Hankins, of the Greek letter by Clive Foss.

: I :

1 Franciscus Philelfus Kyriaco Anconitano sal.

Singularem tuum erga me amorem si non vaehementer amem, ingratus sim. Amo te, inquam, mi Kyriace, cum ob tuam in me benivolentiam, tum ob eam inquisitionem atque diligentiam qua uteris maxima in earum rerum inventione quae vel nimia vetustate vel patrum nostrorum negligentia apud nos perierant. Incumbe igitur, ut facis, in tam liberale tamque laudabile munus renovandae vetustatis, vel ab interitu potius vendicandae. Non enim parum et voluptatis et commodi prae se ferunt istiusmodi eulogia atque epigrammata quae tanto cum studio et labore undique ex universo prope orbe in Italiam advehis. Et horum quidem gratia non solum vivos tibi concilias, sed mortuos quoque reddis obstrictos beneficio sempiterno. Et hac de re satis ac super.

2 Petis a me ut tibi declarem quae Publii Virgilii Maronis senten- tia fuerit in scribenda *Aeneide*. Nam communem illam opinionem quam ludi magistri afferunt, voluisse Virgilium et imitari Homerum et laudare Augustum, nequaquam tibi admodum pro- bari. Non mediocrem profecto rem petis neque brevis orationis opus, a me praesertim, qui hoc tempore otiosus non sum et angor animi non iniuria, tum ob hanc pestilentiae acerbitatem, qua me Venetiis obsessum intueor, tum quia hic inutiliter tempus tero, ab iis delusus a quibus minime conveniebat. Sed ne me difficilem voces aut in amore tibi minus respondentem, dicam brevi quod sentio.

3 Quod Virgilius, uno *Aeneidos* carmine melisigenis Homeri *Iliada Ulysseam*que imitatus, Aeneam laudans Augustum quoque lauda- rit, nequaquam inficior, sed divinum eius ingenium altius

From Venice
December 21, 1427

Francesco Filelfo to Cyriac of Ancona, greetings.   1

I would be ungrateful if I were not strongly affected by the unique affection you bear toward me. Let me say that I love you, Cyriac, both for your kindness toward me and for the great and practical curiosity you have to make discoveries about objects that have perished among us, either through exceeding age or through the neglect of our fathers. Apply yourself, then, as you have been doing, in this liberal and laudable task of renewing, or rather resurrecting antiquity. Projects of this sort provide no little both of pleasure and of profit, as do the inscriptions which you bring back to Italy from around the globe with so much zeal and effort. For their sake you not only reconcile the living to yourself, but you obligate the dead as well with an eternal benefit. Enough, and more than enough, on this subject.

You ask me to explain to you Vergil's purpose in writing the   2
Aeneid. You don't accept the common view that the schoolteachers put about, that Vergil wanted to imitate Homer and praise Augustus. You ask no small thing, nor one that can be briefly answered, especially by me, who have no leisure at present and am distressed, and rightly so, both on account of this bitter pestilence which I watch besieging me in Venice, and since I am uselessly wasting time here, having been disappointed by people who did not keep their agreements. But I don't want you to call me difficult or ungrateful for your affection, so I shall briefly give my view of the matter.

That Vergil in a single poem, the *Aeneid,* imitated the *Iliad* and   3
Odyssey of honey-lipped Homer, praising Aeneas and Augustus as well, I by no means deny. But I am well aware that his divine

suspexisse, nescius certe non sum, quippe qui humanam condicionem contemplative activeque describens, eo cogitatus omnis consiliaque direxerit ut qua via summum bonum in hac vita parari posset, in unius Aeneae sapientia virtuteque ostenderet. Id autem non obscure prima ipsa gravissimi huius sui et elegantissimi operis propositione significat. Ait enim se canere *arma* quo ad virtutes bellicas et activas — nam bellandi pugnandique instrumenta sunt arma. Et *virum* quo ad virtutes urbanas intellectivasque, in quibus sapientia tenet et prudentia principatum; nam sapientia ea mihi virtus sola videri solet qua caeteris animantibus egregie antecellimus. Quod enim animal in terris eam consyderat veritatem quae in caelo est? Hanc sola esr sapientia, quae et inquirit et novit. Prudentia enim sapientiam ita ut ars naturam imitata veritatem quidem inquirit, sed non rerum superiorum atque divinarum, sed inferiorum et humanarum. Nam consultatio eorum quae sint homini emolumenta detrimentave allatura, quid aliud efficit quam ut verum a falso in hac temporali et momentanea mutabilitate decernamus, hoc scilicet sequentes, illud autem aspernantes? In vita igitur civili prudentia sola est quae moralibus cunctis virtutibus dominatur easque sola et moderatur et regit. At prudentia fracta est et debilis nullorumque nervorum, nisi manet ab una sapientia ad eamque tanquam ad principem reginamque referatur. Quare qui prudentiam (a providendo dictam) mediam posuerunt inter moralis intellectualisque virtutes, eamque idcirco perfectam voluerunt esse, virtutem in civili felicitate, quoniam virtutum civilium omnium principium sit et forma, ii nihil sensisse a veritate alienum existimandi sunt.

4   Ita ergo proponit Virgilius Aenean a se canendum, ut virum, hoc est ut sapientem, eundemque prudentem. Quae quidem virtutes aut intellectus sunt ambae, aut intellectus altera et rationis altera. Nam ratio temporalium est, intellectus autem aeternorum,

genius ventured upon something higher. Indeed, as one describing the human condition both in the active and contemplative lives, all his thought and counsel were directed to showing through the wisdom and virtue of Aeneas alone how the highest good could be obtained[1] in this life. This he indicated in the very first proposition of his extremely weighty and elegant work. For he says he is singing about "arms" in respect of military and active virtues, arms being the instruments of warfare and fighting. And he sings of "the man" in respect of civil and intellectual virtues, in which wisdom and prudence keep control of government. Wisdom as a rule seems to me the single virtue by which we exceed markedly the other animals. The earthly animal contemplates heavenly truth. It is wisdom alone that inquires into and knows truth. Prudence too inquires into truth, like wisdom, as an art imitating nature, but not the truth of higher and divine things, but of lower and human ones. Consideration of the things which are going to help or hurt mankind: what else does that do but permit us to distinguish true from false amid all these temporary and rapid changes, following the true and despising the false? Thus in the civil life, prudence by itself dominates all moral and ethical decision making; by itself it measures and controls those things. Yet prudence is weak and broken, lacking in muscle, unless it is lodged in wisdom alone and stays related to it as though to a prince and a queen. Thus those who place prudence (so-called from *providendo* or looking ahead) as a mean between the moral and intellectual virtues and hold it to be for that reason the perfect virtue in the matter of civil felicity, since it is the beginning and the pattern of all the civil virtues— these persons are to be reckoned to believe something not alien from the truth.

Vergil thus proposes that he must sing of Aeneas as a man, i.e., a man both wise and prudent. These are either both virtues of intellect, or one is a virtue of intellect and the other of calculation. For calculation concerns temporal things, intellect eternal ones, so

4

ita ut haec tota in contemplando sit posita, illa autem in consul-
tando. Qua quidem propositione quanquam usus est Virgilius
Homerum imitaturus, non solum quo ad rerum, verum etiam quo
ad ordinis similitudinem, non tamen exequitur eo ordine quo proponit, quippe qui primum virtutes urbanas canit, postea vero bellicas; et id quidem prudentius, mea sententia, quam Homerus, qui
primum de Achillis virtutibus locutus est in *Iliade*, postea vero in
Ulyssea de sapientia prudentiaque Ulyssis. Natura enim fit ut antea
intelligamus, deinde agamus. Itaque in primis sex *Aeneidos* libris
contemplatio maxime et consultatio locum habet. In secundis autem libris sex actionis est laus. Et hoc quidem summatim intelligi
velim de universo *Aeneidos* carmine. Nec tamen negarim et in primis sex libris permulta inveniri quae actionis sunt moraliumque
virtutum, et in alteris quoque sex libris inveniri quaedam non solum consultationis sed contemplationis propria.

5   Et quoniam dixi a Virgilio Marone describi humanam vitam,
hoc ita intelligi cupio, ut moralis, quam ἠθικὴν Graeci nominant,
philosophia, τῇ φυσικῇ, id est naturali, coniuncta sit. Quod eius
rei, ut propius accedam, illuc orditur, cum de Iunone et Aeolo
acutissime fabulatur. Scimus enim Iunonem et regno praeesse et
partui. Quare et 'Lucina' dicta est et 'regina.' Animum trifariam
partitur Plato in rationem, cupiditatem et iram. Rationi locus
datur in cerebro tanquam in arce totius corporis. Haec[1] Aeoli
nomine ideo figuratur quoniam *Aeolus* et 'varium' significat et 'mo-
bilem' et 'agilem' et 'versatilem,' quae quidem omnia rationis sunt
munera. Ira praecordia sibi vendicat, cupiditas autem iecur. At
ventis perturbationes significari, quis est qui ambigat? Praeterea
moralium virtutum formam si quis inquirat, eam nullam inve-
niat nisi rationem esse, perturbationes vero materiam. Versatur,

the latter has to do entirely with contemplation and the former
with consultation [*or* giving counsel]. Although Vergil makes use
of this proposition in order to imitate Homer, not only as regards
things but as regards the likeness of order, he does not however
follow out the order proposed, given that he starts by singing of
the civic virtues, then the military ones. In my opinion this is a
more prudent procedure than Homer used, who in the *Iliad* first
spoke of Achilles' virtues, then of the wisdom and prudence of
Ulysses in the *Odyssey*. For it natural to think before acting. Thus
in the first six books of the *Aeneid* contemplation and consultation
have the largest place. In the following books comes the praise of
action. I would have this be understood as a summary of the
whole *Aeneid*. Yet I would not deny that in the first six books you
find a great many things that belong to action and the moral virtues, and in the last six too certain things having to do with contemplation and consultation.

And since I've said that Vergil is describing human life, I want   5
it to be understood that moral philosophy, which the Greeks call
ethike, is joined together with *he physike*, that is, natural philosophy.
He launches into that subject, to be more specific, when he invents
the very penetrating story of Juno and Aeolus. We know that Juno
took precedence in the kingdom and via her parentage. Hence she
is also called Queen Lucina. Plato divides the soul triply into reason, desire and passion and places reason in the brain, as though
in the citadel of the whole body. This is represented in the name
of Aeolus, since Aeolus means both "many sided" and "mobile" and
"quick moving" and "revolving," which are all gifts of reason; passion he claims for the heart and desire for the liver. Who can
doubt what the disturbances of the wind mean? Moreover, if anyone should ask what the *form* of the moral virtues is, he would find
it to be nothing other than reason, while the "disturbances" are the
matter. The fable is concerned, I say, with the disturbances of

inquam, circa perturbationes moralis virtus, quas ratio ipsa cohibet atque moderatur. Quare non absurde legimus:

mollitque animos, et temperat iras.

Animos eadem ratione pro cupiditatibus poni existimo, qua θυμὸς apud Graecos et 'animum' significat et 'cupiditatem.' Quis enim ignorat nisi tanta esset rationis vis ut perturbationum impetum omnem compesceret, facile futurum ut ab his omne sanum a nobis consilium, omnis recta cogitatio auferatur? Rex igitur his datus est rationis principatus ab omnipotenti Deo, qui rerum omnium et pater est et creator, ea lege, ea potestate, ut et iubere sciat et vetare omnia pro arbitrio iussuque divino.

6   At vide, quaeso, quanta cum brevitate et ordine omnem aetatis humanae cursum Virgilius est complexus. Initium sumit a partu infantis, qui periculosissimus est et ei quae parit et infanti ipsi qui paritur. Itaque turbulentissimi ventorum flatus tempestatesque describuntur quae quidem adversa omnia naufragioque obnoxia idcirco apparente Neptuno continuo cessant, quia cum primum infans e matris utero veluti enatarit, uterque omni periculo liberatur. Nec enim absurdum cuiquam videri debet si *Neptunus* a duobus verbis Graecis νεῖν (quod est 'nare') et πτᾶν (quod 'volare' significat) deduci affirmemus. Nam quemadmodum tarditas parientis periculosa est, ita celeritas et quasi volatus in lucem levationem dolorum affert salutiferamque quietem. Nam quod rursus ad Aeolum spectat, αἰολεῖν 'agitare' significat et 'versare' et 'variare'; quae omnia ac similia humanae vitae competere, ambigat nemo. Vel Aeolus quasi *Aeonolus*, hoc est 'vitae deletio.' Nam αἰών 'aevum' 'vitam'que significat, ὀλεῖν vero delere. Nascentibus enim omnibus vitae discrimen interitusque imminet. Infantia vero, quae in septimum usque tendit annum, tota in alendo versatur; id quod per septem cervos illos quos Aeneas venatus fingitur, non obscure

moral virtue, which reason itself restrains and controls. Hence not absurdly do we read:

He softens souls and tempers passions.[2]

I reckon that "souls" stand for "desires" in the same way that *thumos* for the Greeks signifies both "soul" and "desire." Who doesn't know that if the force of reason were not sufficient to repress all the impulses of the passions, the latter would take away all sanity from our counsels and all correctness from our calculations? The omnipotent God, father and creator of all things, gives us a king for these reasons, as a principle of reason, with the law and power to know how both to command and forbid all things in accordance with his divine will and bidding.

But look how neatly and compendiously Vergil has embraced 6 the whole course of human life. He takes his beginning from the birth of the infant, which is extremely dangerous both to mother and child. Thus are described the turbulent winds and storms which expose everything to risk of shipwreck, and for this reason when Neptune appears they immediately stop, since when the infant first "swims out" as it were from his mother's uterus, both mother and child are free of danger. Nor ought it to seem absurd to anyone if we shall affirm that "Neptune" is derived from two Greek words, *nein*, to swim, and *ptan*, to fly. For just as slowness in giving birth is dangerous, so does swiftness, and, as it were, flying into the light, bring relief of pain and a healthy state of quiet. Going back to Aeolus, *aiolein* means "agitate" and "turn over" and "vary," all of which, and similar words, correspond to human life; everyone knows Aeolus is related to Aeonolus, i.e., "wiping out life"; for *aion* means "age" and "life"; *olein* means "to wipe out." Danger and destruction threaten all things that are born. But infancy, which extends to the seventh year, has entirely to do with nourishment, something that one may understand in no obscure way through the seven stags that Aeneas is imagined as hunting.

licet intelligi. Post infantiam sequitur puericia, quae fabularum
auditione admodum delectari consuevit. Hinc Ilii captivitas vasta-
tioque narratur et Aeneae Troianorumque errores. Deinceps ado-
lescentia est, quae propter vaehementissimum sanguinis augumen-
tum atque ardorem tota est dedita voluptatibus. Unde quanta sit
vis amoris, quantus ignis, iucunda expositione ostenditur. Conse-
quens est iuventa laudis cupida et plane ambitiosa. Quare honori-
fici ludi cum pulcherrimis praemiis referuntur. Post iuventam sequitur aetas gravior, quae in huius vitae consyderatione et in
veritatis perspicientia tota versatur. Quo factum est ut descensus
ad inferos fieret eaque narrarentur quae a Pythagoricis et Platoni-
cis de animis hominum rebusque divinis disputata sunt, et haec
quidem in sexto *Aeneidos* libro.

7   Nam reliqui sex libri, circa vitam activam distributi, quod ad
mores attinet, mirabili artificio complectuntur, ubi quanquam
multa de iusticiae, multa de pietatis munere apparent, fortitudinis
tamen laus in primis floret. Et quemadmodum initium sumptum
est a primo infantiae ortu, ita aetatis humanae finis est mors. Itaque non inepte ultimo loco subdidit:

Vitaque cum gemitu fugit indignata sub umbras.

Turnus enim, qui se iniusticiae fecerat ignaviaeque obnoxium, in
obscuritate nominis moritur sempiterna. Aeneas vero, vir iustus et
fortis, quasi numen in dies magis atque magis diuturnitate gloriae
illustratur.

8   Et haec sunt quae mihi ad tuas litteras in hac temporum difficultate respondenda occurrerunt. Vale. Ex Venetiis. XII Kal. Ia-
nuarias MCCCCXXVII.

After infancy follows childhood, which usually takes delight in hearing myths. Thus the capture and destruction of Troy is narrated, and the wanderings of Aeneas and the Trojans. Then comes adolescence, which is entirely given up to pleasures owing to the most violent increase and burning of the blood. That is why a pleasant account is given of the great power and fires of love. Then comes youth, desirous of praise and openly ambitious. That's why contests of honor with highly attractive prizes are mentioned. After youth comes graver age, which is completely occupied with meditation on this life and the perception of truth. That explains why the descent to Hades happens then and accounts are given by Pythagoreans and Platonists of human psychology and theology. This takes place in the sixth book of the *Aeneid*.

The other six books divide up in relation to the active life. 7 Moral themes are handled with wonderful skill. Although a great deal appears there about the duty of justice and piety, it is the praise of courage that is principally cultivated. And just as he takes his beginning from the first onset of infancy, so the end of human life is death. Thus it is appropriate that he adds in the final passage:

And life fled with a groan, in anger, to the shadows.[3]

For Turnus, who had made himself punishable for injustice and cowardice, died with an eternal blot on his reputation. But Aeneas, a just and brave man, was illumined every day more and more, as though a divinity, with lasting glory.

This is what it has occurred to me in order to respond to your 8 letter in this difficult time. Farewell. From Venice, December 21, 1427.

∶ II ∶

1   Franciscus Philelfus Kyriaco Anconitano salutem.

    Placuisse tibi litteras meas et ea quae de Virgilii Maronis sententia scripsimus in *Aeneida,* gaudeo. Quod autem petis qua ratione Neptunus, ab Ovidio Nasone cognominatus sit 'Amphitrites,' et Fortuna 'Rhamnusia,' paucis accipe.

2   Rhamnusia quidem non est fortuna, ut vulgo exponunt magistri ludi, sed indignationis dea, quam Graeci tui Νέμεσιν vocant. Nam cum Narcisus formae bonitate abuteretur superbius, recte fingitur eiusmodi deam adversus illum indignatam iustis precibus assensisse. Est enim indignatio animi aegritudo adversus eum qui bonis praesentibus sit indignus. *Nemesis,* inquam, 'indignationem' significat. *Rhamnusia* vero dicta est a Rhamnus, qui est Atticae vicus ubi colebatur; cuius quidem deae simulacrum eo in loco pulcherrimum fuisse tradunt, factum a Phidia, ulnarum in altitudinem decem, illudque marmoreum.

3   Neptunus autem nequaquam est *Amphitrites* cognominatus. Dictio illa depravata est apud Ovidium librariorum inscitia. Est enim foeminini generis declinaturque more Graeco, nominativo *Amphitrite,* genitivo *Amphitrites.* Fingitur autem a poetis esse Neptuni uxor. Unde Claudianus *De raptu Proserpinae* ita cecinit.

> Etiam . . . Nereia glauco
> Neptunum gremio complectitur Amphitrite.

Nam *Amphitrite* 'mare' significat, dicta illa quidem ab ἀμφί, 'circum,' et τρεῖν, 'terrere.' Mare enim circum se navigantis pereundi

: II :

From Venice
January 28, 1428

Francesco Filelfo to Cyriac of Ancona, greetings.   1

I'm happy that you liked my letter and what I wrote about Vergil's aims in writing the *Aeneid*. Now receive these few words concerning your question why Ovid gave Neptune the cognomen
"Amphitrites" and Fortune "Rhamnusian."

Rhamnusia is not in fact [Greek for] "fortune," as schoolmasters   2
commonly state; she is the goddess of anger, which your Greeks
call Nemesis. For when Narcissus abused the goodness of beauty
with too much arrogance, it was rightly imagined that a goddess of
this kind would have answered righteous prayers and become angry at him. Anger is a mental sickness directed against someone
who is unworthy of good presentations;[4] and Nemesis means anger. Rhamnusia comes from Rhamnus which is a town of Attica
where she is worshipped. They say there was a beautiful likeness
of the goddess in that place, made by Phidias, ten fathoms high
and made of marble.

Neptune by no means had the cognomen "Amphitrites." The   3
locution has been corrupted in Ovid through the ignorance of
scribes. It is a word of the feminine gender and is declined in the
Greek way; it is *Amphitrite* in the nominative and *Amphitrites* in the
genitive. According to the inventions of the poets she is the wife of
Neptune. Hence Claudian also sings in the *De raptu Proserpinae*:

Amphitrite, daughter of Nereus, holds Neptune
In her sea-green lap.[5]

For Amphitrite means "sea": the expression comes from ἀμφί,
"around," and τρεῖν, to terrify. For the sea assails those sailing

terrore insequitur. Ex Amphitrite autem et Neptuno Triton natus
fingitur a poetis.

4   Si quid est quod aliud a me velis, nunquam frustra requires officium meum.

Vale. Ex Venetiis quinto Kal. Februarias MCCCCXXVIII.

: III :

1   Franciscus Philelfus Kyriaco Anconitano sal.

Vix profecto credi queat, et praecipue ab indoctis, quam ipse
tuis his epigrammatis delectatus quae ex Aegypto in Italiam repor-
taras et in praesentia dedisti ad me. Opto, mi dulcissime Kyriace,
tibi a Deo immortali quamlongissimam et quamfortunatissimam
vitam dari, qui mortuos etiam vivificas. Quod te polliceris brevi ad
nos iturum, perlibenter audio. Non enim minus cupio visitandi tui
quam tu visendi mei. Fac igitur ne differas tuum adventum. Nam
apud me tibi omnia parata offendes quibus maxime delectaris, hoc
est et Musas et libros una cum tuo Mercurio.

2   Interea vero temporis quae verba Graeca Latine exponi a
me vis, breviter accipe. Et primum ξυήλη Laconicus est gladio-
lus, quem Latine 'pugionem' possumus appellare. Ἄμη 'falcem'
significat. Ex quo verbo descendit ἀμητήρ, hoc est 'mes-
sor.' Μάκελλα, μακέλλης est 'ligo.' Πτύον 'ventilabrum' est.
Αὐχήν, αὐχένος 'cervicem' significat. Καταχωρίζειν significat plura: 'partiri,' 'locare,' 'disponere,' 'digerere,' 'distribuere.'
Δεινότης item in plura transit significata; nam et pro 'vi' poni-
tur et pro 'gravitate' et pro 'sollertia' et pro 'acrimonia.' Et δεινὸς
(natura ei diphthongus est Graeca) significat 'terribilem' et

around in it with fear of death. The poets imagine that Triton was born from Amphitrite and Neptune.

If there is anything else you want from me, you will never require my good offices in vain. 4

Farewell. From Venice, January 28, 1428.

: III :

From Bologna
July 7, 1428

Francesco Filelfo to Cyriac of Ancona, greetings. 1

It can scarcely be believed, especially by the unlearned, how much delight you take in those inscriptions of yours that you have brought back from Egypt to Italy and have now given to me. I wish, my dear Cyriac, that you, who bring the dead back to life, may be granted the longest and most fortunate of lives by the immortal God. I hear with great pleasure that you are promising you will visit us soon. My desire to see you equals your desire to visit me. So please don't put off your arrival. You will find everything here ready for you, everything you most enjoy, i.e. both the Muses and books, together with your Mercury.

Meanwhile, here, briefly, are answers to your questions about 2 the meaning of Greek words. First, *xuele* is a small Spartan sword which we can call a dagger. *Ame* means shovel. From that word we get *ameter*, reaper. *Makella, makelles* is "pickax." A *ptuon* is a winnowing fork. *Auchen, auchenos* means "neck." *Katachorizein* means many things: separate, place, order, digest, distribute. *Deinotes* likewise passes into many meanings. It is used in the place of "violence," and for "gravity," and for "shrewdness" and for "acrimony." And *deinos* (it naturally has a diphthong in Greek) means "terrible"

'industrium' et 'acutum' et 'molestum.' Quid multis? Locus notan-
dus est; nam varie eo verbo utuntur Graeci.

3   Vale. Ex Bononia, Nonis Iuliis MCCCCXXVIII.

: IV :

1 Φραγκίσκος ὁ Φιλέλφος Κυριακῷ χαίρειν.

Ἐγώ σου τὴν περὶ λόγους δύναμιν καί πάλαι θαυμάζων,
νῦν οὐκ ἔχ᾽ ὅπως ἂν τοῦτο δράσαιμι προσηκόντως, οὕτω με
τὸ τῶν σῶν ἐπιστολῶν κατὰ τὴν ἑλληνικὴν γεγραμμένων
φωνὴν, ἐξέπληξε κάλλος· καί σε οὐκ ἐν τῇ Κωνσταντίνου
ποτε τοὺς λόγους μαθεῖν, ἀλλ᾽ ἐν Ἀθήναις ἐκείναις
περιφανῶς ἐμήνυεν. Ἡ γὰρ ἐνοῦσα σοι χάρις ἐν τῷ λέγειν,
ἐκεῖθεν.

2 Ἐγὼ μὲν οὖν οἶμαι τὴν τῶν Μουσῶν πρώτην, εἴπερ ἂν
αὐτῇ σωματικῶς ξυνέβαινεν ἐντυχεῖν σοι, διαπορουμένην
τὲ καὶ σου τὸ ἐπαφρόδιτον τῶν λόγων θαυμάζουσαν, τὸ
ὁμηρικὸν ἐκεῖνο ἐρέσθαι·

τίς πόθεν εἶς ἀνδρῶν; πόθι τοι πόλις ἠδὲ τοκῆες;
καὶ γὰρ ἐρῶ σ᾽ ἄγη μ᾽ ἔχει ὡς ὑπὸ θνητοῦ τόσσον
νικῶμαι πασάων θεάων ὑπέρτατος.

3 Ὑγίαινε τοιγαροῦν ὡς ἂν ἡμᾶς τε καὶ τοὺς πρὸς τὴν σὴν
ἀρετὴν ἡμῖν ὁμοίως διακειμένους, τῇ Θεόθεν ἐνούσῃ σοι
εὐμουσίᾳ, καὶ μᾶλλον εὐφραίνειν ἔχοις. Ἐγὼ δέ σοι ἐπὶ
τούτοις, καὶ τὸ τοῦ Νέστορος γῆρας ἐπεύχομαι, ὡς οὐ

and "hard work" and "sharp" and "annoying." In short, you need to pay attention to the context, for the Greeks use this word in various senses.

Farewell. From Bologna, July 7, 1428.   3

: IV :

From Florence
March 7, 1431

Francesco Filelfo to Cyriac, greetings.   1

I have long admired your skill with words, but now I don't know how to express what I feel, so struck am I by the beauty of your letters written in the Greek language. It clearly revealed that you didn't learn the language in Constantinople, but in that famous Athens. The charm in speaking that you have comes from there.

As for me, I think that the first of the Muses — if it ever happ-   2
pened that she should meet you in the flesh — surprised and amazed at the charm of your language, would speak those well-known Homeric words:

What man are you; what your city, your parents?
And I tell you that wonder seizes me how I, the highest of all goddesses, should be so beaten by a mortal.

Stay healthy, therefore, so that by the skill that you have from   3
God you will be able even more to make us, and all those who share our view of your excellence, happy. And beside this, I wish you the long life of Nestor as one who has not yielded the first

μόνον τοῖς καθ' ἡμᾶς ἐπὶ σοφίᾳ, ἀλλ' ἤδη καὶ τοῖς πάλαι
διαπρέψασι, μηδ' ὁπωσοῦν τῶν πρωτείων παραχωρήσαντι.

4   Ἔρρωσω τῶν Μουσῶν τέμενος. καὶ τὸν σὸν Φιλέλφον
φίλει, ὡς εἴωθας, ὃς ὑπέρ σου καὶ τῶν σοὶ συνοισόντων κὺν
εἰς πῦρ ἄλοιτο τὸ τοῦ λόγου προθύμως.

5   Φλωρεντίαθεν ταῖς νώναις μαρτίου, ἔτει α^ωυ^ωλ^ωα^{ωα} ἀπὸ
Χριστοῦ γεννήσεως.

: V :

1   Franciscus Philelphus Antonio Pantormitae ἀνδρὶ ἀρίστῳ καὶ
ποιητῇ καλλίστῳ salutem dicit.

Salve, dimidium animae meae. Si vales, ita est ut opto; ego autem perbelle valeo.

2   Kiriaci Anconitani singulare studium in revocandis ad vitam
mortuis non te latet. Quare, etsi minime sum ignarus quanti hominem facis—facis enim plurimi—velim tamen mea etiam causa
eum tibi carissimum fieri.

place in wisdom to our contemporaries or to those who were outstanding in the past.

Farewell, you shrine of the Muses, and love your own Filelfo as   4
you do, who would readily even jump into the fire for the sake of
you and whatever will be to your advantage in learning.

From Florence, on the nones of March, in the year 1431 from   5
the birth of Christ.

: V :

Filelfo to Panormita

1433 or 1434

Francesco Filelfo to Antonio Panormita, the best of men, greet-   1
ings.

Be well, half of my soul. If you are well, it is as I wish; and I
want you to be well most prettily.

You will be aware of the extraordinary zeal of Cyriac of Ancona   2
in calling the dead back to life. So, though I am quite well aware
how much you value the man — a great deal indeed — I would have
him be extremely dear to you for my sake as well.

APPENDIX IV

Cyriac of Ancona on the Six Constitutions, 1440/1447

This opusculum, which reads like Cyriac's notes to himself and follows up on his interest in political systems expressed in the first letter to Bruni, appears in two manuscripts: Lucca, Biblioteca Capitolare, MS. 555, ff. 470r–71r (L), and Florence, Biblioteca Riccardiana, MS. 996, ff. 55r–56v (R).[1] It was edited from the Lucca manuscript by J. D. Mansi in the eighteenth century, with numerous errors, and published in Fabricius' *Biblioteca latina*, 5:374–75. A fresh text has been prepared for this volume by Ornella Rossi, Assistant Editor of the I Tatti Renaissance Library, based on the two known manuscripts.[2]

The political terminology is based closely on the discussion of constitutions in Book 6 of Polybius' *Histories*, and Cyriac thus counts as the first Western humanist to be demonstrably familiar with this important source of Hellenistic political theory.[3] Polybius' account descends from the philosophers of the classical age, especially Plato and Aristotle, where regimes are classified according to the number of people in power (one, few, or many), and evaluated according to their aims: good governments are devoted to the common interest; bad ones focus only on the interests of an individual or a ruling class. Each system therefore has a "correct" form and a "deviation": for example, one-man rule can be kingship (positive) or tyranny (negative). Cyriac uses the same categories, bringing them up to date with modern examples.

The date of composition can be roughly determined by the coincidence of the reigns of sovereigns whom Cyriac cites as contemporary. The *terminus post quem* is the election of Frederick III as

Holy Roman Emperor in 1440; the *ante quem* is the death of Pope Eugenius IV in 1447.

The English translation is by Clive Foss and James Hankins, the notes by James Hankins and Ornella Rossi.

NOTES

1. Described in *Iter* 1:256 and 1:213, respectively.

2. The spelling of the Lucca manuscript has been followed; punctuation and capitalization have been modernized. Minor misspellings have not been recorded.

3. The key evidence is Cyriac's use of the term *ochlocracy* (mob rule), which was coined by Polybius and used twice in Book 6. See James Hankins, "Europe's First Democrat? Cyriac of Ancona and Book 6 of Polybius," forthcoming in a Festschrift for Anthony Grafton, ed. Ann M. Blair, Anja Goeing, and Urs Leu (Leiden: E. J. Brill).

Sex modi administrandarum rerum publicarum,
tres ad iustitiam et tres ad iniustitiam.
Kyriacus Anconitanus.[1]

1   Monarchia iustum regnum, cui opposita est tyrannis. Aristocratia optimatum potentatus, cui contraria est oligarchia, paucorum violentum[2] imperium. Democratia populi bene administrantis potentatus, cui opposita[3] est ochlocratia, imperitae turbae temeraria potestas.

Monarchia

2   Princeps unus in orbe bonus, ut Caesar vel[4] Augustus, qui ex lege et Senatus Consulto plebisve scito et tribunicia[5] potestate, magistratibus bonis provincias regnaque per orbem moderare curabant, ut hodie Federicus[6] designatus imperator in Germania, nec non in Gallia et Britannica[7] insula Carolus et Henricus nobilissimi reges sua quique regna optime nostro aevo regia potestate gubernant. Sed praeclarius hodie Alphonsus inclytus ille Ausoniae rex Tarraconensem[8] Hispaniam, Balearum Sicanorumque insulas Ausoniamque sua praeclarissima regna insigniter propagata gubernat, Eugenio optimo maximoque annuente pontifice, qui sanctius divini[9] iuris ordine Christicolis toto orbe imperat universis.

Tyrannis

3   Principis unius in urbe regnove dominatio, ut Athenis Pysistratus et Syracusis Dionysius, qui fortiter sine lege, absoluta potestate populis imperitabant et ad libitum eos sua quaeque iussa mandatave sequi pro impetu cogebant. Ut hodie potissimum inter

Six ways of administering states:
three tend to justice, and three to injustice.
Cyriac of Ancona.

Monarchy is a just kingship; its opposite is tyranny. Aristocracy is   1
the rule of the best; opposed to it is oligarchy, the violent command of the few. Democracy is the rule of the people when it ad-
ministers [the state] well; its opposite is ochlocracy, the irrespon-
sible power of the ignorant mob.

Monarchy

Monarchy is a single good prince in the world, like Caesar or Au-   2
gustus who by law and decrees of the Senate or by resolutions of
the People and the tribunician power took care to administer the
provinces and kingdoms with good magistrates throughout the
world, as today Frederick, the emperor-designate, does in Germany. It includes as well Charles and Henry, most noble kings in
France and the British Island: they each govern their respective
kingdoms excellently with royal power in our age. But today Alfonso, the famous king of Italy,[1] is the more outstanding, governing as he does Aragon,[2] the Balearic and Sicilian islands and Italy,
having markedly enlarged his glorious realm. He does this with
the approval of the great and best pontiff Eugenius, who gives holy
commands to all Christians throughout the globe under the order
of the divine law.

Tyranny

The domination of a single prince in a city or kingdom, like Pisis-   3
tratus in Athens or Dionysius in Syracuse; they used to order their peoples about boldly, lawlessly, with absolute power,
and they used arbitrary force to make them follow each of their
orders or mandates. In this way today, especially among the

barbaros homines Murath Begh in Bythinia et Thracia, in Aegypto vero et Syria Sultanus ille Memphiticae Babylonis princeps insolentissime servant.

Aristocratia

4 Optimates cives delecti, ut Lacedaemonum xxviii virorum virtute bona consilium[10] et Romanorum patrum senatus. Quorum[11] optimam politiam nostra hac[12] aetate Veneti per Italiam, sed aliis posthabitis omnibus externis una inter Illiricos Ragusaeorum civitas laudatissime servat.

Oligarchia

5 Paucorum civium in urbe regimen vel dominium, ut decemviri qui in Urbe perinde ac tyrannidem magistratum gerere contendebant, ut Bononiae et Genuae nostro aevo saepe nonnulli audaces insurgere conantur suis cum sectatoribus cives.

Democratia

6 Populi municipumque mixtum in civitate principatum, ut Athenienses servasse comperimus, quamquam saepenumero perinde ac aristocraticum opportune optimum Areopagitarum consilium habuissent. Hodie vero ex Italis Florentia in Thuscia, in Piceno autem Ancon, et Ricinatum Colonia servare videntur, et hae quidem alma sub pontificia Dei vicaria potestate protectae et[13] moderatae sunt.

Ochlocratia[14]

7 Plebis urbanae turbaeve multorum in civitate dominium, ut in Urbe quandoque a patribus segregata plebs, concitave tribunis ex

barbarians, men like Murad Bey[3] in Bithynia and Thrace, and in Egypt and Syria the sultan, prince of Memphitic Babylon, arrogantly maintain their power.

Aristocracy

In aristocracy the best citizens are chosen, as in the Council of the Twenty-Eight Good Men of the Spartans[4] and the Senate of the Roman Fathers. Their excellent constitution in our day is preserved by the Venetians in Italy, but leaving aside all other foreign cities, one city of the Illyrians, Ragusa [Dubrovnik], maintains it in the most praiseworthy fashion.[5]

Oligarchy

The rule or the domination of a few citizens in a city, like the Decemvirs,[6] who strove to exercise their magistracy in Rome exactly like a tyranny; just as in Bologna and Genoa in our time some reckless citizens have tried to rise up with their partisans.[7]

Democracy

A mixed regime of the people and townsmen in a city, such as we learn the Athenians maintained, although very often they used to employ the excellent counsel of the Areopagites at suitable moments, just like an aristocratic regime. Today among the Italians, Florence in Tuscany, Ancona in Picenum and the colony of Recanati seem to maintain this [type of regime]. These indeed are protected and regulated beneath the fostering pontifical power of the vicar of God.

Ochlocratia

The domination of the urban plebs or a mob of the many in the state, as in Rome whenever the plebs was separated from[8] the

impetu multitudinis eorum absoluta voluntas, ut perinde ac lex haberetur, instabat, eamque sequi magistratus omnes cogere pertendebat.[15] Ut et nostro tempore Bononiensis populus et Asculanus et quandoque[16] conciti Genuenses magni perniciose [quandoque] tumultuarieque conspirasse videntur.

Iratus recole, quod nobilis ira leonis
    In sibi prostratos se negat esse feram.[17]

senate, or [whenever], incited by the tribunes, their will, unshack-led by a rising of the multitude, strove to be considered the equivalent of law, and pressured all the magistrates to obey itself. As in our time the people of Bologna and Ascoli and from time to time the great Genoese were ruinously stirred up and appear to have conspired in tumult.

When angered, remember that the rage of the noble lion
  refuses to be bestial toward those who bow down before it.[9]

APPENDIX V

IMMORTALI DEO

1 Antonius Leonardi Felici Feliciano amico suo salutem dicit.

Litterae tuae apud nos perlectae nobis maximam attulerunt laetitiam quia amatorem ac restauratorem oblitarum antiquitatum his nostris perditis diebus reperimus. Quum adeo rari ac perditi sint ut vix inter mortales pauci inveniantur, maxime igitur penes omnis laudandus es, quum ex infinito hominum grege quasi solus supersis.

2 Multa in tuis litteris de Kiriaco nostro Anconitano scribis: qui utinam extaret, nam superioribus annis natura vitae suae finem fecit. Habeas ⟨quod⟩ vir ille inter antiquos antiquissimus fuisset, beneque in variis rebus eruditus, litteris praesertim Graecis atque Latinis; nam opuscula ab eo edita quae vagantur testes sunt ⟨de eo⟩ qui, ne longius quam statui sim, totum ferme peragravit mundum. Nam aedificia, templa deorum marmorea, statuas, epigrammata, antiquitates omnes hic propriis oculis conspectus est; nec huic unquam nocuit itineris asperitas, nec pelagi saevitia neque longae peregrinationis lassitudo; omnia ob virtutem, ob antiquitates inveniendas facillima, suavia, iucundaque fuerunt.

APPENDIX V

*A Letter to Felice Feliciano about Cyriac**
1457

TO THE IMMORTAL GOD

Antonio di Leonardo sends greetings to his friend Felice Feliciano.   1

It was a great joy to read your letter to me, because I discovered from it that you are a lover and renewer of forgotten antiquities in this degenerate age of ours. Such men are so seldom met with and are so scarce among us that hardly any are to be found among mortals. You are therefore universally to be praised, since you are, as it were, the sole survivor of an infinite company.

You write a good deal in your letter about our Cyriac of An-   2
cona. Would that he were still alive! But Nature, some years ago, put an end to his life. He may be considered as a man who, among the ancients, would have been most ancient: a man well learned in sundry matters, especially in Greek and Latin literature, as his *opuscula* that are now circulating bear witness: a man, in short, who traveled over almost the whole world. With his own eyes he inspected buildings, temples of the gods, marble statues, inscriptions, and all manner of antiquities. Nor was he ever daunted by the harshness of the way, the cruelty of the sea, or the weariness of long journeying: everything was most easy, agreeable, and pleasant to him on account of his courage and the antiquities to be discovered.

---

* For the circumstances, see Note on the Texts, p. 306. For the Latin text and critical apparatus, based on Treviso, Biblioteca Capitolare, MS 2A/1, see Scalamonti, 196–98 (Appendix 4).

3   Sed inter alia haec tibi narrare de patientia huius viri libet. Quum provintiam quandam Graeciae perscruptasset, postea sarcinullae navim impositae ac vela ventis dedissent, quum per XXC milia passuum abesset, ab amico suo audivit epigramma quoddam vidisse post moenia civitatis nuper ab eis relictae, Kiriacus ob hoc summo affectus dolore, postquam terram applicuit, relicta trireme, redivit ut epigramma videret ac pernotaret, qui minime, ut dixi, longiorem viam metuit.

4   Ipse etiam apud omnes ferme nationes notus carusque fuit. Nam apud Theucros plurimum claruit, unde genitor huius qui Byzantium nuper delevit cheirographum suo signatum nomine optumo Kiriaco donavit, qui tutus per civitates, oppida, loca, ac villas sine offensione, vectigale, et ulla laesione ire posset ac si unus ex familia suae domus esset.

5   Quapropter haec pauca ex multis ad te scribere haud ingratum fuit, quum vestigia huius hominis te approbare videar, quae erga omnes virtuti deditos probanda amplexandaque sunt.

6   Igitur huius Kiriaci nostri clarissimi facta lauda, inquire, dilige, ama, atque cole, nec ignobilem aut obscurum aemulaveris hominem sed clarum sanguine, postea clariorem virtute.

7   Postremo si quid humanitatis apud nos dignum fore aspicies, petas amice atque illico obtinebis. Vale, antiquitatum amator decusque. Ex Venetiis IIII Nonas Octobris MCCCCLVII.

8   Et quia, ut hominem eruditum decet, antiquitatis delectatione teneris, mitto ad te epigrammata Torcelli reperta nec non Muriani. Hac in re iudicium tuum expecto.

Let me give you one example among many of this man's patient 3
endurance. After he had investigated a certain region in Greece, he
put his little pack on board a ship and they set sail. But when they
had sailed eighty miles, he heard from a friend that he had seen a
certain inscription behind the walls of a city they had just left.
Cyriac was greatly upset by this, and when they made landfall, he
left the ship and returned to see and note down the inscription.
He had no fear, as I said, of the longer route.

He was also known and welcome in almost every country, and 4
was particularly esteemed among the Turks — so much so that the
father [Murad II] of the recent destroyer of Byzantium [Sultan
Mehmed II] gave him a document signed by his own illustrious
hand, enabling Cyriac to travel safely through cities, towns, locali-
ties and villages without vexation, taxation or any other injury, as
if he were one of the sultan's own household.

So it has been a pleasure to tell you these few things among the 5
many I could have mentioned, since I see that you admiringly follow in Cyriac's footsteps, which are to be commended and ap-
proved by everybody dedicated to virtue.

Praise, therefore, the achievements of our brilliant Cyriac; in- 6
quire into them, value, love, and cherish them. For you will be
emulating no mean or unknown person, but a man illustrious by
birth who afterward became more illustrious by his manly worth.

To conclude: if your eye falls on anything in my house that is 7
worthy of your humane erudition, ask for it, my friend, and it
shall immediately be yours. Farewell, lover of antiquities and their
ornament. From Venice, October 4, 1457.

And since, as befits a man of learning, you are seized by a relish 8
for antiquity, I am sending you these inscriptions found in Torcello and Murano and I look forward to your remarks on them.

[*There follow three Latin inscriptions, labeled "At Torcello, near Venice,"
"In Venice," and "At Murano, near Venice."*]

303

Note on the Texts

❧❦❧

Of Cyriac's early life and travels, our knowledge rests uniquely—apart from the few early letters included in this volume and his long retrospective epistle, familiarly known as the *Itinerarium*, addressed to Eugenius IV¹—on the materials for a *Vita* put together by his friend and fellow citizen Francesco Scalamonti, which largely reproduces Cyriac's own records and carries his biography down to late 1434 or early 1435. This *Vita* survives in a single manuscript, now in Treviso (Biblioteca Capitolare, MS 2 A/1, *olim* I 138), which was published with certain omissions and emendations in 1792,² and again by Mitchell and Bodnar in Scalamonti (see Abbreviations). Except for a very few clarifications and corrections, the present edition reproduces that of Scalamonti, 26–100, which was based on a fresh collation of the Treviso manuscript.

The Treviso manuscript was written, illuminated, and assembled by Cyriac's enthusiastic disciple, the Veronese antiquary and scribe Felice Feliciano (1433–ca.1479).³ The first section contains the *Vita* proper, on ff. 22r–108r, to which was prefixed Scalamonti's dedicatory letter (ff. 10v–21v) to Lauro Quirini.

The second section (ff. 108v–198r) comprises a substantial, though chronologically disordered and sometimes fragmentary, miscellany of Cyriac's writings—opuscula, extracts from his travel journals, letters, vernacular poems, occasional pieces, extracts and translations from antique authors, ancient inscriptions, modern epitaphs, etc.—that span his career from 1435 to 1449, along with at least one posthumous eulogy of him. It is noteworthy that the first item (ff. 108v–119v) in this second section, immediately following the *Vita*, is Cyriac's *Naumachia Regia*, describing the naval battle at Ponza on August 5, 1435, in which the Genoese defeated King Alfonso of Naples; the dedication of this piece to Scalamonti suggests that it was perhaps appended to the *Vita* when the latter came into Felice's hands to transcribe. Eleven folios of this section have been torn out. The partial remains of one of them suggests that the lost folios were adorned with drawings, since it contains two of Felice's colored copies of drawings Cyriac made of beasts he saw in Egypt — a giraffe on the recto and an elephant on the verso.[4]

The third section (ff. 198v–220r) — to which somebody, not Felice, tacked on extraneous inscriptions from Mantua and Brescia (ff. 220v, 221r) — is in effect a vivid testimony of Felice's devotion to Cyriac's memory and example. It opens with a letter about Cyriac, dated 1457, from a certain Antonio di Leonardo that forms a connecting link between the strictly Cyriacan and the Felicean matter in the volume, and thus gives a unity to its whole tripartite structure. (The letter is given in Appendix V.)

The manuscript concludes (ff. 201v–220v) with Felice's well-known account (the *Memoratu digna* and the *Jubilatio*), couched in flowery Cyriacesque language, of the trip he made in company with his friends Andrea Mantegna, Samuele da Tradate, and Giovanni Marcanova round the southern shores of Lake Garda on September 24–25, 1464, to which is appended a little sylloge of inscriptions from the Garda and Veronese regions.

The subsequent history of the manuscript is obscure until the end of 1774 or the beginning of 1775, when the manuscript came into the hands of Girolamo Tiraboschi, who incorporated a detailed *précis* of Scalamonti's *Vita* into his chapter on the fifteenth-century discovery of antiquity in his *Storia della letteratura italiana*.[5] Tiraboschi did not in fact publish the manuscript himself. It was published with omissions, emendations, and a good deal of rearrangement toward the end, together with a long introduction and notes, by Giuseppe Colucci in volume 15 of his *Delle antichità Picene* (1792) from a copy, as he noted, supplied to him by Tiraboschi. Colucci apparently never saw the original codex, and he relied heavily on Tiraboschi in preparing his edition of it.

For the convenience of the reader, we have punctuated the text and divided it into paragraphs according to sense, and not according to the rather arbitrary punctuation and paragraphing of the manuscript. To facilitate comparison between the text and our translation, we have numbered the paragraphs in both.

Anyone experienced in Cyriac's stylistic mannerisms can see them in Scalamonti's prose, which often appears to be nothing more than the transcription of passages from Cyriac's diaries, changed from the first person to the third. Therefore, in determining whether the misspelling of a Latin word is Felice's or Scalamonti's (i.e., Cyriac's) we have been guided by the surviving autographs of Cyriac's writings. Misspellings and incorrect grammar, whether the products of Cyriac, Scalamonti, or Felice, have been tacitly corrected here. For full details of the manuscript variants, see the footnotes in the Mitchell-Bodnar edition of Scalamonti.

The texts of the inscriptions are given for the most part as they occur in the manuscript, despite numerous errors. A few of the more banal scribal errors have been corrected and the corrections indicated in square brackets. Translations are based as far as possible on Cyriac's text of the inscriptions; however, in a few cases where Cyriac's text cannot yield a coherent translation, recourse has been had to modern editions of the inscriptions. The reader should be aware that modern texts of the inscriptions sometimes differ substantially from the texts found in Cyriac's manuscripts.

In translating the inscriptions, words added in roman script within square brackets represent editorial realizations of conjectural letters; words in italics within brackets are added by the editor to clarify the sense. References to modern editions of the inscriptions are given in the Notes to the Translation. Photos and/ or squeezes of a growing number of the original stones and manuscripts are now visible via the website of the *Corpus inscriptionum latinarum* (cil.bbaw.de).

CORRESPONDENCE, 1423–38

1. Cyriac to Bonarelli, March 15, 1423, *inc.* Cum Venetiarum ad urbem. First published by Morici, "Dante e Ciriaco d'Ancona," 74–77; see also Pittaluga, "Ciriaco d'Ancona e i poeti latini." Bodnar's edition is based directly on the unique manuscript, Vat. lat. 8750, ff. 125v–128r.

2. Cyriac to Leonardo Bruni, December 13 [1432], *inc.* Cum hisce diebus. Cyriac's first letter to Bruni occurs in three manuscripts: (1) Milan, Biblioteca Ambrosiana R 21 sup., f. 174r, fifteenth century; (2) Venice, Biblioteca Marciana, Marc. Lat. XIV 12 (4002), f. 25r, fifteenth century; (3) and an eighteenth-century apograph of the letter made by Jacopo Morelli, preserved in the same library, Marc. lat. XIV, 221 (4632), ff. 174v–175r. For the manuscripts and earlier editions, see Scalamonti, 189n1. The text was first published in Luiso, *Studi*, 177–78, based on the two fifteenth-century manuscripts; Bodnar's edition in Scalamonti, 181–82, followed here, was based on the fresh collation of the same two manuscripts.

3. Bruni to Cyriac, after May 31, 1433, *inc.* Melius erat, o Kyriace. The letter was published in Mehus 1741, 2:57–61 (Ep. 6.9 = Luiso, *Studi*, 121, Ep. 6.13). For the numerous manuscripts, see Gualdo Rosa, *Censimento*. The text printed here is that given in Scalamonti, 182–89, based on Mehus and a selection of four manuscripts; for details of the manuscripts used, see Scalamonti, 190n3.

4. Cyriac to Bruni, January 30, 1436, *inc.* O quam hodie. We follow the excellent text of Cortesi, "La *Caesarea laus*," with commentary, with some adjustments in the punctuation. The anno-

tated text produced independently by Hankins, "Addenda to Book X," 396–406, has also been consulted. The notes are indebted to those of Cortesi and Hankins.

5. Cyriac to Bruni, shortly after April 7, 1436, *inc.* Ἐπίγραμμα εἰς Ἀθήνας. This letter was published, without indicating the source, by Giovanni Targioni Tozzetti, "Notizie di alcune lettere odeporiche di Ciriaco Anconitano," in *Relazioni d'alcuni viaggi fatti in diverse parti della Toscana*, vol. 5 (Florence, 1773), 414–16. Bodnar, *Cyriacus and Athens*, p. 45, quoted the letter from the transcription of Targioni Tozzetti. The manuscript source was later identified as Florence, Biblioteca Nazionale Centrale, MS. Pal. Targioni 49 (*olim* 53), ff. 23r–24r, a paper manuscript of the fifteenth century. On this manuscript, see *Later Travels*, 379–80. The scribe is almost certainly Niccolò di Ugolino, who seems to have copied the letters in the manuscript from Cyriac's original, probably sometime in the 1470s (see Di Benedetto, "Il punto," 21–22). The present edition is based directly on the manuscript and not on Targioni Tozzetti's inaccurate version.[6]

6. Poggio to Bruni, March 31, 1438, *inc.* Oblata est mihi nuper. Our text follows that of *Poggio Bracciolini Lettere. II. Epistolarum familiarium libri*, ed. Helene Harth (Florence: Istituto Nazionale di Studi sul Rinascimeto, 1984), 298–301.

THE KING'S NAVAL BATTLE

The text is preserved in eleven manuscripts, two of them in Cyriac's own hand and two others with his corrections. The oldest was written by Cyriac in November 1435. A revised version of January 1436 is the basis of the admirable edition of Liliana Monti Sabia, *Kyriaci Anconitani Naumachia regia* (Pisa: Istituti editoriali e poligrafici internazionali, 2000), whose text we reproduce here with her gracious permission. Full details of the manuscripts and their variant readings may be found in that volume.

NOTES

1. To be included in the projected third I Tatti volume of Cyriac's travels, covering the years 1435–44.

2. Giuseppe Colucci, in *Delle Antichità Picene* 15 (1792): 50–100.

3. See Mitchell, "Felice Feliciano."

4. See van Essen, "Cyriaque d'Ancône en Égypte," with reproductions of the torn drawings on f. 173r–v; compare Lehmann, *Cyriacus of Ancona's Egyptian Visit*, fig. 30.

5. Tiraboschi, *Storia*, 6:156–77.

6. We thank Ornella Rossi for helping us obtain a digital copy of the manuscript from the library and verifying its reading *in situ*. The recent *Censimento dei codici dell' Epistolario di Leonardo Bruni*, compiled by an international team of scholars (see Gualdo Rosa, *Censimento*) — which in principle also includes letters directed *to* Bruni — has not disclosed any further witnesses to the text.

Notes to the Texts

❦❧❦

1. *Corrected:* Bonifacio XI pont. DXLIII olympiadis anno II *MS.*

2. *The text from the beginning of §5 down to* educavit *is missing from the MS. but has been supplied thanks to the discovery of Di Benedetto, "Il punto," p. 21.*

3. Ciucio: *sic MS.: see Notes to the Translation ad loc. (n. 10).*

4. VII *MS.: see Notes to the Translation ad loc. (n. 48).*

5. Ciucio *MS.; see above, §16.*

6. hinc et: *modern texts of Ovid read* inque.

7. *Modern texts of Vergil read* accipite; *but the variation may be intentional.*

8. Manto *and* Mantuam *supplied from Cyriac's source, Isidore of Seville,* Etymologiae 15.59.

9. *In the MS. the* c *is written directly above the first* V.

10. *In the MS. the* c *is written directly above the second* I.

11. *fol. 104 of MS. is missing; fol. 105r preserves the following Greek inscription.*

CORRESPONDENCE

Leonardo Bruni to Cyriac, after May 31, 1433

1. id est: *MS., corrected following modern texts of Sallust.*

Cyriac to Leonardo Bruni, January 30, 1436

1. I.e., contentionem

2. gestarum *Hankins:* vestrarum *Cortesi*

3. *Following a correction in Cyriac's hand noted in Hankins' apparatus:* contemptionibus *Cortesi; see also the relevant note (26) to the translation.*

4. I.e., expressis

5. more *Hankins, who reports the reading as a correction to* sermone *in the earlier MS.*: sermone *Cortesi.*

6. rem p. *MSS., with* et *added superscript in the earlier MS.*: rem et publicam *Hankins*: rem et populum *Cortesi. See also the relevant note (56) to the translation.*

7. tot rogatas *Hankins*: tot constitutas ue rogatas *Cortesi*

8. ignava *Hankins*: ignavi *Cortesi*

9. εἴδολα *MSS.*

10. *Conjectural addition of E. W. Bodnar.*

11. suis = eius. *Cyriac regularly uses the reflexive pronoun/adjective where classical Latin requires* eius *or* eorum.

12. *Cyriac, misreading the word* taedia *in the text of CIL 9:1589 as* tabedia, *in effect created a word that he adopted into his vocabulary. See Maas, "Ein Notizbuch," 13, n. 2.*

Cyriac to Leonardo Bruni, after April 7, 1436

1. *An* s., *presumably for* salutem, *has been erased or has become faded with time.*

2. σήμ^{ην} *MS.*

3. ΑΙΤΟΛΩΝ *MS.*

APPENDIX III

1. Haec: *a conjecture*: Nec *De Keyser*

APPENDIX IV

1. *om.* L, Mansi

2. *post* imperium R

3. contraria *Mansi*

4. ut R

5. tribuni *Mansi*

6. Fridericus *Mansi*

7. Britannia *R*

8. Taraeonensem *Mansi*

9. divinis *Mansi*

10. xxviii . . . consilium *om. Mansi*

11. vero *after* Quorum *crossed out in L*

12. ac *Mansi*

13. ac *R*

14. Ochilocratia *R*

15. praetendebat *Mansi*

16. quoddammodo *L, Mansi; but the second* quandoque *is probably to be excluded as a dittography.*

17. *It is not clear that this couplet is actually part of the* Sex modi; *it stands in this position in L, but in R appears earlier in the MS, on f. 26r.*

Notes to the Translations

❧❦❧

ABBREVIATIONS

Bodnar 1960
Edward W. Bodnar, S. J., *Cyriacus of Ancona and Athens* (Brussels-Berchem: Latomus, 1960).

CIG
Corpus Inscriptionum Graecarum, ed. August Böckh et al., 5 vols. (Berlin: G. Reimerus, 1828–77). Republished in 15 volumes (Berlin: Akademie der Wissenschaften, 1863–1905).

CIL
Corpus Inscriptionum Latinarum, ed. Theodor Mommsen et al., 17 vols. (Berlin: [various publishers], 1862–2012); online guide at cil.bbaw.de

DBI
Dizionario biografico degli Italiani (Rome: Fondazione Treccani, 1960–), and online at www.trecccani.it/biografie

Fragmenta
Fragmenta Notis Illustrata. Pesaro: In aedibus Gavelliis, 1763.

IG
Inscriptiones Graecae, consilio et auctoritate academiae scientiarum Berolinensis et Brandenburgensis editae (Berlin: [various publishers], 1913–2001); online guide at ig.bbaw.de

Iter
Paul Oskar Kristeller, *Iter Italicum*, 7 vols. (London-Leiden: E. J. Brill, 1963–97).

Itinerarium
Kyriaci Anconitani Itinerarium nunc primum ex ms. Cod. in lucem erutum ex bibl. illus. clarissimique Baronis Philippi Stosch, editionem recensuit, animadversionibus ac praefatione illustravit, nonnullisque eiusdem Kyriaci epistolis partim editis, partim ineditis, locupletavit Laurentius Mehus. Florence: ex novo typographio Joannis Pauli Giovannelli, 1742.

Later Travels	Edward W. Bodnar, with Clive Foss, *Cyriac of Ancona: Later Travels* (Cambridge, MA: Harvard University Press, 2003).
Mehus 1741	*Leonardi Arretini Epistularum libri VIII*, ed. Lorenzo Mehus, 2 vols. (Florence: Bernardus Paperinius, 1741). Reprint, with an Introduction by James Hankins (Rome: Storia e letteratura, 2007).
Nova	Annibale Olivieri degli Abati, Commentariorum Cyriaci Anconitani Nova.
Scalamonti	Francesco Scalamonti, Vita viri clarissimi et famosissimi Kyriaci Anconitani, ed. and trans. Charles Mitchell and Edward W. Bodnar, S. J. (Philadelphia, PA: American Philosophical Society, 1996).

THE LIFE OF CYRIAC OF ANCONA

1. The deified name of Romulus.

2. For the principal dates in Cyriac's life up to 1435, see Appendix I.

3. Michele Steno became doge on December 1, 1400. Therefore, Cyriac was in Venice on April 13, 1401, at the earliest. If he was nine years old at the time, he must have been born after April 13, 1391.

4. Francesco da Carrara the younger, lord of Padua (1391–1404).

5. Giacomo di Marzano, duke of Sessa, and Roberto di Marzano, count of Squillace and grand admiral of the *regno*.

6. Charles III of Durazzo, king of Naples (1381–86), assassinated at Buda on February 27, 1386.

7. The Latin text here uses the antique terms *seviri* and *treviri* for their Anconitan equivalents, the boards of six *anziani* and three *regolatori*; the latter were among the chief civic magistracies governing the town.

8. Mercury was Cyriac's patron "saint," to whom he prayed when embarking on a journey.

9. Cyriac was elected senator by exception to the minimum age requirement.

10. Thus the manuscript, but perhaps the name Cinzio is meant: Tiraboschi, *Storia*, 6:159, gives "Cincio de' Pizzicolli."

11. I.e., a yellow marble: see Pliny the Elder, *Natural History* 36.49, and Juvenal 7.182.

12. The column dedicated to Diocletian. Cyriac wrongly took the fragmentary words [. . .]OKPAT[. . .] and AΛEΞANΔP[. . . .] in its inscription to refer to Dinocrates, the architect of Alexandria, and to Alexander the Great, whereas they actually refer to the emperor and to the city: [AYT]OKPAT[OPA] and AΛEΞAΔP[EIAS]. See Fraser, *Ptolemaic Alexandria*, 1:27, 2:89–90.

13. Faraj (r. 1403–14). The next sultan, ruling in 1414, was Sheik al Muayyad.

14. The condottiere Galeazzo Malatesta, lord of Pesaro (1385–1461), known as "the Inept," attacked Ancona on the night of October 6, 1413.

15. Cyriac's Italian account of this action seems to be lost.

16. Cyriac addressed a letter to *Franciscus eques* (probably Scalamonti) and Crassus from Arta, December 29, 1435 (*Itinerarium*, 58–65).

17. For the vernacular poet Alberto Orlandi da Fabriano, see E. Lamma, "Rime inedite di Alberto Orlandi," *Archivio storico per le Marche e per l'Umbria* 4 (1889): 494–517.

18. Leonardo Giustiniani (1388–1446), Venetian humanist and statesman, was also a famous vernacular poet and singer of the time.

19. Ancient Senia, the port south of Rijeka on the Liburnian coast, now in Croatia; also mentioned in §98, where the name was misinterpreted as Siena in Scalamonti, 130.

20. Created count of Monteserico and marquis of Gerace in Sicily by Alfonso V; *signore* of Bitonto; captain-general of the Church and viceroy, he accompanied Alfonso of Aragon on his expedition to the island of Djerba in 1432 and was taken prisoner with Alfonso at the naval battle of Ponza in August 1435.

21. The text suddenly shifts here from the third-person singular to the first-person plural — probably because Scalamonti neglected to alter

his source, Cyriac's own diary, at this point as he would normally have done.

22. Presumbly the fortified town of Alcamo, fifty-four kilometers southwest of Palermo.

23. See n. 21 above. Here the text wavers in a single sentence from "they" (*venissent*) to "we" (*convenimus*), then back to the third plural again (*perceperant*).

24. Loredan commanded the forces that recovered Venetian strongholds in Dalmatia from the Turks in 1416.

25. Oddone Colonna, elected Pope Martin V at Constance, November 11, 1417; his election put an end to the Great Schism in the Western church that had begun in 1378.

26. Since there is no "Suasna" on this coast, it seems probable that the strategic island of Saseno, which commands the Gulf of Valona, is intended.

27. Compare Vergil, *Aeneid* 3.291.

28. Filippo degli Alfieri was elected Anconitan consul of Constantinople and of Romania in 1419 at the instance of the Byzantine emperor, Manuel II.

29. For Cyriac's description of Constantinople, see Vickers, "Mantegna and Constantinople," who believes that Cyriac "must have made profuse illustrations of what he saw" and that these hypothetical drawings are reflected in the background of Mantegna's *Agony in the Garden.*

30. Either at this time or later, he made at least seven drawings of Hagia Sophia: see Appendix II.

31. The equestrian statue of Justinian, destroyed in 1540. According to Vickers, "Theodosius, Justinian or Heraclius?" 281, the popular identification of the statue as one of Heraclius goes back at least to 1204.

32. The "convex arrangement of marble columns and architraves at the head" seen by Cyriac must be the large hemicycle adorned with a colonnade of thirty-seven columns. The *spina* of the racecourse was originally adorned with seven monuments, among them the monolithic obelisk

brought from Heliopolis to Constantinople by Theodosius and erected with great effort by Proculus in thirty-two days, as the Latin and Greek inscriptions on its base declare. Cyriac (or perhaps his guides) are portrayed as being able to read these inscriptions in 1419. As in the case of the Hagia Sophia drawings, the Parma manuscript (see Appendix II) has on folios 66v and 67r headings for two drawings of obelisks with blank spaces left unfilled.

33. The spiral columns of Theodosius in the Forum Tauri, and of Arcadius in the Forum of Arcadius, were both inspired by the column of Trajan in Rome.

34. The nine-hundred-foot span of Constantinople's main aqueduct, built by Valens in 368 CE, is still standing, but it is built of stone, not brick. The *nymphaea* were reservoirs into which the various aqueducts were emptied.

35. Cyriac's rhetorical *Laus urbis Galatae*, written in epistolary form in 1446, is printed in *Later Travels*, 256–72.

36. For the inscription naming her, see *CIL* 5:50. Her name was actually Postuma.

37. This is the first mention in the *Vita* of Cyriac recording inscriptions. *CIL* 5:3–4 lists a number of inscriptions from Pola recorded by him.

38. The *Nova Fragmenta*, consisting mainly of Cyriac's *commentaria* on his northern Italian journey of 1442–43, includes at the beginning a record that Cyriac was *podestà* of Varano, a township near Ancona, in 1420, at a time when citizens of Ancona had fled there to escape the plague. This notice is preceded by the inscription Cyriac supposedly composed on that occasion (*Nova Fragmenta*, 2–3). Considering, however, Scalamonti's clear statement (§53) that Cyriac began to study Latin only in 1421, it seems most likely that this inscription is to be dated later, perhaps to 1442, where it appears in the *Nova Fragmenta*.

39. Gil (Egidio in Italian) Alvarez Carillo de Albornoz, born in Cuenca, Spain, circa 1295; archbishop of Toledo (1338–50); created cardinal December 17, 1350, at Avignon; made legate in Italy in June 1353 by Innocent VI, with extensive powers to prepare the Papal States for the return of

the popes; author of a model constitution for Ancona, which was later extended to all the Papal States and remained in force until 1816—hence he came to be called their "second founder." He died near Viterbo, Italy, on August 22 or 23, 1367, while escorting Pope Urban VI to Rome.

40. Condulmer arrived in Bologna on August 16, 1423, to replace Cardinal Alfonso Carillo as papal governor.

41. Compare Petrarca, *Canzoniere* 90.1.

42. Vergil. That "to me his voice sounds distant far" may allude to Cyriac's ignorance of Vergil in Latin at this date, or to knowing his work only by reputation.

43. Tommaso Seneca da Camerino (ca. 1390–1472) was a humanist teacher and poet, later secretary to Sigismondo Malatesta in Rimini. Camerino is a town in the mountains south of Ancona; the town still honors its native son with a Viale Tommaso Seneca.

44. On Cyriac's records of Trajan's arch, and particularly the kindred accounts of it in his *Anconitana Illyricaque laus et Anconitanorum Raguseorumque foedus* (June 1440) and in the *Itinerarium*, dated October 1441, see Campana, "Da codici del Buondelmonti."

45. On Cyriac's putative equestrian statue and its heraldic use, see ibid., 496–98. The *podestà* was the chief judicial officer of an Italian town, usually a foreign judge with a doctorate in civil law.

46. CIL 9:5894.

47. In March 1423, Cyriac stopped at Fano and Rimini on the way to Venice, a journey not recorded by Scalamonti but documented in Cyriac's letter to Pietro de Bonarellis (see below, 174). It may have been at this time that Cyriac translated and interpreted for the people of Fano the inscriptions on their prominent ancient monument, the arch of Augustus.

48. The manuscript reads VII, i.e., *septimo*, the seventh year of Martin's pontificate, but De Rossi, "De Cyriaco," 2:357, emends to *octavo*, the eighth year, because Condulmer ceased to be legate in Bologna on June 9, 1423, and did not arrive in Rome before about the middle of that year.

49. The first mention of Cyriac's *commentaria* in the *Vita*; they are later mentioned five more times (§§76, 105, 113, 166, 199).

50. For Antonio Colonna (d. 1472), see *DBI* 27 (1982).

51. Luigi dal Verme (ca. 1390–1449), condottiere; see *DBI* 32 (1986).

52. The last two lines of *CIL* 6:1033.

53. The poem also survives independently in another manuscript, Florence, Biblioteca Riccardiana, Ricc. 2732, ff. 68r–69r, under the title *Ciriacho danchona, chanzona morale*; see *Iter* 1:222.

54. Pagliaresio di Simone de' Pisanelli. He was a supporter of Condulmer in Ancona from 1418 to 1419, and soon after Condulmer's election as Eugenius IV, Ancona sent him as ambassador to Rome to ask the pope to restore its castles of Monsanvito and Fiumescino, seized by Galeazzo Malatesta of Pesaro, a request Eugenius granted in 1432. A Pagliaresio di Simone de'Pisanelli was on a board of six, along with Cyriac, appointed May 14, 1440, to negotiate a new treaty between Ancona and Ragusa.

55. Janus Lusignan, king of Cyprus, Jerusalem, and Armenia (1398–1432).

56. Unidentified.

57. Benvenuto Scotigolo also is mentioned as the Anconitan captain of the ship that carried Cyriac to Egypt circa 1436 (*Itinerarium*, 49). Perhaps he is the same person as the ship captain, Benvenuto di Filippo Scottivolo (or Scottivoli), mentioned in contemporary records of sailings from Ancona to the Levant in 1439 and 1440.

58. Francesco Ferretti, appointed *podestà* of Ancona in 1425, became senator of Rome in 1429.

59. Andreolo Banca of Genoa: like most other administrators and shareholders of the Genoese *Maona* (company of merchants) in Chios, he took the name of Giustiniani. Twenty-eight letters from Cyriac to Andreolo are published in *Later Travels*.

60. For the Syrian inscriptions, *CIL* 3:160, 206, 17*, see De Rossi, "De Cyriaco," 2:258a, n. 1, who asserts that *CIL* 3:160 constituted headings of lost drawings of Vespasian and Bacchus.

61. I.e., Timur, known as Tamerlane, who sacked the city in 1400.

62. The ungrammatical character of the Latin text at this point (*sunt* with predicates in the accusative— *vicum, casam, arcem*) is an indication that Scalamonti was working from a first-person record of Cyriac's, which he converted, awkwardly and unsuccessfully in this instance, into a third-person account.

63. Since 1383 the Genoese had enjoyed political and commercial jurisdiction in Famagusta; all ships trading with Cyprus were compelled to call there, except those coming from Turkey, which might put in at Kyrenia, on the north coast of the island.

64. *Physicus* might also mean "medical doctor."

65. Sir Badin de Nores, marshal of Jerusalem, appointed a royal counselor by Janus in 1425.

66. An important passage for dating Cyriac's visit to Cyprus. The king's "recent misfortunes" were at the hands of the Mamelukes, who invaded Cyprus on July 1, 1426, and defeated and captured Janus on July 7, when Badin de Nores (see preceding note) was in command of the left wing. Nicosia was sacked on July 15, and the king and six thousand of his men and women were carried off to Cairo. Janus was ransomed on May 12, 1427, and returned to Cyprus. His restoration of the ravaged island, commemorated in Cyriac's inscription, included the building of a new royal palace to replace the one burned by the invaders. Allowing time for the restorations to become noticeable, Cyriac's arrival in Nicosia must have been well after May 12, 1427, and probably not until some time in 1428. Two additional bits of information can then be fitted into the last part of 1427: (1) On May 13, 1427, Cyriac finished copying Ovid's *Fasti*, which he later carried with him on his journey to the Levant (see n. 76 to §76), so he was still in Italy on that date; moreover, (2) a letter from Francesco Filelfo to Cyriac, dated Venice, December 21, 1427 (Appendix III), may imply that Cyriac did not depart for the Levant until the beginning of 1428, since it seems likely that the encounter between Cyriac and Filelfo occurred while the traveler was in Venice, getting his commission from Zaccaria Contarini, and that Filelfo sent his reply to Cyriac's questions to

the traveler while he was still in Ancona, preparing for the journey to the Levant, early in 1438.

67. The italicized phrases in the Latin echo, respectively, Vergil, *Aeneid* 4.151, 4.143–44, 1.498.

68. Theodosius, author of a work on nouns and verbs, apparently lived in the third or fourth century CE.

69. Apianus and Amantius, *Inscriptiones sacrosanctae vetustatis*, 506.

70. In 1428, the knights of Rhodes turned the island of Nisyros over to Fantino, who soon added Kos, Kalymnos, and Leros to his domain. He was deposed and imprisoned as the result of a revolt in 1453.

71. Leoni, *Ancona illustrata*, 1:218–19, 2:274–75, reports that Cyriac gave the senate of Ancona many manuscripts, which perished on September 21, 1532, when Clement VII seized the city. He adds: *Fra le altre cose portò una superba statua di Venere al naturale, mancante le coscie e le gambe; lavoro del famoso Fidia, ed aciò ogn'uno ne godesse la pose in una nicchia sopra la porta di sua casa, che per lungo tempo fu la delizia degli intendenti; ma invaghitosene il cardinal di Mantova, non potendola ottenere con preghiere ed oro, di notte armata mano la tolse dalla nicchia, e la spedì al marchese di Mantova suo fratello nel 1503; donando agli eredi Pizzecolli ottanta ducati d'oro.* (Among other things, he brought a superb statua of Venus nude, missing thighs and legs, a work of the famed Phidias. And so that everyone could enjoy it, he put it in a niche above the door of his house where it was the delight of connoisseurs for a long time. But when the cardinal of Mantua became enamored of it, not being able to get it with prayers or gold, he removed it from the niche at night by force of arms and sent it to the marquis of Mantua, his brother, in 1503, giving eighty gold ducats to the Pizzicolli heirs.)

72. The Latin translation of the life of Euripides mentioned here in the *Vita* seems to be lost.

73. Salonica was captured by the Turks on March 29, 1430. It follows that Cyriac's purchase in Adrianople of manuscripts plundered from there occurred in April 1430 at the earliest. Since Cyriac is described as having spent the winter (*per hiemem*) in Adrianople, this must have been

the winter of 1429–30. Thus, the period of almost a year passed in Cyprus (*nondum expleto anno*) must have been 1428 to 1429, and the progress from Ancona to Cyprus (leisurely though it was, via Constantinople, Chios, Beirut, and Damascus) could not have begun any earlier than January 1428 (see above, n. 66 on §68).

74. Probably Niccolò Ceba, of the Grimaldi family, to whom Filelfo wrote many letters, including one of 1441 referring to a voyage of his to Persia (Tiraboschi, *Storia*, 6.1:163; Filelfo, *Epistolae*, 1502, 31r).

75. The Latin term used here, *peranterea scapha*, may be derived from the Greek word, *peran*, and could possibly mean "ferry boat."

76. For the buying and selling of slaves by Italian merchants in Cyriac's time and the probability that they purchased slave girls to serve as their concubines, see Ashtor, *Levant Trade*, 408; and in reference to Cyriac's Clara, see Colin, *Cyriaque d'Ancône*, 52–64 and 184–85. Murad II had swept down into Epirus and Albania after his capture of Salonica (March 29, 1430). It seems likely that Cyriac's "Chaonian" (i.e., Epirote) slave girl had been caught up in that campaign.

77. See n. 10, above.

78. CIL 3:647 and 3:7337

79. Compare Ovid, *Fasti* 3, 707–8. In his own copy of the *Fasti* (Vatican Library, MS. Vat. lat. 10672), which he copied out himself (signed May 13, 1427), Cyriac added inscriptions of Philippi in the margin of fol. 31v (see Banti, "Iscrizioni," 213–20, and Berra, "Per la biografia," 461–62).

80. For Cyriac in Salonica, see Vickers, "Cyriac of Ancona at Thessaloniki," 75–82.

81. It is unlikely that a triumphal arch would have been erected in the provinces as early as the time of Aemilius Paullus (victor at nearby Pydna in 168 BCE). Vickers, in a review of H. P. Laubscher (see Bibliography), decided that the Arch of Galerius must be meant, even though it is on the eastern edge of the ancient city and not in its center. The same scholar (Vickers, "Cyriac of Ancona at Thessaloniki," 76–77) identified the "temple of Diana" as an elaborate portico (known as *Las Incantadas*,

owing to its numerous statues of deities on its architrave), which stood in the center of the city on the southern edge of the ancient forum until 1864.

82. St. Demetrius, just north of the ancient forum, was the metropolitan church of Salonica in 1431, when Cyriac visited it. The walls Cyriac saw are from the fifth century CE, and the extant inscriptions that contain the name Lysimachus (*IG* 10.2.1, nos. 27, 97, 113, 243, 635), refer to private individuals and not to the Hellenistic king. See Vickers, "Cyriac of Ancona at Thessaloniki," 78–79.

83. I.e., to the fact that the two poets were contemporaries; compare *Anthologia Palatina* 7.53; see Vickers, "Cyriac of Ancona at Thessaloniki," 79–80.

84. See n. 74, above.

85. The letter survives only in this fragmentary form. Cyriac presumably met Cardinal Giordano Orsini (d. 1439) and may have met Leonardo Bruni of Arezzo (1370–1444) when he visited Rome in 1424. A visit by Bruni to Rome in 1424 is not recorded, but it is known that he served as ambassador to Martin V in Rome in 1426, and he may have been used in that role on other occasions in those same years; see Hankins, "Addenda to Book X," 371–72.

86. The epithet occurs repeatedly in Vergil, at *Aeneid* 1.65, 2.648, 10.2, 10.743.

87. One of five bastard sons of Carlo I Tocco, count of Cephalonia. He had received only one-fifth of Acarnania on Carlo I's death in 1429 and had appealed to Sultan Murad II for aid in recovering what he considered to be his whole heritage, most of which had gone to his cousin, Carlo II, the nephew of Carlo I. After the fall of Salonica in 1430, the Sultan used Memnon's appeal as a pretext for sending an army to Ioannina, which capitulated and thenceforth became part of the Turkish Empire.

88. Babilano Pallavicini (d. 1488) was one of the leaders of the Genoese commercial colony in Galata Pera, which he later saved from destruction when he paid homage to Mehmed II in 1453.

89. "Canuza" Bey is the same person as Hamza Bey, statesman and military commander, and governor of Anatolia under Murad II (1421–51).

90. Pliny the Elder, *Natural History* 36.98.

91. Cyriac visited Cyzicus again in 1444, when he lamented the further ruin of the temple since his first visit. Today there is nothing left of the temple except its vaulted foundations, barely discernible in the brambles that cover and surround it.

92. Ashmole, "Cyriac of Ancona," 187–88.

93. Ovid, *Tristia* 1.10.29–30.

94. The inscription on the lintel of the south gate (*CIG* 3748) states that the arched structure was erected under Claudius Gothicus at the end of 268 CE, not by Tiberius Claudius Germanicus.

95. Cyriac may have been shown the Church of the Fathers, where the First Ecumenical Council supposedly met in 326 CE (it actually convened in the imperial palace); the church has not been identified. Or, he may have seen the Church of Hagia Sophia, still standing in the center of the city, where the Seventh Ecumenical Council of 787 may have met. See Foss, *Nicaea*, 101–4, 110–14.

96. Scutari (Uskudar) is not the actual site of Chalcedon, which is the nearby district of Kadiköy.

97. Pasqualino Mucciarelli. An evaluation of the ships of Ancona, drawn up in 1430, names Pasqualino as the owner of a *navetta* worth two hundred scudi.

98. The lord of the island of Lesbos at this time was not Giorgio, but his uncle, Dorino I Gattilusio, who ruled from 1428 to 1455.

99. Part of the text of *CIL* 3:450. Other inscriptions of Lesbos copied by Cyriac are *CIG* 2171, 2173, 2190, 2211, 2194, 2172 (see Kaibel, "Cyriaci Anconitani . . . sylloge," 1–24); and *CIL* 3:455, 456.

100. Cyriac actually means "theaters," of which there are two in Pergamum.

101. Cyme as the birthplace of Hesiod: a dubious inference from *Works and Days* 1.640.

102. These coins Cyriac later showed to Ambrogio Traversari in Venice, who mentioned them in a letter to Niccolò Niccoli (see Traversari, *Epistolae* 2:412 [Book 8, ep. 45]).

103. The events here narrated occurred after October 31, 1431, when the Genoese government learned of the Venetian preparations, and before November 6, when the Venetian fleet arrived off Chios.

104. Astorgio Agnesi, consecrated bishop of Ancona on March 6, 1419.

105. *CIL* 14:3607.

106. Probably the so-called temple of Vesta (or the Sibyl), the dedication being to Hercules Saxanus (see Dessau's note on *CIL* 14:3543).

107. *CIL* 14:3543.

108. *navistatium*: possibly a coinage by Cyriac, from *navis* + *stare*; or possibly related to the Greek *naustathmon*.

109. Sigismund (1361–1437), king of Hungary, arrived in Siena on July 8, 1432, and remained there until April 25, 1433. For further discussion of his expedition to Italy in these years, see the notes to the correspondence with Leonardo Bruni, below. For arguments that the events narrated in §§204–16 (southern Italy) belong chronologically between §96 and §97, see Scalamonti, 165, nn. 250–51, 253; and below, n. 269 to §217.

110. Gaspar Schlich (or Schlick), chancellor, and Francesco Bossio, bishop of Como (1420–1435).

111. Lucio Conti, protonotary apostolic; created cardinal (1411), died in 1437.

112. In 1444 Cyriac also gave a silver coin of Vespasian to Raffaelle Castiglione to remind him of the destruction of the Temple in Jerusalem in 70 CE, which avenged the death of Christ, and in 1445 he gave a Rhodian Greek silver coin to Bandino of Rhodes: *Later Travels*, 84f., 194f.

113. Brunoro della Scala, a scion of the former lords of Verona and an imperial diplomat, died in Vienna in 1434.

114. Battista Cicala (1407–51), a Genoese nobleman who served as ambassador of Genoa at the imperial court, later imperial representative in Poland.

115. Cyriac probably remained in Sigismund's court from this point on until the coronation, accompanying the emperor-elect on his journey to Rome (April 25, 1433), and participating as one of his honorary courtiers in the ceremony in St. Peter's on May 31, 1433.

116. See above, §31, and n. 19.

117. Correcting the translation of *Phrygipenates* in Scalamonti, 130 ("?Frangipani") — though the Frankopans were supposedly descended from the medieval Roman patrician clan of the Frangipani. Among other titles, members of the Frankopan family held the county of Senj from the king of Hungary. The Stjepan Frankopan referred to may be the son (d. 1481) of Ban Nikola Frankopan. The name *Phrygipenates* likely represents a fanciful Cyriacan etymology of the name of the powerful Croatian family.

118. Even after Eugenius officially transferred it to Ferrara on September 18, 1437, it continued on in Basel as a "rump" council, defying Rome, and eventually appointed its own anti-pope, Felix V.

119. Vergil, *Aeneid* 4.611.

120. Cyriac's visit to Florence probably occurred before Cosimo de'Medici's exile from the city (September 1433–October 6, 1434) and thus before the exiles of Palla Strozzi and Filelfo in November and December 1434, respectively; see the notes to §102. Yet Niccolò da Uzzano had died on April 20, 1431, so it is hard to explain Cyriac's desire to see him in 1433. Throughout the paragraphs on the Florentine visit, there are imprecisions in chronology, suggesting that the account was composed later from reminiscences rather than compiled from contemporaneous notes. See also nn. 121 and 123, below.

121. Filippo Brunelleschi, the architect of the cathedral and a famous artist. The name of the old cathedral, Santa Reparata, was used until the new one, Santa Maria del Fiore, was given to it at its reconsecration in 1436. Brunelleschi's dome was still under construction in 1433; it was not finished until 1436, though Scalamonti's narrative makes it sound as though Cyriac had seen the completed cupola.

122. *marmoream ornatissismam cienceriam turrim:* evidently the campanile, though the meaning of *cienceriam* is obscure. The campanile was designed by Giotto and was built between 1334 and 1359.

123. The erroneous tradition that the Baptistery (actually built between 1059 and 1150) was originally a Roman temple of Mars rededicated to St. John the Baptist is echoed in Dante's *Inferno* 13.143–46, 19.17, *Paradiso* 16.22, and many other contemporary sources, including Book 1 of Bruni's *History of the Florentine People;* the tradition lasted until the nineteenth century.

124. Of the three bronze doors, Andrea Pisano's south door was set up in 1338, Ghiberti's present north door was installed in 1424, but the panels of his second door were not cast until 1436 or 1437, its frame not until 1445, and the completed door was not set up until the summer of 1452; see Krautheimer, *Ghiberti,* 3–9. Hence a problem is created by Scalamonti's reference to *three* bronze doors on the occasion of Cyriac's visit to Florence in 1433. If the chronology of the doors given above is correct, the third door could not have been seen by Cyriac in 1433; it was not installed until after the last of his recorded visits to Florence, in 1441. This anachronism, apparently introduced into the text by Scalamonti and not based on Cyriac's notebooks, seems to indicate that this part, at least, of the *Vita* was not written until after 1452. Another possibility is that Cyriac saw models of the third set of doors in Ghiberti's workshop (see §103); the design process (which involved, among others, Leonardo Bruni) had been begun in 1425 and was the subject of much discussion among humanists and art lovers in the city.

125. I.e., Lorenzo Ghiberti. Nencio is the diminutive form of Lorenzo, Ghiberti's first name.

126. Presumably the Palazzo Vecchio and the Bargello.

127. Cyriac's earliest recorded encounter with Leonardo Bruni; but see n. 85, above.

128. Carlo Marsuppini (1390–1453), from Arezzo; member of the Florentine circle of humanists and particularly close to the Medici. He succeeded Filelfo in the chair of Greek at Florence in 1431, served for a time

as a papal secretary, and, at the end of his life, succeeded Bruni as chancellor of Florence. Highly respected for his command of Greek, he translated Book I of the *Iliad* into Latin. Marsuppini also composed a poem in praise of Cyriac, which occurs frequently in the manuscripts.

129. Francesco Filelfo (1398–1481), born in Tolentino in the March of Ancona, taught in Florence between April 1429 and December 1434.

130. Cyriac here compares Niccoli, who left his large collection of manuscripts to the library of San Marco, to the founder of the library of Alexandria. Cyriac later sent Niccoli a copy of the hieroglyphs on the biggest pyramid he saw in Egypt (*Itinerarium*, 52).

131. The expression, *cavata ex Nicolo*, is obscure. *Cavata* by itself can mean "concave," "hollowed out," "excavated," or "carved in relief." Taking *ex Nicolo* as expressing agency, it could mean either that Niccoli discovered it by excavation (our translation) or, perhaps, that he himself engraved lettering on the ancient gem, as Ghiberti did on a cornelian showing Apollo and Marsyas, which he also thought was the work of Pyrgoteles (see Krautheimer, *Ghiberti*, 1:13, citing from Ghiberti's autobiography).

132. The codex was captured in the siege of Pisa in 1406 and kept in the chapel of the Signoria as a civic trophy. It was believed by humanists down to the time of Poliziano to be the original codex compiled by Justinian's editor Tribonian in the sixth century CE.

133. The Certosa di Galuzzo just south of Florence, built by the Acciaiuoli family in the fourteenth century.

134. Most of the inscriptions of Milan and Brescia also appear in *Nova fragmenta*, Cyriac's northern Italian journal of 1442–1443; full references in Scalamonti, 159–61, nn. 166–208.

135. I.e., Cisalpine Gaul, the area north of the Apennines in the Po river valley.

136. Scipio Mainente of Ferrara (d. 1444), for whom see the Introduction, p. xiv, and Cyriac's 1436 letter to Bruni, below, nn. 7–8.

137. *CIL* 11:832.

138. *CIL* 11:863.

139. *CIL* 11:884.

140. *CIL* 11:830.

141. *CIL* 11:855. Cyriac's copy of the side-by-side inscriptions was accompanied by his drawing of the portrait heads on the stones.

142. *CIL* 11:839.

143. Cyriac interpreted the tomb of the philosopher Biagio Pelacani of Parma (d. 1416) as the tomb of Macrobius, to which he thought the remains of Pelacani had been added. The tomb had on it busts of Pelacani and Macrobius, who was believed to have been born in Parma. For the inscription see *CIL* 11:1122.

144. "Panormita" is Antonio Beccadelli (1394–1471), so called because he was a native of Palermo [*Panormus*]. He taught at the Studio in Pavia in 1430–1431 and again in 1432–1433; later, he became principal secretary to Alfonso V of Aragon. This dates Cyriac's arrival in Pavia to the end of 1433, since Panormita left there for Naples at the beginning of 1434 to enter Alfonso's service. He composed this distich as an epitaph of Cyriac's mother:

ANCONIS SPLENDOR IACET HOC MASIELLA
SEPULCHRO
UNA PUDICITIAE KYRIACIQ(ue) PARENS

Masiella, glory of Ancona, lies in this tomb,
parent at the same time of modesty and of Cyriac.

145. Both in the Church of San Pietro in Ciel d'Oro, formerly the Cathedral of Pavia.

146. The Insubres were a Celto-Gallic nation that settled in Lombardy and were said to have founded Milan around 600 BCE.

147. Filippo Maria Visconti (1392–1447), duke of Milan (1412–47).

148. *CIL* 5:6099.

149. *CIL* 5:6037.

150. A prominent merchant of Milan, later one of the ruling junta under the so-called Ambrosian Republic (1447–50); this corrects the translation in Scalamonti, 133.

151. *CIL* 5:6069.

152. *CIL* 5:6008.

153. *CIL* 5:5896.

154. *CIL* 5:6039.

155. *CIL* 9:5931; actually from Ancona.

156. *CIL* 5:6276.

157. *CIL* 5:5940.

158. *CIL* 5:6024.

159. *CIL* 5:5061.

160. *CIL* 5:6045; the Latin is hard to construe, as the dedication is to a son, but the name of the dedicatee is female.

161. *CIL* 5:5893.

162. *CIL* 5:5859.

163. *CIL* 5:5959.

164. *CIL* 5:6041, translating Cyriac's mistranscription rather than the modern text.

165. *CIL* 5:5905.

166. *CIL* 5:5906.

167. *CIL* 5:6083.

168. *CIL* 5:5956.

169. *CIL* 5:5895.

170. *CIL* 5:5762.

171. *CIL* 5:5942.

172. *CIL* 5:640*; possibly not genuine.

173. *CIL* 5:6019.

174. *CIL* 5:5771.

175. *CIL* 5:6006.

176. *CIL* 5:6100; the names differ slightly in the *CIL* text.

177. *CIL* 5:5853.

178. *CIL* 5:5911; the inscription is fragmentary.

179. *CIL* 5:5776.

180. *CIL* 5:7386.

181. *CIL* 9:5927; actually in Ancona, not Milan.

182. *CIL* 5:5634.

183. *CIL* 5:679; a medieval, not classical, inscription whose meaning is unclear.

184. *CIL* 5:6128; the scansion of the hexameters breaks down after line 5. On the stone itself the hexameters are arranged to fit the stone and are not in verses.

185. *CIL* 5:5927.

186. *CIL* 5:7385.

187. Filippo Maria Visconti's father was Gian Galeazzo Visconti, duke of Milan (1395–1402).

188. *CIL* 5:4403.

189. *CIL* 5:4639. Translation uncertain, but "C. M. I." may be the initials of the owner of the plot (an interpretation kindly suggested by Dr. Roger S. O. Tomlin).

190. *CIL* 5:4367.

191. Later manuscripts locate this inscription "at the church of St. Andrew outside the walls near the entrance to the aforesaid church" (see Mommsen's note in *CIL*, *ad loc.*).

192. *CIL* 5:4340.

193. *CIL* 5:4470. Mommsen found this inscription buried beneath a pile of ruins (*sub aggere*) in an ancient temple to Diana. Only the three lines copied by Cyriac stuck out (*eminuisse*) from the wall.

194. *CIL* 5:4332; Cyriac copied only the last two lines of this dedication to a high imperial official.

195. Later manuscripts, from Feliciano's onward, locate this inscription "in the Church of SS. Faustinus and Lovita near the altar of St. Honorius at the foot of the bell-tower (*sub campanile*)" (see Mommsen's note on *CIL, ad loc.*).

196. *CIL* 5:4368.

197. *CIL* 5:4501.

198. *CIL* 5:4369.

199. *Nova Fragmenta*, 67, no. 190, gives the location: *Cippus Brixiae ad S. Georgium* (a pillar in the Church of San Giorgio in Brescia).

200. *CIL* 5:4463.

201. *CIL* 5:4416.

202. *CIL* 5:4676.

203. *CIL* 5:4370.

204. *CIL* 5:4766.

205. *CIL* 5:4460.

206. This is the only recorded occasion when Cyriac investigated the antiquities of Verona.

207. See the medieval lexicon of Papias, s.v. *Athesis: Athesis flumen Veronae*.

208. *Pharsalia* 1.403.

209. Scalamonti's source for these topographical remarks about the Adige in Verona—as well as for his tedious accounts of legends about the foundation of Mantua and the origin of its name (below, §192) and his murky calculations about the date of Mantua's foundation (§193); his confused summary of legends about Genoa's foundation, name, and date (below, §§198–202); and his jumble of lore about the foundation and original name of Benevento (§214)—was probably one of Cyriac's notebooks of *parerga* and extracts from ancient and medieval sources about the particular places he was visiting, which the traveler kept *pari passu* with his journals, occasionally entering a few of the ancient *testimonia* into the journals themselves at the appropriate places. At this point it begins to look as if Scalamonti, growing tired of his task and perhaps despairing

of ever reaching the end of it, figuratively emptied out his Cyriacan files, including the traveler's notes on Verona, Mantua, and Genoa garnered from ancient and medieval sources.

210. Verona was in Gallia Cisalpina, not Liguria, which is on the northwest coast of Italy.

211. Faenza, Biblioteca Comunale, MS 7, is a much fuller *sylloge* of Veronese inscriptions, with drawings of most of the monuments on which they appear; it is in the hand of Felice Feliciano, who seems to be copying Cyriac's own lost *sylloge*, without any connecting narrative, of the stones he inspected during this visit (see Mitchell, "Felice Feliciano," 214–15, pls. XXVIIb, XXIVb, XXXVIIIa). Cyriac copied only the last two lines of this dedication to a high imperial official.

212. *CIL* 5:3329.

213. *CIL* 5:3221.

214. *CIL* 5:3338; the relationship of Marcellina to Sollers is established by another inscription, *CIL* 5:3337.

215. *CIL* 5:3830.

216. *CIL* 5:3281.

217. *CIL* 5:3340.

218. *CIL* 5:3689; CIL gives the location: *Veronae in contrata S. Andreae antiqui* (At Verona in the contrada of Sant'Andrea the Elder).

219. *CIL* 5:3257.

220. *CIL* 5:3643.

221. *CIL* 5:3387.

222. *CIL* 5:3734. In later manuscripts, this inscription is located *prope Sanctum Salvatorem ubi coria conficiunt* (near San Salvator where leather objects are made).

223. *CIL* 5:3748.

224. *CIL* 5:3460.

225. *CIL* 5:3677.

226. *CIL* 5:3657.

227. *CIL* 5:3627.

228. *CIL* 5:3628.

229. *CIL* 5:3419.

230. *CIL* 5:3382.

231. Ibid.

232. Ibid.

233. Ibid.

234. *CIL* 5:3393. Later manuscripts locate this stone *in moenibus vetustissimis S. Michaelis a porta loco privato* (in the ancient walls of San Michele by the gate, on a private site).

235. When Scalamonti says he found the following material (§§192–93) in Cyriac's *commentaria*, he may be referring to one of the traveler's commonplace books, such as the one he kept *pari passu* with his journal of the visit to mainland Greece in 1435–36 (see above, n. 209 on §165).

236. Isidore of Seville, *Etymologiae* 15.59.

237. Vergil, *Aeneid* 9.59–60.

238. Compare Vergil, *Aeneid* 10.198–200, and *Eclogues* 9.59–60, with Servius' commentary on both passages, identifying Ocnus and Bianor; see also Isidore, *Etymologies* 15.59; Paul the Deacon, *Historia Langobardorum* 2.14, 2.23; Statius, *Thebaid* 4.406.

239. Orosius, *Historiae adversus paganos*, 7.3.1 (date of the foundation of Rome); Augustine, *City of God* 16.17 — not Book 18, as in the text — (date of the birth of Abraham). The references to Jerome and to the chronicles of Miletus and Eusebius are too vague to identify with precision.

240. *CIL* 5:3827.

241. *CIL* 5:4066.

242. *CIL* 5:4072. The inscription appears within a drawing of an arch.

243. *CIL* 5:4073.

244. Pliny, *Natural History* 3.5.48–49.

245. *Historia Langobardorum* 2.16.

246. Solinus 2.5.

247. Albarium, Galiganum, Serzanum: none of these place-names appear in Graesse's *Orbis Latinus*; they are probably zones in or near the city of Genoa: Albaro (formerly S. Francesco Albaro), the hill of Carignano in the center-east, and the esplanade of Sarzana. The etymology of Sarzana is now thought to be from *Arx Jani* rather than from Cyriac's more fanciful *saltus Jani*.

248. The statements attributed to Jerome (on Moses and the foundation date of Rome) and Bede and Methodius (on the founding of Genoa) could not be verified. The legend of Bellovesus, the son of a Celtic king, who was led by augury to found Mediolanum, is told by Livy 5.34, but he does not speculate on the date.

249. Livy 28.46.7.

250. Livy 21.32.5.

251. Livy 30.1.10.

252. A secretary and chancellor of Filippo Maria Visconti, son of Giacomo Barbavara; see *DBI* 6 (1964).

253. Cyriac saw the famous emerald crater, a spoil from the sack of Caesarea in Syria, in the treasury of San Lorenzo in Genoa (*Itinerarium*, 17, n. 4). In a letter written in August 1446 (*Later Travels*, 268), Cyriac also mentions Francesco Spinola, Benedetto Negrone, and Giovanni Grillo in connection with the bowl of precious green stone, which he said he recorded in his *per Ligustiam commentaria*.

254. Paolo Imperiale (ca. 1390–ca. 1460), Genoese humanist and diplomat, later governor of Caffa; see *DBI* 62 (2004). Giacomo Bracelli (d. ca. 1466), lawyer, later chancellor and secretary of the Republic of Genoa, friend of Francesco Barbaro, Biondo Flavio, and Poggio Bracciolini. Nicolaus de Camulio (d. after 1457), humanist, colleague of Bracelli in the Genoese chancery, father of the better-known Prosper Camulio (or Camogli).

255. On Pagliaresio di Simone de' Pisanelli, see above, §61, n. 54.

256. A folio (104) is missing at this point. This torn-out leaf presumably referred to Cyriac's welcome by Joan as a grandson of Ciriaco Selvatico, his obligation to Giovanni Caracciolo, and his visit to the temples of Cas-

tor and Pollux, as described in the *Itinerarium* (see text in Scalamonti, 205, no. 11b). Perhaps there was a drawing of the temple, which would account for the removal of the folio. For the inscription on the temple, see Campana, "Ciriaco d'Ancona e Lorenzo Valla."

257. Translation from CIG 5791; IG 14:714; see also CIL 10:184. Cyriac's transcription is badly garbled.

258. CIL 9:1558.

259. CIL 9:1589.

260. Not found in CIL 9.

261. As with Mantua and Genoa, this intercalated "historical" section indicates that Scalamonti was utilizing Cyriac's *parerga*.

262. Solinus 2.10.

263. Papias, s. v. Diomedis, Samnis, Samnium, Samnitae.

264. Paul the Deacon, *Historia Langobardorum* 2.20.

265. The archbishop of Benevento was Gaspar Colonna, consecrated in 1429, and he did have twenty-two suffragans.

266. References to Miletus and Jerome not found.

267. Off the coast of Tunisia. Alfonso attacked the sultan's forces in the summer of 1432. The king of Tunisia was Abu Fâris ʿAbd al-Aziz II, who reigned from 1394 to 1434. Alfonso's naval war against the sultan of Egypt, Barsbay, went on until the summer of 1435, when Alfonso, in an all-out effort to gain the throne of Naples, withdrew his ships to Gaeta, where they were engaged by the Genoese on August 5, 1435, off the island of Ponza, and Alfonso was captured; see Cyriac's *Naumachia Regia*, below, 234–53.

268. Maria d'Enghien (ca. 1370–1446), queen of Sicily, wife of Raimondo del Balzo Orsini and then of King Ladislas of Naples. Taranto, which was her fief, she passed on to her son, Giovannantonio del Balzo Orsini, who sided with Alfonso of Aragon in the latter's attempt to gain the throne of Naples.

269. As previously remarked (n. 208 to §165), this last part of the *Vita* seems fragmentary and patched together, and it appears to stop rather

than to come to a conclusion. Even if we re-date §§204–17 back to the year 1432, bringing Scalamonti's account to an end with Cyriac still in Genoa (§203), followed by the one-sentence valediction to Lauro (§218), the ending feels abrupt and unfinished.

CORRESPONDENCE

Cyriac to Pietro De' Bonarelli, March 15, 1423

1. On Pietro di Liberio Bonarelli, scion of an ancient mercantile family from Ancona and a figure of some weight at the Council of Constance, see *DBI* 11 (1969).

2. For the italicized phrases, compare Vergil, *Aeneid* 10.215–16 and 8.405–8.

3. For the italicized phrases, compare Ovid, *Fasti* 1.455–56; Vergil, *Aeneid* 7.26, 5.42, 2.270, 5.295.

4. The lad was Sigismondo Malatesta, son of Pandolfo Malatesta (d. 1427), lord of Fano. Sigismondo (b. 1417) was only six years old in 1423.

5. Vergil, *Aeneid* 6.34.

6. The *Aeneid*.

7. Ibid. 5.713–14.

8. The phrase occurs nine times in the *Aeneid*, for example, at 1.60, 1.65.

9. Ibid. 6.117.

10. An epithet of Faunus; a play on the name of the city, Fano.

11. Mercury.

12. For the italicized phrase, see Vergil, *Aeneid* 4.239–40.

13. Ibid. 1.521.

14. Ibid. 2.604–6.

15. The sun.

16. Vergil, *Aeneid* 6.724–29.

17. Ibid. 8.351–54.

18. Ibid. 6.660–63.

19. Ibid. 6.566–72.

20. Vergil, *Eclogues* 4.4, 6–7.

21. Vergil, *Aeneid* 6.748–51.

22. Macrobius, *Saturnalia* 3.9.16.

23. Dante, *Purgatorio* 6.118–20.

24. Vergil, *Aeneid* 4.278 and 9.658.

25. Ibid. 2.302.

CYRIAC TO LEONARDO BRUNI, DECEMBER 13, [1432]

1. For the date, see Scalamonti, 189nn., and Hankins, "Addenda to Book X," 421.

2. Sigismund of Luxembourg (1368–1437), king of Hungary and Croatia (1387), later king of Bohemia (1419) and Italy (1431), was elected king of the Romans in 1410/11 on the death of King Rupert of Germany. Election as king of the Romans gave Sigismund the right to petition the pope to be crowned Holy Roman Emperor. At the end of 1432 and in early 1433, Sigismund was in Siena, negotiating for his coronation with Pope Eugenius IV. He was crowned Emperor Sigismund III in Rome on May 31, 1433 (see next letter).

3. For the meaning of *ex Fluentinis scaenis*, an archaizing touch, see Fiaschi, "Inediti," 340ff. "Fluentia" was the original name of Florence according to Leonardo Bruni's *History of the Florentine People*, ed. and trans. J. Hankins, 3 vols. (Cambridge, MA, 2001–7), 1:11 (1.3).

LEONARDO BRUNI TO CYRIAC, AFTER MAY 31, 1433

1. This letter is dated by its reference to the coronation of Sigismund III as Holy Roman Emperor, which took place in Rome on May 31, 1433. The letter appears in Mehus 1741, 2:57–61 (VI, 9).

2. Bruni uses the term *princeps* for emperor, in accordance with ancient usage. In contemporary, that is, medieval Latin, the word *imperator* was used for the Holy Roman Emperor. For the issues at stake in Bruni's discussion of political terminology, see the Introduction, pp. xiii–xvii.

3. Sigismund III (1368–1437). See n. 2 to the previous letter.

4. For the most important ancient sources for the famous contrast between the laughing Democritus and the weeping Heraclitus, see Cora E. Lutz, "Democritus and Heraclitus," *The Classical Journal* 49.7 (1954): 309–14.

5. Suetonius, *Augustus* 52.

6. Suetonius, *Julius Caesar* 76, 79–80.

7. Sallust, *Bellum Iugurthinum* 85.35.

CYRIAC TO LEONARDO BRUNI, JANUARY 30, 1436

1. This paragraph echoes a number of phrases in the previous letter of Bruni but turns the laughter of the wise against the barbarism imputed to Poggio.

2. The Latin echoes Vergil, *Georgics* 4.192 and *Aeneid* 6.831.

3. The phrases italicized in the Latin are from Vergil, *Aeneid* 3.78.

4. Giorgio Begna, a Dalmatian humanist who lived in Zadar; called, with some exaggeration, "the Poggio of Dalmatia," for his literary discoveries in that region. From November 9 to 26, 1435, as Cyriac began writing the present letter, Cyriac was Begna's guest. See Praga, "Indagine e studi . . . Il cod. Marciano," 214.

5. Triton's "trumpet" was a conch shell: Vergil, *Aeneid* 6.171–74. The inscription was identified by Mommsen as *CIL* 3:55211. For further bibliography on these inscriptions, see Cortesi, "La *Caesarea laus*," 44, n. 31.

6. *CIL* 3:2922. See Cortesi, "La *Caesarea laus*," 44, n. 31.

7. Possibly Marino de' Resti, with whom Cyriac later negotiated a commercial treaty between Ancona and Ragusa (May–June 1440). See Praga, "Indagini e studi . . . Ciriaco de' Pizzicolli." *Soloneus* is an alternative form of Saloneus, as Cortesi notes in her edition (54, note to l. 29).

8. The passage was from Poggio's letter to Scipio Mainente mentioned in the Introduction, p. xiv. Cyriac was acquainted with Scipio as well, since the latter acted as Cyriac's sponsor in Modena, when he passed through that city late in 1433; see *Life* §105.

9. Poggio's letter to Scipio Mainente begins as follows (Bracciolini, *Opera omnia* 1:357–58): *Rem sane arduam et imparem meis viribus postulas tibi a me scribi, suavissime Scipio, uter scilicet vir praestantior atque elegantior fuerit, et pluris aestimandus, superiorne Aphricanus, aut C. Iulius Caesar. Multa enim a veteribus rerum scriptoribus de utroque tradita sunt summa gloria et laude digna, ut difficilimum sit inter tales principes et tantos sententiam ferre. Quamvis de altero factum iam praeiudicium esse per Plutarchum videatur, qui Caesarem Graecorum omnium excellentissimo magno Alexandro comparārit. Sed credo illum res militiae gestas et belli gloriam secutum esse, non virtutes.* (You ask me, dear Scipio, to write on a really difficult subject for which my powers are inadequate, whether a man was more outstanding or elegant, and to be more greatly respected — that is, whether Africanus or Julius Caesar was superior. Much about both of them that is worthy of glory and praise has been handed down by ancient authors so that it is very difficult to have an opinion about such great leaders. However it seems that a judgment has been made about the latter by Plutarch who compares Caesar with the most outstanding of all the Greeks, Alexander the Great. But I believe that Caesar gained glory for his achievements in the military and war, not from his virtues.)

10. The Latin text (*antea . . . diem*) borrows language from Ovid, *Fasti* 1:455–56; see also Ovid, *Metamorphoses* 11.597.

11. Adapted from Homer, *Iliad* 2.23–24. Cyriac was elected an *anziano* (counselor) of Ancona at an unusually early age. Dream (Oneiros) is a personification that appears frequently in Homer and other Greek literary works.

12. Cortesi, "La *Caesarea laus*," 55, note to line 52, reports that Bodnar suggested to her an identification of this personage with the sea nymph Kymodoke, or Cymodocea, for whom see the indexed passages in *Later Travels* and pl. III, as well as Neuhausen, "Cyriacus und die Nereiden."

13. The italicized phrase in the Latin is from Vergil, *Aeneid* 4.177, 10.767.

14. The Muses, who were born in Pieria in Thessaly and lived on Mount Helicon. Cyriac regularly confuses them with the nymphs. Polyhymnia is the muse of sacred poetry, dance, and eloquence; she appears in Dante's *Paradiso* 23.56.

15. The italicized phrase in the Latin is from Vergil, *Aeneid* 1.521.

16. The Cumaean Sibyl. Compare Statius, *Thebaid* 4.488: *Phoebea virgo*.

17. The italicized phrase in the Latin is from Vergil, *Aeneid* 2.790–91.

18. The muse of epic poetry, daughter of Zeus and Mnemosyne.

19. The italicized phrase in the Latin recalls Vergil, *Aeneid* 9.5.

20. Perhaps meant as a reminiscence of Vergil, *Aeneid* 6.847–53.

21. The language sounds Neoplatonic, as it locates ideas within "deep mind," likely the hypostasis of Nous, but the allusion is too general to associate with any one passage in a source.

22. The passage in ancient Greek echoes Homer, *Iliad* 2.761; see also *Odyssey* 1.1.

23. The italicized phrase in the Latin recalls Vergil, *Aeneid* 6.117.

24. The italicized phrases in the Latin recall language in Vergil, *Aeneid* 10.3, 7.251 = 12.939, and 7.756.

25. Venus and Diana.

26. Or, following the reading preferred by Cortesi, "having spurned the quarrels of the Paphian and Delian goddesses," and assuming the rare word *expretis* is derived from *ex-sperno*. This reading seems unlikely, as Caesar is traditionally said to be descended from Venus, who acts as his divine patron.

27. For the italicized phrases in the Latin, see Vergil, *Aeneid* 4.222–23 and 4.242.

28. See *Aeneid* 4.239–40.

29. See *Aeneid* 5.810.

30. See *Aeneid* 6.55 and 1.521.

31. The goddess Roma. See above, §§10 and 11.

32. For the italicized phrase in Latin, see Vergil, *Aeneid* 2.604–6.

33. I.e., Plato's δημιουργός; see Plato, *Timaeus* 29c. See also Mussini Sacchi, "Per la fortuna," 299–310. Plato's demiurge (craftsman) was often identified with the creator God by Christian theologians. The corruption into "demogorgon" was popularized by Boccaccio in his *Genealogia deorum*

gentilium, 1.1–14, where the demogorgon becomes the founder of the race of the gods; see Mussini Sacchi, "Per la fortuna."

34. See Cyriac's opusculum on the six constitutions for his understanding of this Aristotelian political terminology (Appendix IV).

35. Compare Orosius 1.1.6.

36. The view that the *pax romana* initiated by Augustus was part of God's providential plan to prepare the world for the incarnation of Christ was a staple of Christian historiography since at least the fourth century.

37. Matthew 22:21, Mark 12:17, Luke 20:25. That God and Caesar held coordinate rule over heaven and earth was a basic doctrine of Byzantine political theory, first enunciated in Eusebius' famous *Life of Constantine* of the fourth century.

38. The traditional iconographic symbols for the four evangelists are a winged man or angel (Matthew), a lion (Mark), an ox (Luke), and an eagle (John). The eagle is not included here, since the saying of Christ's quoted appears only in the synoptic gospels (as in n. 30), and not in the Gospel of John.

39. Lucan, *Bellum civile* 1.128.

40. The eagle. Metonymy for the Roman standard, by itself the eagle stood for Roman military power and its *imperator*, Caesar, and his successors. See Vergil, *Aeneid* 1.394 and 12.247, and frequently in Dante, for example, *Purgatorio* 33.38 and *Paradiso* 6.1–2.

41. Plutarch, *De Alexandri Magni fortuna aut virtute* 1.9; 2.2 = *Anthologia Palatina* 16.120 (last line).

42. The italicized phrase in the Latin is from Vergil, *Aeneid* 9.106 = 10.115.

43. Reading πᾶν ἐδάνεις, θεόφραδε Ἑρμῆς as a mistaken imitation of πάντ' ἐδάης, Μουσαῖε θεόφραδες, as in John Tzetzes, *Chiliades* 12.399, v. 149 (= p. 445 κ). Μοναρχόφιλος is apparently a Cyriacan coinage.

44. Leonardo Bruni and Carlo Marsuppini, both from Arezzo.

45. Not identified.

46. For the phrase *magno sub axe*, see Ovid, *Fasti* 3.106; *Ex Ponto* 4.15.36.

47. See n. 3 above.

48. In accordance with the usual Renaissance view, the Roman *imperium* (empire) here is held to begin with the end of the kingdom (509 BCE), i.e. under what moderns call "the republic," but which Cyriac specifies as *sub regimine consulum* (under the consular regime); whereas what moderns refer to as "the empire" and date from the battle of Actium in 31 BCE, Cyriac refers to as the time *sub principibus* (under the emperors)" See see J. Hankins, "Exclusivist Republicanism and the Non-Monarchical Republic," *Political Theory* 38.4 [2010]: 452–82.

49. The argument that the Roman Empire flourished because of political liberty under the consuls but declined under the emperors (*sub principibus*) was first made in Leonardo Bruni's *History of the Florentine People*, Book 1. The first six books of this history were already published in 1428/29 and were probably known to Cyriac; see J. Hankins, "Notes on the Composition and Textual Tradition of Leonardo Bruni's *Historiarum Florentini populi libri XII*," in *Classica et Beneventana: Essays Presented to Virginia Brown on the Occasion of her 65th Birthday*, ed. F. T. Coulson and A. A. Grotans (Tournhout: Brepols, 2008), 87–109.

50. For the italicized phrases in the Latin, see Vergil, *Aeneid* 1.254 and 12.829; *Georgics* 3.553 and 4.415.

51. Compare Vergil, *Aeneid* 10.501.

52. Compare ibid. 7.621.

53. Compare ibid. 9.516.

54. I.e., the transfer of the capital from Rome to Constantinople under the emperor Constantine in 330 CE. Bruni was again the first to have identified this event as having precipitated the fall of the Roman Empire. See Patricia Osmond, "'The Idea of Constantinople': A Prolegomenon to Further Study," *Historical Reflections* 15.2 (1988): 323–36.

55. Or, "the best principate." The term *principatus* in the Middle Ages and early Renaissance was often used for regime or constitution but can

also refer to the type of government set up by the Julio-Claudian emperors. Later in the Renaissance the term comes to mean "sovereignty" or "sovereign prince."

56. *Sub consulibus* is the commonest language in Roman sources for the type of regime modern historians refer to as "republican," i.e., a system for sharing power among members of an elite, led by magistrates and having a measure of popular support. *Res publica* in the fifteenth century does not refer to a period of Roman history (see "Exclusivist Republicanism").

57. Perhaps a reference to the concept of *anacyclosis*, the natural process of constitutional degeneration, found in Polybius' *Histories*, Book 6; see the introduction to Appendix IV.

58. Compare with the harpy in Vergil, *Aeneid* 3.211, 233, 365, a symbol of ruin and death.

59. The italicized phrases in Latin are from ibid. 8.333–35.

60. Sophocles, *Ajax*, 125–26.

61. In ancient pagan theology, a *daimon* is a creature of the air, generally invisible, of lower status than a god; but Cyriac here seems to use the word interchangeably with *deus* (god).

62. I.e., the spring of Hippocrene, on Mount Helicon, so called because it was said to have been created by a blow of Pegasus' hoof. For the Latin phrase, see Persius, *Satires*, Prologus 1.

63. Some phrases in the preceding sentences are borrowed from Pliny the Elder, *Natural History* 7.25.91.

64. Siccius: possibly Lucius Siccius (or Sicinius) Dentatus, celebrated as the "Roman Achilles." Sergius, a military tribune at the siege of Veii, was the boast of the patrician family of the Sergii in historical times. Both are mentioned in Cyriac's source, Solinus 1.106.

65. Phrases in this paragraph are borrowed from Pliny the Elder, *Natural History* 7.25.92, interwoven with Solinus 1.106.

66. For these sentences, see Pliny the Elder, *Natural History* 7.94.

67. Suetonius, *Julius Caesar* 44.

68. Vergil, *Aeneid* 6.789.

69. Ibid. 3.515.

70. Ibid. 4.278 and 9.658.

71. Presumably the date on which Cyriac sent off copies of this draft to Bruni and Marsuppini.

72. This is apparently the date and place (November 20, 1435, Zadar) at which Cyriac began to compose the letter. Cyriac was in Zadar from the November 9 to 26, 1435: see Bodnar 1960, 25. The probability that Cyriac circulated the letter to different recipients is supported by the last remark in Poggio's letter to Bruni (see below, 231).

CYRIAC TO LEONARDO BRUNI, AFTER APRIL 7, 1436

1. In an unpublished note found among his papers, Fr. Bodnar dates the letter to "shortly after April 7, 1436." His reasoning was as follows: "Since Ciriaco mentions, and gives inscriptions from, Delphi and Athens, the letter was written after his visit to Delphi (March 21–27, 1436) and after or during his visit to Athens (April 7–22, 1436)."

2. CIL 3:549.

3. CIG 1694. This is a fragment; the complete text is published in *Fouilles de Delphes* 3.1:50 no. 87.

POGGIO BRACCIOLINI TO LEONARDO BRUNI, MARCH 31, 1438

1. Scythians, a nomadic people vaguely located to the north and east of the Greco-Roman world, were regarded by the ancients as a byword for wild and barbarous behavior.

THE KING'S NAVAL BATTLE

1. Ancient name of Marsala in Sicily.

2. Alfonso laid siege to Gaeta in April 1435.

3. A famous condottiere in the service of the Visconti, Torelli rose to become admiral of the Genoese fleet, driving the Aragonese from Naples in 1424. He died in Milan in 1449.

4. Military commander, diplomat, and humanist, Assereto was Chancellor of Genoa from 1423 to 1435, when Milan lost control of the city. He was active in Milanese politics until his death, in 1456.

5. A member of one of the four leading families of Genoa, Spinola played an active role in his city's political life. He favored the conquest of Genoa by the Milanese as well as the revolt that expelled them in 1435; he held high office in Genoa until his death, in 1442.

6. Of an ancient Roman family long settled in Naples, Queen Joan II named him Protonotarios and Logothete of the kingdom, an office he maintained under the Aragonese.

7. Scion of a powerful Roman family, he settled in Naples, where Joan II named him captain general. After her death, he served Alfonso V of Aragon as military commander and diplomat, dying in 1456.

8. Unidentified.

9. Brother of Alfonso and king of Navarre from 1425, he succeeded Alfonso as king of Aragon and Sicily in 1458 but died the next year.

10. Giovanni Antonio Orsini del Balzo, the most powerful feudal lord in the kingdom of Naples, supported Alfonso, who made him duke of Bari. He was murdered in 1463 after revolting against Ferdinand I, king of Naples.

11. Youngest brother of Alfonso, Henry was master of the religious-military order of St. James, based at the Basilica of Compostela. The title Infante was reserved for legitimate sons of the Spanish king.

12. Favorite brother of Alfonso, killed at the Aragonese siege of Naples in 1438.

13. Genoese shipowner of the family that ruled the island of Chios.

14. Member of a family that had provided leaders to Genoa since the tenth century.

15. Antonio Colonna, prince of Salerno and duke of Istria, possessed his own fleet of galleys. After the death of Alfonso, whom he supported, he switched sides to the Angevins, then back to the Aragonese; he died in 1471.

16. Ruggero Caetani, nephew of Christopher, made chamberlain by Queen Joan II.

17. Illegitimate son of the condottiere Giovanni Colonna, Ludovico, following his father's profession, successively served Queen Joan II, Pope Martin V, Filippo Maria Visconti, and Alfonso V of Aragon. After Ponza, he supported Pope Eugenius IV against members of his own family, one of whom killed him in 1436.

18. Giovanni Antonio Marzano, member of a family that traditionally held the offices of grand admiral and grand chamberlain under the Angevins; in 1435 he took the side of Alfonso, who made him grand admiral of the kingdom and gave him his own daughter in marriage.

19. Supporter of Alfonso who, when he had taken Naples, was restored to the Acquaviva family lands he had previously lost. In 1459, with the support of Giovanni Antonio Orsini, he got the rest of his properties from King Ferdinand; he died of the plague after supporting the revolt against Ferdinand in 1462.

20. Known alternatively as Menicusso or Menguzo, in 1437 he was in the service of Alfonso as captain general.

21. Maria of Castile, daughter and sister of successive kings of Castile and Leon, married her cousin Alfonso in 1417.

22. Of an old Milanese family, Lampugnani was adviser, treasurer, and ambassador of Filippo Maria Visconti.

23. So called because of the viper on his coat of arms.

APPENDIX III

1. Or, "prepared for"; the ambiguity of *paro* is significant theologically and may be intentional.

2. Vergil, *Aeneid* 1.57.

3. Ibid. 12.942.

4. The language is Stoic; *boni praesentes* is likely to be Filelfo's rendering of προλήψεις.

5. Book 1, lines 103–4.

APPENDIX IV

1. Italy: *Ausonia*, the region of the Italian peninsula south of the Apennines, bordering on the Tyrrhenian Sea.

2. The Kingdom of Aragon is surely meant, but it is an imperfect equivalent for the ancient Roman province of Tarraconensis Hispania.

3. Sultan Murad II, the Ottoman sultan (1421–51).

4. I.e., the Gerousia, which consisted of twenty-eight men, all over the age of sixty, plus the two Spartan kings. Cyriac's language seems to assimilate the Spartan magistracy to the government advisory councils, often called *Buonuomini*, found in Italian city-states in his own day.

5. The reference to Ragusa show the close relationship between this text and another short work by Cyriac, dated June 18, 1440, called *Anconitana Illyricaque laus et Anconitanorum Raguseorum foedus*, published in Praga, "Indagini et studi . . . Ciriaco de' Pizzicolli," 270–78. In the latter work, Cyriac presents Ancona and Ragusa as sister cities, each historically free, under democratic and aristocratic regimes, respectively.

6. Cyriac means the Decemviri, who ruled Rome with consular power from 451 to 449 BCE and who were deemed to have acted tyrannically; see Livy 3.33–58.

7. Cyriac refers here and in §5 to the frequent changes of regime between oligarchic and popular factions in Genoa in his time.

8. I.e., whenever the plebs withdrew from participation in the community, as it did many times in early Roman history, as recorded by Polybius and Livy.

9. *CIL* 6:5. First recorded in Niccolò Signorili, *Descriptio urbis Romae* (ca. 1425), who considered the lines to be ancient. They were later copied in numerous manuscripts and printed collections of inscriptions and ancient poetry, including those of Felice Feliciano and Giovanni Marcanova. They are considered to be medieval in the modern epigraphical literature.

Bibliography

ॐᏘᏘॐ

Apianus, Petrus, and Bartholomaeus Amantius, eds. *Inscriptiones sacrosanctae vetustatis, non illae quidem Romanae, sed totius fere orbis, summo studio ac maximis impensis terra marique conquisitae.* Ingolstadt: in aedibus Petri Apiani, 1534.

Ashmole, Bernard. "Cyriac of Ancona and the Temple of Hadrian at Cyzicus." *Journal of the Warburg and Courtauld Institutes* 19 (1956): 179–91.

Ashtor, Eliyahu. *Levant Trade in the Later Middle Ages.* Princeton: Princeton University Press, 1983.

Babinger, Franz. "Veneto-kretische Geistesstrebungen um die Mitte des XV. Jahrhunderts." *Byzantinische Zeitschrift* 57 (1964): 62–77.

Banti, Luisa. "Inscrizioni di Filippi copiate da Ciriaco Anconitano nel codice vaticano latino 10672." *Annuario della R. Scuola Archaeologica di Atene e delle missioni italiane in Oriente* n.s. 102 (1940): 213–20.

Belozerskaya, Marina. *To Wake the Dead: A Renaissance Merchant and the Birth of Archeology.* New York: W. W. Norton, 2009.

Berra, Luigi. "Per la biografia di Ciriaco d'Ancona." *Giornale storico della letteratura italiana* 63 (1914): 461–62.

Bertalot, Ludwig, and Augusto Campana. "Gli scritti di Iacopo Zeno e il suo elogio di Ciriaco d'Ancona." *La Bibliofilia* 41 (1939): 356–76. Reprinted in Ludwig Bertalot, *Studien zum italienischen und deutschen Humanismus*, ed. Paul Oskar Kristeller (Rome: Storia e letteratura, 1975), 2:311–32.

Bertalot, Ludwig, with A. Wilmanns. "*Lauri Quirini Dialogus in Gymnasiis Florentinis*, ein Nachklang zum 'Certame Coronario' (1442)." *Archivum Romanicum* 7 (1923): 478–509 (= Bertalot. *Studien*, ed. Kristeller, 1:339–72).

Bodnar, Edward W. *Cyriacus of Ancona and Athens.* Bruxelles-Berchem: Latomus, 1960.

351

Bodnar, Edward W., and Charles Mitchell, eds. *Cyriacus of Ancona's Journeys in the Propontis and the Northern Aegean, 1444–1445.* Philadelphia: American Philosophical Society, 1976.

Bracciolini, Poggio. *Epistolarum familiarium libri.* Edited by Helene Harth. 2 vols. Florence: Olschki, 1984.

——. *Epistolarum liber ad Nicolaum Nicolum.* Edited by Helene Harth. Florence: Olschki, 1984.

——. *Opera omnia.* Edited by Riccardo Fubini. 4 vols. Turin: Bottega di Erasmo, 1964–69.

Brown, Beverly Louise, and Diana E. E. Kleiner. "Giuliano da Sangallo's Drawings after Ciriaco d'Ancona: Transformations of Greek and Roman Antiquities in Athens." *Journal of the Society of Architectural Historians* 42 (1983): 321–35.

Campana, Augusto. "Ciriaco d'Ancona e Lorenzo Valla sull'iscrizione greca del tempio dei Dioscuri a Napoli." *Archeologia classica* 25–26 (1974): 84–102.

——. "Da codici del Buondelmonti." In *Silloge Bizantina in onore di Silvio Giuseppe Mercati,* 33–42. Rome: Associazione Nazionale per gli Studi Bizantini, 1957.

Canfora, Davide. *La controversia di Poggio Bracciolini e Guarino Veronese su Cesare e Scipione.* Florence: Olschki, 2001.

Casu, Stefano G. "Travels in Greece in the Age of Humanism: Cristoforo Buondelmonte and Cyriacus of Ancona." In the exhibition catalogue *In Light of Apollo. Italian Renaissance and Greece (22 December 2003–31 March 2004),* edited by Mina Gregori, 2 vols., 1:139–42. Milan: Cinisello Balsamo and Athens: Hellenic Culture Organization, 2003.

Ciriaco d'Ancona e la cultura antiquaria dell'Umanesimo, Atti del convegno internazionale di studio, Ancona, 6–9 febbraio 1992. Edited by Gianfranco Paci and Sergio Sconocchia. Reggio Emilia: Diabasis, 1998.

Colin, Jean. *Cyriaque d'Ancône. Le voyageur, le marchand, l'humaniste.* Paris: Maloine, 1981.

Colucci, Giuseppe. *Delle antichità Picene.* 32 vols. Fermo: Dai torchi dell'Autore, 1786–97.

Cortesi, Mariarosa. "La *Caesarea laus* di Ciriaco d'Ancona." In *Gli umane-simi medievali. Atti del II Congresso dell'Internationales Mittellateinerkomitee, Firenze, Certosa di Galluzzo, 11–15 settembre 1993,* edited by Claudio Leonardi, 37–65. Florence: SISMEL, 1998.

Crevatin, Giuliana. "La politica e la retorica: Poggio e la controversia su Cesare e Scipione." In *Poggio Bracciolini, 1380–1980, nel VI centenario della nascita.* Istituto Nazionale di studi sul Rinascimento, Stud e testi 8, edited by Riccardo Fubini, 281–342. Florence, 1982.

Cyriac of Ancona. *Later Travels.* Edited by Edward W. Bodnar with Clive Foss. Cambridge, MA: Harvard University Press, 2003.

De Keyser, Jeroen. "*Nec tibi turpe tuum ducas audisse poetam:* Francesco Filelfo all'amico Antonio Beccadelli il Panormita." *Schede umanistiche* n.s. 22 (2008): 40–68.

De Rossi, Giovanni Battista. "De Cyriaco Pizzicolli Anconitano." In *Ins-criptiones christianae urbis Romae septimo saeculo antiquiores,* 2 vols., 2.1:356–87. Rome: Libraria Pontificia, 1888.

Di Benedetto, Filippo. "Il punto su alcune questioni riguardanti Ciriaco." In *Ciriaco d'Ancona e la cultura antiquaria,* 17–46.

Fabricius, Johann Albert. *Bibliotheca latina mediae et infimae aetatis.* First Italian edition by Joannes Dominicus Mansi. 6 vols. Padua: Apud Joannem Manfrè, 1754.

Fiaschi, Silvia. "Inediti di e su Ciriaco d'Ancona in un codice di Siviglia (Colombino 7.1.13)." *Medioevo e Rinascimento* 25/n.s. 22 (2011): 307–68.

Foss, Clive. *Nicaea, A Byzantine Capital and Its Praises.* Brookline, MA: Hellenic College Press, 1996.

Fraser, Peter Marshall. *Ptolemaic Alexandria.* Oxford: Clarendon Press, 1982.

Gorni, Giuseppe. "Storia del Certame Coronario." *Rinascimento* n.s. 12 (1972): 135–81.

Graesse, Johann Georg Theodor, Friedrich Benedict, and Helmut Plechl. *Orbis Latinus.* Dresden, 1861. Reprint, Braunschweig, 1971.

Gualdo Rosa, Lucia, ed. *Censimento dei codici dell' Epistolario di Leonardo Bruni.* 2 vols. Rome: Istituto Storico Italiano per il Medio Evo, 1993–2004.

Hankins, James. "Addenda to Book X of Luiso's *Studi su l'Epistolario di Leonardo Bruni.*" In Gualdo Rosa, *Censimento*, 2:352–422.

Kaibel, Georg. "Cyriaci Anconitani Inscriptionum Lesbiacarum Sylloge Inedita." *Ephemeris Epigraphica* 2 (1875): 1–24.

Krautheimer, Richard. *Ghiberti's Bronze Doors.* Princeton: Princeton University Press, 1971.

Krautheimer, Richard, with Trude Krautheimer-Hess. *Lorenzo Ghiberti.* 2 vols. Princeton: Princeton University Press, 1970. Reprint, 1982.

Krautter, Konrad, Paul Oskar Kristeller, Agostino Pertusi, Giorgio Ravegnani, Helmut Roob, and Carlo Seno, eds. *Lauro Quirini umanista: Studi e Testi.* With a presentation by Vittore Branca. Civiltà Veneziana, Saggi, 23. Florence: Olschki, 1977.

Lehmann, Phyllis Williams. *Cyriacus of Ancona's Egyptian Visit and Its Reflections in Gentile Bellini and Hieronymus Bosch.* Locust Valley, NY: J. J. Augustin, 1977.

Leoni, Antonio. *Ancona Illustrata.* Ancona: Tipografia Baluffi, 1832.

Luiso, Francesco Paolo. *Studi su l'Epistolario di Leonardo Bruni.* Edited by Lucia Gualdo Rosa. Rome: Istituto storico italiano per il Medio Evo, 1980.

Maas, Paul. "Ein Notizbuch des Cyriacus von Ancona aus dem Jahre 1436." *Beiträge zur Forschung. Studien und Mitteilungen aus dem Antiquariat Jacques Rosenthal, München,* 1 Folge, Heft 1 (1915): 5–15.

Mancini, Girolamo. *Vita di Leon Battista Alberti.* Florence: Carnesecchi, 1911.

Mitchell, Charles. "Felice Feliciano Antiquarius." *Proceedings of the British Academy* 47 (1961): 197–221.

Monti Sabia, Luciana. *Kyriaci Anconitani Naumachia regia.* Pisa: Istituti editoriali e poligrafici internazionali, 2000.

Morici, Medardo. "Dante e Ciriaco d'Ancona. (Per la fama di Dante nel primo trentennio del '400)." *Giornale dantesco* 7 (1899): 70–77.

Moroni, Carlo. *Epigrammata reperta . . . a Cyriaco Anconitano.* N.p., n.d. [Rome, ca. 1650].

Mussini Sacchi, Maria Pia. "Per la fortuna del Demogorgone in età umanistica." *Italia medeovale e umanistica* 34 (1991): 299–310.

Neuhausen, Karl August. "Cyriacus und die Nereiden. Ein Auftritt des Chors der antiken Meernymphen in der Renaissance." *Rheinisches Museum für Philologie*, n.f. 127 (1984): 174–92.

Oppel, John W. "Peace vs. Liberty in the Quattrocentro: Poggio, Guarino, and the Scipio-Caesar Controversy." *Journal of Medieval and Renaissance Studies* 4 (1974): 220–65.

Pade, Marianne. "Guarino and Caesar at the Court of the Este." *La Corte di Ferrara e il suo mecenatismo 1441–1598. The Court of Ferrara and Its Patronage*, edited by Mariane Pade, Waage Petersen, and Daniela Quarta, 75–92. Copenhagen: Museum Tusculanum, and Modena: Panini, 1990.

——. *The Reception of Plutarch's Lives in Fifteenth-Century Italy.* 2 vols. Copenhagen: Museum Tusculanum, 2007.

Pall, Francisc. "Ciriaco d'Ancona e la crociata contro i Turchi." *Academie Roumaine, Bulletin de la section historique*, 20 (1938): 9–68.

Pittaluga, S. "Ciriaco d'Ancona e i poeti latini." In *Ciriaco d'Ancona e la cultura Antiquaria*, 210–18.

Pontani, Anna. "I Graeca di Ciriaco d'Ancona (con due disegni autografi inediti e una notizia su Cristoforo da Rieti." *Thesaurismata* 24 (1994): 37–148.

Praga, Giuseppe. "Indagini e studi sull'umanesimo in Dalmatia: Ciriaco de' Pizzicolli e Marino de Resti." *Archivio storico per la Dalmazia* 13 (1932–33): 262–80.

——. "Indagini e studi sull'umanesimo in Dalmazia. Il cod. Marciano di Giorgio Begna e Pietro Cippico." *Archivio storico per la Dalmazia* 13 (1932): 211–18.

Rabil, Albert, Jr., trans. *Knowledge, Goodness and Power: The Debate over Nobility among Quattrocento Italian Humanists.* Binghamton, NY: Medieval and Renaissance Texts and Studies, 1991.

Rangone, G. "Umanesimo e 'filologia geografica': Ciriaco d'Ancona sulle orme di Pomponio Mela." *Geographia antiqua*, 3–4 (1994–95): 109–87.

Ronconi, Giorgio. *Le origini delle dispute umanistiche sulla poesia (Mussato e Petrarca).* Rome: Bulzoni, 1976.

Saraina, Torello. *De origine et amplitudine civitatis Veronae.* Verona: Antonius Putelletus, 1540.

Scalamonti, Francesco. *Vita viri clarissimi et famosissimi Kyriaci Anconitani.* Edited and translated by Charles Mitchell and Edward W. Bodnar, S. J. Philadelphia, PA: American Philosophical Society, 1996.

Schadee, Hester. "Caesarea Laus: Ciriaco d'Ancona Praising Caesar to Leonardo Bruni." *Renaissance Studies* 22 (2008): 435–49.

Smith, Christine. "Cyriacus of Ancona's Seven Drawings of Hagia Sophia." *Art Bulletin* 69 (1987): 16–32.

Spadolini, Ernesto. "Il biografo di Ciriaco Pizzecolli." *Le Marche*, disp. 5, a.1 (1901): 70–72.

Tiraboschi, Girolamo. *Storia della letteratura italiana.* 9 vols. Rome: Luigi Perego Salvioni, 1763.

Traversari, Ambrogio. *Ambrosii Traversari Generalis Camaldalensium aliorumque ad ipsum et ad alios de eodem Ambrosio latinae epistolae.* Edited by Petrus Cannetus. Florence: ex typographio Caesareo, 1759.

Van Essen C. C. "Cyriaque d'Ancône en Égypte." *Mededelingen der koninklijke Nederlandse Academie van Wetenschappen. afd. Letterkunde* n.r. 21,12 (1958): 293–306.

Vickers, Michael. "Cyriac of Ancona at Thessaloniki." *Byzantine and Modern Greek Studies* 2 (1976): 75–82.

——. "Mantegna and Constantinople." *Burlington Magazine* 118 (1976): 680–87.

——. Review of H. P. Laubscher, *Der Reliefschmuck des Galeriusbogens in Thessaloniki. Journal of Roman Studies* 67 (1977): 224–30.

——. "Theodosius, Justinian or Heraclius?" *Art Bulletin* 58.2 (1976): 281–82.

Index

Gnaeus Servilius Syrus (freed-
man), 147; Hermia (freedwoman),
129; Julia Eutychia (freedwoman),
125; Julius Marcellinus, 141; Juvenis
(slave), 113; Laelia, 89; Laetilius
Blandus, 107; Leo (slave), 113; Livia
Venusta (freedwoman), 149; Lucia
Peducea Juliana, 97; Lucifera (freed-
woman), 99; Lucius, 101; Lucius
Annius Diomedes, 159; Lucius
Annius Diphilus (freedman), 159;
Lucius Arulenus Anoptes, 119;
Lucius Caelius Arrianus, 131;
Lucius Caelius Firmus, 145; Lucius
Caelius Statura (freedman), 143;
Lucius Camurius Pandarus (freed-
man), 129; Lucius Cassius Nigri-
nus, 143; Lucius Cominius, 129;
Lucius Cornelius Prosodicus, 135;
Lucius Graecinus Pompeianus, 119;
Lucius Lucilius Florus, 121; Lucius
Nonius Ver[us], 99; Lucius Novel-
lius Rhodanus, 149; Lucius Parius
Hermes, 125; Lucius Poblicius
Hebenus, 135; Lucius Reynus Phi-
letus, 119; Lucius Statius Diodorus,
141; Lucius Turpilius Dexter, 89;
Lucius Valerius Marcellinus, 133;
Lucius Valerius Virillio, 107;
Lupula, 119; Lupus (slave), 113;
Lutatia Crispina, 111; Macrina
Secunda, 117; Macrinus Primus,
117; [. . .]Mag[. . .] (Oufentina
tribe), 103–5; Magius Pardion, 105;
Marcellinus, 101, 151; Marcus
Acilius, 159; Marcus Aurelius
Maximus, 101; Marcus Avena
Macer, 153; Marcus Fabricius
Hilarus, 145; Marcus Gavius Cor-
nelius Agathemerus Avenianus,

151–53; Marcus Gavius Serenus
(freedman), 151; Marcus Gavius
Severus, 149–51; Marcus Hortensius Paulinus, 141; Marcus Junius,
109; Marcus Licinius Pusillio, 145;
Marcus Livius Fortunatus, 149;
Marcus Maecius Rufus, 89; Marcus Nonius Arrius Paulinus Aper
(Fabian tribe), 131; Marcus Sacidius, 147; Marcus Sulpicius Acastus,
121; Marcus Sulpicius Acceptus,
121; Marcus Valerius Maximus, 111–
13; Marcus Vergilius Antiochus,
157; Maria Festa, 107; Maria Fes-
tiva, 107; Marina, 101; Marius Hip-
polytus, 107; Marius Montanus,
107; Mascellio Felix, 111; Maternia
Benigna, 101; Maturus (freedman),
111; Maximia Maxima, 115; Messalla
(freedman), 111; Modestus (freedman), 111; Mortaria, 111; Murranus
(slave), 145; Musolamius, 101;
Nicephorus (freedman), 147; No-
vellia Fusca, 109; Novellius Aequalis, 111; Novellius Verus, 109; Octavia Hilara (freedwoman), 143;
Oppia Valeriana, 105; Optata Mulvia, 135; Pamphilus, 157; Pelagon
(imperial freedman), 167; Photinus, 147; Plutia Hermione, 105;
Publius, 101; Publius (Palatina
tribe), 117; Publius Clodius Sura
(Fabian tribe), 133; Publius Clodius
Turpio, 145; Publius Furius, 159;
Publius Graecinius Laco (Publilia
tribe), 143; Publius Julius Apollonius, 145; Publius Plautius Pulcher,
87–89; Publius Plotius Urbanus
(freedman), 101; Publius Sacidius
(Publician tribe), 147; Publius

Publication of this volume has been made possible by

The Myron and Sheila Gilmore Publication Fund at I Tatti
The Robert Lehman Endowment Fund
The Jean-François Malle Scholarly Programs and Publications Fund
The Andrew W. Mellon Scholarly Publications Fund
The Craig and Barbara Smyth Fund
for Scholarly Programs and Publications
The Lila Wallace–Reader's Digest Endowment Fund
The Malcolm Wiener Fund for Scholarly Programs and Publications